GW00319233

Atyeo: The Hero Next Door

Atyeo

The Hero Next Door

Tom Hopegood
John Hudson

First published in 2005 by Redcliffe Press Ltd.,
81g Pembroke Road, Bristol BS8 3EA

© Tom Hopegood and John Hudson, 2005

ISBN-10 1-904537-41-3
ISBN-13 978-1-904537-41-0

British Library Cataloguing-in-Publication Data
A catalogue record for this book is available from the British Library

Design by Stephen Morris Communications, Bristol and Liverpool,
smc@freeuk.com
Typesetting by MFK Mendip, Frome
Printed by MPG Books Ltd, Bodmin, Cornwall

FOREWORD

In Bristol City's history of more than a hundred years, well in excess of eight hundred players have represented the club's first team. None, with perhaps the exception of Billy Wedlock long ago, has won the well-deserved acclaim accorded to John Atyeo. That both these heroes have stands named after them at Ashton Gate is testament to their worth to the club and the esteem in which they are still held.

I am delighted to write the foreword to this, the first book to be published about John's footballing career. My association with Bristol City coincided with the latter part of his playing days, and of course, my late husband Harry was instrumental in ensuring that he chose to join Bristol City rather than Portsmouth in 1951. The ensuing years brought many highs and lows for both the club and John, and in this day and age it is quite remarkable that someone who possessed so much talent chose to remain a one-club man. His record while playing for his country, five goals in six games, would now be hailed universally, and it would be very unusual for a second division player to be considered worthy of selection for the national side. Even today I hear older supporters saying 'Big John would have got that one' or 'Oh for another Atyeo'. This tells us what a wonderful player he was and still is to the followers of Bristol City and everyone who values the very best in football.

Marina Dolman

President, Bristol City Football Club

CONTENTS

CHAPTER 1

350 TIMES A WINNER

In the autumn of 2005, when Bristol City were making one of their worst starts to the season in living memory, a fan took to wearing a club shirt with 'John Atyeo' emblazoned across the back. Not 'Stewart' or 'Murray' or 'Bridges', or any of the other names of the day, but 'John Atyeo'.

It drew plenty of comment:

'Aye, he'd have been the one to get us out of this mess.'

'We want to know your favourite player, mate, not which stand you sit in.'

'That'd be the day. You wouldn't catch him playing for this lot, these days.'

'Get a life, man, that's ancient history.'

At the same time, the shirt left questions hanging in the air:

'What was it about this John Atyeo that makes old guys still bang on about him?'

'He wasn't really that great, was he?'

'What was he doing, a part-timer just up from the Third Division South, playing for England?'

'If he was so wonderful, why wasn't he banging 'em in for Chelsea or Liverpool?'

Good questions, these, as are many, many more; this book will try to answer all of them.

* * *

John Atyeo was an ordinary man and an extraordinary footballer. He was ordinary for the same reason that most people are ordinary: through his birth, his upbringing and the way in which he led his life. He was an extraordinary footballer for two reasons. He was conventionally extraordinary in that he could quite simply play the game more brilliantly than almost anyone else of his generation, and in the most glamorous and eye-catching position on the pitch; and unconventionally because he let the everyday side of him hem in his career to such an extent that even today, for all his achievements, some people see him as a player of unfulfilled potential. It is a rare footballer who limits his sporting ambitions, prizing security and familiarity above dreams of glory; it is a rare sportsman who is well known among his acquaintances for having a regard for money and being careful with it, yet spurns the chance to exploit the one great talent that makes him stand out from the crowd.

'Unfulfilled' is not a word you will hear applied to John Atyeo very often by Bristol City followers. The respect, admiration and adoration that flowed down on him from the terraces and stands of Ashton Gate year-in, year-out for fifteen seasons marked him as a hero unequalled in the club's history. Billy Wedlock, two generations earlier, was the sole idol of comparable status, but as a centre-half, dear old 'Fatty' could never set the pulses racing in the way Big John did, with his hundreds of goals. The only question that remains is whether he might have set tens of thousands more pulses racing at Highbury, Anfield or Stamford Bridge – or, indeed, at Wembley, in the extended run in the England team that his playing among the giants would surely have given him. To which the only possible answer, in South Bristol at least, is: 'Who cares?'

All through his career and into his later years, Atyeo clearly took pride in his loyalty, and swore that, given his time over again, he would play it in exactly the same way. He is to be believed. Looking back in 1970, he pinpointed City's indifferent Division Two form in the seasons following their thrilling Third South championship of 1954-55 as one reason why the England camp turned against him, along with his continued insistence on part-time status, and mused: 'That was the time when I should probably have been thinking of moving to a bigger club'; but note that even after years to think about it, it was only 'probably', and there is much more conviction in his assertion that he never did 'think too much' about leaving Bristol City. His early team-mate and best man at his wedding, Jack Boxley, is among close friends who remain convinced that the inner dynamics of his relationship with the Bristol club – in perhaps too simple terms, his sense of belonging there – could not have been replicated in London, Liverpool or Manchester. Put simply, he would never have felt settled and happy at one of the

major clubs. There is no doubt at all that a key element of his content-
ment lay in his sense of being the biggest fish in the pond. His
managers and fellow players at Ashton Gate admired his unassuming
manner and unselfish style of play, but after his early apprenticeship
he quickly took his supremacy at the club as a fact of life, and tacitly
expected others to do the same. He liked the ethos of a team game, and
his modesty was genuine, but it was still essential that others should
recognise his worth. That recognition would almost certainly have
been harder to come by in more ego-laden dressing rooms.

So Atyeo of the Arsenal, with 50 England goals under his belt? We
shall never know, but in the meantime, the facts, rather than the 'what
ifs', speak for themselves. His 597 Football League appearances for
Bristol City brought him 315 goals, both figures a club record. Thirty
goals in the FA Cup and another five in the then infant Football
League Cup took his total senior tally up to a round 350, while keen
followers of the City put his grand total of goals at 397 in some seven
hundred games when the Welsh Cup, Gloucestershire Senior Cup and
friendlies are taken into account. Ponder, momentarily, those thirty
goals in the FA Cup; they were achieved for a team that never aspired
in his time to any greater heights than Division Two, yet all the stars of
the top division, with their frequent lengthy forays through the competition to the sixth round, semi-final and final, could not equal it until
Denis Law came along. On the other side of the coin, it could be
argued that City themselves in their Third Division days were the
giants in the early rounds of the Cup – and in truth, the fair-minded
Atyeo was almost embarrassed by some of the goals he was allowed to
score against hapless non-League clubs.

Of eleven players who have scored three hundred-plus League
goals, John Atyeo, joint seventh in that roll of honour, is the only one
whose career total is for a single club. The two games he played for
Portsmouth as an amateur in season 1950–51, in which he did not
score, mean that for the purist he is not a one-club man; but as a goal
scorer he most certainly is, the third most prolific in the country for a
single club after Dixie Dean and George Camsell, who netted more for
Everton and Middlesbrough respectively than John did for Bristol
City, as well as getting a few more for other clubs.

Top of the list is the amazing Arthur Rowley, a near-contemporary
of Atyeo in that he notched his 434 League goals between 1946 and
1964 (and never won an international cap); Dixie Dean came next with

379, followed by Jimmy Greaves with 357, Steve Bloomer, 352, George Camsell, 345 and John Aldridge with 330. Atyeo shares his seventh place on 315 goals with Joe Smith, who won fame with Bolton Wanderers in their 1920s heyday but also played for Stockport County. The other members of the three hundred club, all pre-Second World War, are Vic Watson on 312, Harry Bedford, 308 and Harry Johnson, 307.

The other vital Atyeo statistics are his five goals in six full internationals for England, in which he never played on a losing side; and the fact that not once in his career was he cautioned or sent off. This latter achievement was not quite as remarkable then as it was in the early 1990s, when Gary Lineker emulated it; in the climate of John Atyeo's time, good honest pros (or even semi-pros) did not often find themselves in the referee's notebook, and those who had built up their sportsmanlike credentials over the years were increasingly likely to be given the benefit of the doubt in fifty-fifty incidents. To the credit of John Atyeo, 'the Referee's Friend', even a 'benefit of the doubt' situation did not arise more than a handful of times in his career; those with a taste for the blood and thunder of the game sometimes wished it had done so a little more often, and the City manager of the late 1950s, Peter Doherty, was among those who would have been happy if there had been a dash more 'devil' about him.

Maybe, but you do not get on the end of 350 goals, with the skulls, elbows, legs, studs and sweat flying around your head in the six-yard box, without being courageous, resourceful and, even from your tenderest years, as tough as old boots. John Charles, another legendary gentle giant, knew all about the dilemmas faced by the rare Atyeos of this world. One afternoon in the black and white stripes of Juventus in Serie A, upended for the umpteenth time by the same defender, he turned to his less fastidious inside-right Boniperti and sighed: 'You see to him, Boni. You know I can't.' There must have been times when John Atyeo could legitimately have made a similar plea to Bobby Etheridge or Bert Tindill. Instead, he would just smile that slow, wry countryman's smile, dust himself down and walk away, another free kick duly won for his side.

He was certainly physically equipped to look after himself – a touch over six feet tall and a few pounds above twelve stone in his prime, which began prodigiously early in life. Lean, hard and fit, he had speed and drive and more important still he had phenomenal balance, one of the main attributes that set him apart. 'He could send the entire crowd the wrong way with a swivel of the hips,' according to John Cleese, a Clifton College boy who worshipped him from the terraces before going on to find a greater fame of his own. With both his head and his feet, Atyeo had the presence, power and co-ordination to dispatch a ball into the net with clinical accuracy and force – and inside that head there was a footballing brain that put him in precisely the right place to make the best of the chances that came his way. A lesser player can spend the afternoon chasing shadows, stretching for through balls that skid off the end of his toes and leaping a fraction of a second too soon or too late for crosses that skim off the top of his head to safety. John Atyeo could make passes and crosses look pre-ordained goals from the second they left his team-mates' boot. Those team-mates loved him for it, the crowd loved him for it, and John never lost his appetite for that certain feeling he got when leather swished into netting – particularly when he found himself labouring through the occasional barren spell.

There comes a time in a biographer's life when he has to decide whether or not he likes and admires his subject. In the case of John Atyeo, one of the writers of this book was never in serious doubt. He had idolised him from the terraces as a child and when, for a number of seasons towards the end of the great man's life, he found himself sitting close to him in the grandstand at Ashton Gate, he very soon realised he was modest though far from shrinking, mischievously funny in his manner, full of good sense and oddly courtly in an old-fashioned, rural way. Through it all, he was proud of being John Atyeo of Bristol City and England.

What convinced the other author of Atyeo's personal merits, having watched him play often enough but never having come remotely close to knowing him, was the testimony of those who did. In footballing terms these range from Stanley Matthews downwards, but what arguably speaks most highly of the man, and explains all we need to know about the extraordinary choices he made in his life and career, comes from his former pupils of Kingdown, the Warminster secondary school at which he taught for almost a quarter of a century. These are not star-struck youngsters grown up into lifelong keepers of the flame. They have clearly never read about him on the sports pages in their lives; in their written recollections, one calls him 'Ateyo', unconsciously repeating the mistake of the printers of the Portsmouth programme when he made his League debut in 1950, while a young woman begins her account with 'Mr Atyeo (is that how you spell it?)'; but she goes on to describe him as 'the best teacher I ever had, and a great bloke, too', while asking 'did he really play for Bristol City with those funny shaped legs?' One of her schoolmates saw him as 'one of the most caring persons ever to grace the halls of Kingdown... he practically dragged some students into passing their maths O Levels'; and just to prove how far removed he was from the days when he was a household name, another ex-pupil describes how he was 'quite surprised one day when I was browsing through an encyclopaedia of football and stumbled across a photo of him'. There is also the story of how he conspired with senior colleagues to summon a Liverpool fan pupil to the deputy head's room with a stern warning, only to hand him the ultimate present anyone could have given him a few days before an F.A. Cup final. The students knew him as just plain John – behind his back, at least; he was too handy with a ruler on the wrist to be taken liberties with, though caring and gruff kindness were the cornerstones of his teaching career.

More of school life in due course. In short, these recollections tell us that John Atyeo was a good man, a dedicated worker within a small, unpretentious community and most of all, someone who off the field – and after all, most of even the most prodigious sportsman's life is lived off the field – was simply happy to merge in with the crowd. 'I've not got much to tell you about John. He was so ordinary': the writers of this book have heard the phrase time and time again, before the reluctant informant goes on to relate an act of athletic prowess of which few others of his day were capable, or the time he told the League Champions Pompey they could keep their trip to Sunderland because he was playing for Westbury United in the Amateur Cup qualifiers, or the time at the wicket when he majestically headed a rearing ball away for four byes and wondered why everybody else on the ground was lying on the floor laughing.

He was not ordinary in that unlike many other footballers of his ability after the lifting of the maximum wage in 1961, he did not drive an E-type or even a Capri and go chasing the birds down at Tiffany's. He was not ordinary in that, for all his talent, he never really thought full-time football was a proper job for a grown man, tried to make sure he always had another string to his bow and was thoroughly miserable in the few seasons when he did not. He was not ordinary when, after his playing days were over, he did not fully capitalise on media offers to which the door was already half-open. He was not ordinary in craving the ordered, predictable everyday life he helped thousands of people escape for a couple of hours every winter Saturday afternoon for fifteen years. In the end, the cheery banter with old admirers at Ashton Gate once a fortnight was the perfect counterpoint to a week in the workaday classrooms and corridors of a country comprehensive school. It was enough of the not-quite-ordinary to make him slump back into his car with relief at five o'clock, let the traffic clear a bit as he tuned in to the results and then drive cheerfully home to Ruth and reality in Warminster.

This is not a book about sporting plain-sailing. John Atyeo was an outstanding servant of Bristol City Football Club but never a pushover. Those two descriptions equally applied to Harry Dolman, the club's long-time chairman, and there were several differences of opinion between the two of them over the years, usually concerned with the terms of John's contract and, to sum it up in a word, money. In retrospect, there must clearly have been times when the club would willingly have traded John's services for a £30,000 cheque from one of the giants, justifying the move with bland but not wholly unreasonable talk of 'not wanting to stand in the lad's way'; running a medium-sized football club, after all, has a lot to do with paying the bills and keeping the bank manager happy, and in this respect, the legendary Atyeo loyalty was not always to Bristol City's immediate advantage. Another point of controversy was the dressing-room turmoil when Peter Doherty was manager, and there were those who looked in vain to Big John for leadership in healing the rift of the notorious split camp of season 1959-60. He was a strong enough man in every way to have helped point the way forward; the club he loved was certainly in need of a way forward; but this time, at least, he could not or would not deliver in that disastrous relegation season. These were dark days, both off the field and on, and some of the things that happened haunted John Atyeo for the rest of his life.

After he had retired, with high ambitions to do well in a demanding new career and the responsibilities of a growing young family that by 1970 would add up to five children, there was a spell when he had little time for Ashton Gate, and there was every reason to believe that the new regime at the club had little time for him. For several seasons he found himself watching what little football he did get to see some distance from Bristol but towards the end of his life, there he was back again, up in the stand among the men and women in red to whom he was more special than any other footballer in the world. If it was simply his old Kingdown pupil Rob Newman who had brought him back, that was a happy coincidence; his relationship with City was rather different from what was happening at Stoke, Preston and Bolton, where those clubs' home-grown idols and his former England team-mates Stanley Matthews, Tom Finney and Nat Lofthouse were cosseted and feted as national treasures and matchday VIPs; but as far as his admirers in the stand were concerned, John Atyeo was back at the Gate, they hung on his every word, God was in his heaven and all was right with the world.

CHAPTER 2

DEPRESSION YEARS BABY

For hundreds of years, records showed Atyeos living only in mid-Somerset, with slightly later forays into Dorset and Devon. In medieval times the clan was concentrated in the neighbouring communities of Langport, Othery, Stoke St Gregory, Middlezoy and Weston Zoyland, the 'yeo' part of their name taken from the local pronunciation of 'ea', which was the Old English word for 'river'. Various Yeo rivers and streams still flow in these parts, not least the one that passes through Yeovil. By coincidence, the first known of these 'dwellers by the river', recorded in the Somerset Subsidy Roll of 1327, was John atte Yo (or Yoo). A Roger atte Yo was living across the border in Devon at much the same time as him and was noted there in 1333. To the football world our hero was forever 'At-ee-o', but here, history tells us that the apparently casual and lazy 'Atyo' pronunciation is far nearer the mark.

The word 'yeoman', an antiquated term for farmers, tradesmen and other members of the early English middle classes in country districts, comes from a different source: the Oxford Dictionaries, not wholly convincingly, surmise that it is a corruption of 'young man'. However, the term also brings to mind someone upright, sturdy, honest and trustworthy, and there is no doubt at all that in his playing days, John Atyeo, the big man from the West, seemed to epitomise all the finest qualities of yeoman service. Plain John with a trusty, reliable name as rustic as russet apples and haystacks: that is how football fans all over the country learned to know and admire him.

Not many out-and-out mysteries will be found in the John Atyeo story. The major one, without a doubt, centres on his reluctance to spread his wings from Bristol City and the lower divisions. Another lies in his reasons for leaving Portsmouth; and a third is why he allowed the myth to perpetuate that he was a Wiltshire man, born, bred and resident well into his adult life at Dilton Marsh, a straggling village a couple of miles to the west of Westbury. 'The second largest village in Wiltshire', they used to say of it, though the spread of new housing developments in the county in recent years has thrown such traditional certainties into disarray. Bred there and resident there John most certainly was, but his place of birth was Standerwick, less than two miles away from Dilton Marsh on the Frome side. Less than two miles away, but rather importantly, on the other side of the boundary between Wiltshire and Somerset; the fact is that for all his Moonraker credentials, his county sporting honours and his intimate ties with Westbury, Trowbridge and Warminster, John Atyeo, true to his name, was a native son of Somerset.

Peter John Walter Atyeo was born the only child of Walter and Effie Atyeo, née Noad, at their cottage home in Marsh Road, Standerwick on Sunday, February 7, 1932, in the depths of the Depression years. His three names were the first intimation that here was a sportsman coming into the world; cricket-loving Walter dreamed from the start that he would bat for Somerset, and he knew those three initials on the scorecard would give him equal billing to the toffs who were prominent in the game at that time. When John was in his sporting prime, the England cricket captain was the Charterhouse-educated P. B. H. May; P. J. W. Atyeo would have had an equally distinguished ring to it.

Effie was well into her thirties when little Peter came along, old to be having her first child in those days – an 'elderly primigravida' in the unforgiving language of the medical profession – and this made his arrival all the more special for the couple, even though the only birth deemed to be of interest to readers of the *Somerset Standard* that week was a baby girl born on the 12th to Robert Cathcart Bruce of Kent and his wife, who was one of the Hendersons of Berkley House. Walter originated from deep in Atyeo country, the Charlton Mackrell and Charlton Adam area near Somerton in Somerset, and so did Effie; they had moved to the far east of the county with his work as a (then) relief signalman with the Great Western Railway, and only rarely had contact with the folk back home after that. Many of the couple's new neighbours worked on the land, or would have done if the jobs had been there; in the month Peter was born, the local paper was urging unemployed men and women to think about going out to Jersey for six weeks in May to join the three thousand casual workers needed for the potato harvest: return fares would be paid, accommodation was free and 'good wages can be earned'; so many people grew their own vegetables and kept some sort of livestock in rural England at that time that there was still food of sorts on the table come early February – potatoes, turnips, maybe carrots, to go with the bread – but meat was by now a luxury for many families, and at least one local butcher was slashing his prices and urging shoppers to compare them with what he was charging a year previously. Pigs' heads were fourpence a pound. 'Better leave the eyes in, because it's got to see us through the week...'

The Atyeos saw the deprivation around them, and learned to value even more Walter's steady, regular income. Living in Somerset, Peter first went to school in Standerwick's neighbouring village of Berkley, at the small Victorian schoolhouse there, a stone's throw from his home, with a picturesque little Georgian church as its immediate neighbour. It is strange that, as a bright and intelligent child well capable of remembering the pre-Dilton Marsh years, he later chose to expunge both Standerwick and Berkley from his public recollections, particularly as they were always there on his doorstep to remind him and Somerset, after all, was his beloved father's county. Perhaps just as odd is the fact that so few Somerset people, bombarded by endless talk of Atyeo the Wiltshire Moonraker in his years of glory, did not occasionally pipe up and say 'now hold on a minute...' In Berkley itself there are still people who have clear memories of his school days there, and can point out the cottage where he lived. It is also part of Atyeo family folklore that the little boy broke his leg in the garden there, at the age of five, when playing around the hen coop. He never suffered a similar injury throughout his playing career.

It was very shortly after Dilton Marsh Halt was opened in 1937 that the Atyeos moved east across the Wiltshire border to Glenthorne, the house on Dilton's High Street in which John Atyeo would live for much of his life. Yes, Peter Atyeo was John, all of a sudden. At the village school at Berkley his little class-mates simply followed their teacher's lead and called him by his proper name, but by the time he was seven or eight at Dilton Marsh, Effie was upset to hear his new pals addressing him as 'Pete'. She would not have her Peter suffering that indignity, so she simply moved one step to the right in his string of names and started calling him John. They would not shorten that. As it turned out, they did not lengthen it much, either, throughout his life. There would be talk of 'Johnny' this and 'Johnny' that on the terraces, but only extremely rarely in print was he anything other than John.

The halt, apart from being closely allied to Walter's work, also played a significant role in his son's life. Many of his footballing adventures would begin and end there, right through to his England days, while it was on the ten-minute journey between there and school in Trowbridge that he met the girl who was to become his wife. Ruth Harraway lived five minutes down the line at Warminster and was a pupil at his school's sister girls' high. In the early years they did not have too much to talk about apart from maths homework and nasty teachers, but as time went by he would be boarding the train with ever more exciting news from the morning's post as county and schoolboy international honours came his way. Dilton Marsh Halt opened as part of the Great Western's inter-war policy of siting small stations close to growing communities – but as was often the case with the G.W.R., it was not all that close, being right on the fringe of the village at the Westbury end. The walk there would have been quite a burden to older people living in the heart of the village or on the Frome side, but of course to Big John it was simply an easy five-minute lope away, with the added bonus of a glimpse of the Westbury White Horse on a distant hillside. The poet laureate John Betjeman wrote a short poem about Dilton Marsh Halt, a pleasant fact diminished by the truth that it was produced in old age and very possibly the worst thing he ever did. The two platforms, separated by the road bridge, have been rebuilt since John's time and are no longer made of sleepers, but they are still resolutely stark and utilitarian. Now simply Dilton Marsh, it is a request stop station where passengers signal to the driver to let them on as if hailing a bus. Bristol Temple Meads is fifty-eight minutes to the north, the Portsmouth suburban station of Fratton all of an hour and forty minutes to the south. That latter journey seemed a long, long way to the Atyeo family more than half a century ago.

John would talk lovingly about the big orchard beside his home, which created the impression of a rambling farmhouse of a building. In fact Glenthorne is a semi-detached house that would not look out of place in a late Victorian or Edwardian city suburb and unusual, for this red-brick village, in having a stone-clad facade. It looks smaller than average from the road, but stretches back a good way to provide more than adequate accommodation for an average-sized family. The orchard was sold in 1990 for half a dozen homes to be built on it in two terraces, with plenty of communal space around them, and the development could only be known as Atyeo Close. Here young John's school was just a minute's walk away, in the heart of a village which in his childhood days consisted of the massively four-square St Mary's church, with a great squat Norman tower which in reality, like much of the rest of the village, dates from no longer ago than the middle years of the nineteenth century; the King's Arms pub, now just a memory, but with its brewery's sign clinging resolutely to it still; the small post office; and, just a little way beyond, the Dilton Memorial Hall, with a foundation stone laid on New Year's Day, 1921, to record that it was 'erected in memory of the brave lads of Dilton who served in the Great War'. It was unusual in those times – and is in these times, for that matter – for memorial stone inscriptions to be couched in such unassuming, everyday terms, and it tells us much about the unpretentious community in which the Atyeos found themselves; there was a tannery there, for instance, for two hundred or more years, and there are rarely any airs and graces about tanning folk. A brick and tile works, iron quarries and a cloth mill added further to Dilton's hard-working credentials.

Facilities there these days include a Chinese chip shop and the Crowning Glory hair salon. The Prince of Wales free house out on the Standerwick side is small, cosy and welcoming, but there are no mementoes of the local hero on its walls. Neither does the village Internet website feel the need to record his links with the community. John Atyeo might have loved the place – 'I weighed up the prospect of living in a city like London or Liverpool, but Dilton had a kind of hold on me', he reflected in 1970 – but it must be said that his name is only occasionally invoked there today. The feeling is that had he not done that smart piece of business with the orchard in 1990, there would not even be an Atyeo Close to record that once a giant walked there.

The player would look back on that orchard with particular affection. Apart from growing apples, his mother kept hens there, and to the end of his playing days he would take eggs and fruit in to Ashton Gate to sell to the lads from the boot of his car after training. Doubtless the cash for them went to her, but that was a subtlety lost on the players, who laughingly regarded it as another sign of his money-minded ways. More important, John saw that orchard as 'sacred ground', since it was there that he was given his first tuition in both football and cricket by his parents. 'I know every inch of it,' he recalled in 1970. 'I have spent countless hours there, and even today I go out there quite often, getting the kind of practice you need for every kind of sport.' When John's prowess as a hurdler led him to county and national recognition, Walter put up three makeshift hurdles in the orchard, all the correct height and with the right number of strides between them; the only way they would fit in was by putting them on a curve. The boy very nearly became English schools champion on this kind of preparation.

The cricket coaching also came from Walter, who, by repute at least, at one time swore he would rather John played the summer game for Somerset than football for England; he was not heard to say that very often after a foggy afternoon of glory under the floodlights at Wembley in November, 1955, but there is no doubt that cricket was always his first love, and when John was a boy he would bowl tirelessly at him in the orchard, hour after hour. Effie, on the other hand, had novel ways of sharpening up the lad's football skills, with the simplistic but admirable thought in her mind that all the game is really about is banging the ball into the back of the net as hard and as often as possible. She would prop an old tin tray against an apple tree and encourage John to shoot at it from all angles and distances. He claimed that for all his early promise as a schools, local league and county and international youth player, he received no real professional coaching until he joined Portsmouth in 1950: 'It just came naturally to me.' Naturally, with more than a little help from mum.

There is also a playing field in Dilton Marsh on which young boys today, more than a hundred of them, all told, take part regularly in organised soccer. It speaks of the forethought that now goes into childhood football, and the enthusiasm and dedication of large numbers of parents, teachers and youth workers, and we can be sure that if there is another John Atyeo out there he will not spend his first couple of senior years as a boy in the rough, tough man's world of Westbury United. He will have been signed up by Arsenal, Manchester United or Chelsea before he has reached his ninth birthday. In John's younger years, however, the playing field was still a place for kickabouts with coats for goals, while throughout his career he would trot around it on training runs in his gym shoes, long shorts and an old sweater. 'We would kick a ball about until it was dark,' he recalled of his boyhood at the height of his fame, 'and always I was the last to leave. Some of the others would get tired and drift away home. Others would lose interest and go off to the pictures in town, but I never got tired and I never lost interest. It wasn't until it was too dark to see any more that I reluctantly gave up chasing and booting our ball about.' Another of the kids on the park, a couple of years older, was John's neighbour Ivor Compton, who was later a team-mate at Westbury United and went on to play for Trowbridge and Yeovil Town.

No one at Dilton Marsh School or indeed at home at Glenthorne was surprised when John passed his scholarship to go to Trowbridge Boys' High School in September 1943. He was a keen and good-natured scholar and an only child on whom the Atyeos lavished care and attention far above and beyond their games with him in the orchard. Like all youngsters graduating from tight-knit village class-rooms, he was bewildered by what awaited him at the 'big school' for a term or two, and it is not until the Christmas of his second year, 1944, that his name appears in the school magazine *The Wing* for the first time, listed as right-half in Farleigh house's junior football team. In the summer 1945 issue he is recorded as fourth in the under-15s high jump at the school sports, and there is no reason to suppose that he is any kind of athlete or leader at all until the summer of 1946, by which time he has risen to the modest heights of Farleigh house's junior cricket captain. For a boy who would be playing centre-forward for the Football League champions in four years' time, pulling on the white Three Lions shirt in youth internationals and representing his county in four major sports, these were remarkably low-key formative years.

The tempo begins to quicken in 1947 when, still only 15, he has graduated to the school's first cricket XI and is singled out for special praise in *The Wing* for the first time. In a house match for Farleigh against Brooke, he took five wickets for eight runs and 'played a valu-able innings' in scoring thirty-four not out. In the school sports he won the under-16s long jump with a leap of sixteen feet two inches, as well as the hurdles, and the writer of the Farleigh notes, the source of some of his earliest rave reviews, called him a 'tower of strength' at full-back in the house soccer team. That phrase was to be applied to him in three different sports at Trowbridge High before his time there was through. Indeed, it was with him for the rest of his sporting life. In rugby, too, he was beginning to excel, and *The Wing* of Christmas 1947 reported that 'Atyeo has impressed tremendously as centre-threequarter, and his kicking and tackling have been of a very high order'. This was the time Westbury United were inviting him along to taste life at their Meadow Lane ground, and his horizons were about to widen in ways he would not have believed possible even twelve months earlier. Now the sky was the limit – and that was the way it stayed until the time, in the next decade, when he opted to apply limits of his own making and choosing.

Those who were at school with boys who went on to become League footballers will know that by and large they fell into two categories. Feckless, skinny, pimply youths forever being caned for smoking (and worse) behind the bike sheds or glorious, strapping, Corinthian games captains. For those caught in between these two extremes at the age of sixteen, the one kind could be just as nauseating as the other, and come 1948 there must have been plenty of non-sporty types who muttered into their Vimtos about Atyeo-this, Atyeo-that all over the school magazine, as well as having to read about his deeds of derring-do for Westbury United and Frome Cricket Club in the local rag every week. Who did he think he was? Captain Marvel or somebody?

In the Wiltshire County Schools Athletics Championships at Nelson Haden School in Trowbridge in June 1948 he became the county's champion hurdler, as well as finishing second in the high jump. Wiltshire being a small rural county without endless resources of talent, his time in the hurdles was not of the kind that would have prompted the men in blazers to send him to the national championships if they had been in Manchester or York, but they were not. They were at the Recreation Ground in Bath, so he went along for the ride, found himself battling into the final and eventually came from complete also-ran to take second place and the silver medal. In the national elite at athletics and on the verge of representing his country at football: 1948 was the year in which John Atyeo's name became known beyond the confines of Wiltshire.

That silver medal in the All England Schools Athletics Championships remained one of his proudest sporting mementoes until the end. 'I really owe it to my old P.E. master, Jock Burns,' he recounted years later. 'It was really won by gamesmanship. I was always keen on athletics and did practically every event possible. I was essentially a sprinter and a jumper, and hurdling was my speciality. Jock Burns was a hurdler of international standard, and he coached Johnny Adlam, a younger boy from the same village as me, to win at the All England championships at Hull in the previous year. Warming up before the race at Bath, I wore an old cricket sweater and a pair of flannels. All the other fellows had smart tracksuits with the names of their clubs emblazoned all over the place. They were drinking all sorts of secret potions, and it didn't do my confidence much good, but I struggled through the first round and managed to get in second place. Then, in the semi-final, the chap who was leading hit a hurdle and fell, so I finished second again. The final was a couple of hours later, after torrential rain. There were six of us and Jock said: "You'll finish last. You're the worst of the six", and of course I was. But then he said he had studied the starter very carefully; he allowed no gap between the "set" and the "off" – "So when he says set, you get going." That's exactly what happened. I was off like a hare with a two or three yard lead. When you're in front you can always perform better, and I ran the race of my life. I led until the last hurdle, when I was overtaken, but I finished second, beaten by a yard.' The winner was Dave Kay, who went on to become an athletics coach for the West Country. 'He's been to my school in the last year or so and we talked about the race,' Big John reminisced in 1970. 'But he never mentioned that dodgy start!'

In cricket in 1948 he was described as 'the outstanding player of the year', with much of the burden of bowling and batting falling on him. Once more he was declared 'a tower of strength'. That having been said, Trowbridge High was a fiercely competitive sporting school, and he topped neither the batting nor bowling averages; he ran up the best individual score of the season, however, with fifty-six in a drawn game against Chippenham Grammar School. He was now captain of the Farleigh house cricket XI, and took six for ten against Gaunt after top scoring with thirty-six. In rugby, *The Wing* reported, 'Atyeo has been a tower of strength. His defensive kicking has gained yards for his forwards, but his strong running, elusive swerve and cutting-through have brought him and his team-mates many tries. Moreover, his place kicking and drop kicks have been invaluable. Atyeo has scored eighty-three points in ten games – a most remarkable feat.' A year on, at Christmas 1949, it was a very similar story, although by now it was noted that he was the rugby team's star performer only in 'all games in which he has played'. Other pressures, both sporting and academic, were clearly beginning to home in on him. Nevertheless, he was still notable in the first XV for his fast running, swerve and a sidestep that was making him 'quite a master' of selling the dummy. Once again, his strong and accurate kicking had 'saved his forwards lots of work and made yards for his side in defence'. Another factor in his favour was obviously his size and strength – almost grown to his full six feet before he was sixteen, which was a rarer phenomenon in the post-war austerity years than it is today.

The school played rugby before Christmas and football in the spring term. When John first went to Trowbridge High he was as anti-rugger as a soccer man could be, but of course his kicking skills and beautiful balance caught the eye of the masters who organised the oval ball game, and he was sucked in. Apart from taking all the place kicks, he used to love running with the ball and was just as proud of that 'dummy-selling' technique as the magazine writer was impressed by it. 'I'm sure that's how I developed my body swerve for football,' he recalled. 'I developed a technique of throwing my weight one way and darting off in the other direction. This used to give me an easy passage past the full-back and give me dozens of points at school. Once I started playing professional football, I used it. Many people who watched me in my early days will remember it, I'm sure – but it all came from playing rugby for the school, and then for the county. I needed room to do it at City, and I often got it. In those days the defenders weren't so adept at grabbing you or standing in your path as they seem to be today. I was rather sorry to pack up rugby, because I began to enjoy it. I was something of a manufactured player – I played in the soccer way, I would fly-kick the ball into touch, for example, and I never did fancy dropping on the ball! I've got into quite a few arguments about the respective merits of soccer and rugby over the years. There are a lot of similarities between the two, but I'm convinced soccer is the more difficult game to master.'

In the summer of 1949 the football notes in *The Wing* were written by the school football captain, P. J. Atyeo. By this time, of course, he had been John for years, but in his early days at the High, before he was known, he was P. Atyeo in the magazine. There was no danger of that now. His long report of the season's events is an early insight into the essential Atyeo – unremittingly modest, but leaving no-one in any doubt about his place in the firmament. First of all the three teachers in charge of the team are thanked for their efforts. There is then special mention of 'our faithful linesman, Jones, who never failed to turn up in all winds and weather to carry out his tricky job', and the article continues: 'It is hard to single out any particular player as outstanding, as the team spirit was so predominant.' John then goes through the team player by player – the reliable and safe keeper, the fast and fearless full-backs, the 'tower of strength' – yet another – at centre half, and two wing-halves who helped assure that 'much of the success of the first XI was due to a great half-back line'. Then there were the forwards: 'The wingers were fast and elusive, seldom wasting an opportunity, and they centred accurately. The inside men were great schemers, never failing to keep the forward line moving with well-judged ground passes, enabling the centre-forward to round off the good work started by the rest of the team.' There are no prizes for guessing the name of the centre-forward in question, but a list is helpfully appended, detailing the team's full programme for the season, with all goalscorers credited. Ten games were won and two lost, and of fifty-eight goals scored, Atyeo netted twenty-six of them. He scored in eleven of the twelve games, with two four-goal tallies, two hat-tricks and five braces. For all the glories to come, he never again managed a goal average of more than two a game for an entire season. Who would?

Maybe John would have been happy to end the report at this point – though since he was more than human enough to revel in the recognition of his talents, maybe not – but whatever, the editor of *The Wing* added this glowing postscript:

On reading these notes, it will be obvious from glancing down the list of goal scorers that Atyeo was the inspiration of the school XI. His scheming, ball control and leadership were of tremendous value to the team, but his most outstanding asset was his powerful shooting, which brought him many goals and scared quite a few goalkeepers. The success of the first XI was due, to a large extent, to Atyeo's capabilities as a player, his keen captaincy and loyalty to his team.

That loyalty stayed true to the end of his school days, as the Atyeo brand of loyalty would so famously do in the years to come, and in his final year at Trowbridge High, when he was school captain, he represented Wiltshire in the full hand of football, rugby, cricket and athletics. By this time, however, the school realised it had unearthed a gem which could no longer be confined to the playing fields of Wingfield Road, with the faithful Jones running the line. John always talked appreciatively of the school giving him a more free rein in his outside sporting activities than it might have done had it kept strictly to the book, but then again, how could it have handled such a force of nature any differently? Like all good schools, it strove to be even-handed and restrained in its praise of pupils' endeavours, making scant distinction between the efforts of the brave sloggers and the feats of the outstandingly gifted. The editor's addition to that report in the summer of 1949, however, was an admission that sometimes, maybe just once in a lifetime, all the teaching staff could do was hold up their hands and bask in the reflected glory of a seventeen-year-old genius.

The Boys' High School is no more, in name at least. It merged with the adjacent girls' school in 1969 to form a combined but still selective high school, which in 1974 was relaunched as the comprehensive John of Gaunt School, the largest of three in the town. The old boys' school's original Victorian block, with its distinctive tower, lives on, however, and so do the sports fields on a 25-acre campus that also includes tennis courts, a floodlit all-weather pitch and community sporting provisions. Big John would still have been in his element there.

Outside school, his senior football began on the village playing field with Dilton Athletic, and by the time he was fifteen he was battling it out in the tough Wiltshire League with Westbury United. In his mind's eye, at least, he would play three games a day on a Saturday – for school in the morning, for Westbury in the afternoon and for Dilton in the evening, in matches especially timed to fit in with his plans. It is hard to imagine that this was the state of affairs week-in, week-out, but his memory of such Saturdays was so clear that they really must have happened, on the odd occasion at least. In his first game for Westbury he put four past the Calne goalkeeper before going off with cramp. With twenty minutes to go it was one-all, and John was trying hard to succeed without feeling he was quite making it. Then came those four goals in six minutes and everyone on the ground agreed the kid deserved his early bath after that. Even at the height of his senior England career, he could reel off the names of the Westbury players who had looked after him when he was not much more than a child among them – Charlie Hodgson, Harold Dudley, Jack Smith, the pre-war Portsmouth player Wilf Alford: 'I shall always remember their help, and be grateful.'

Looking back on his time with the club he echoed the generous spirit of his report in *The Wing* by saying: 'Westbury had a very powerful side in those days, and this gave me the chance to score plenty of goals.' That having been said, he always insisted 'the school came first for me', just as, a couple of years later, Westbury came first when Portsmouth called him up to lead their line at Sunderland. It was a golden age for Westbury. In his brief spell there John won two Wiltshire League championship medals, and on the day he was not at Roker Park he helped them reach the first round proper of the F.A. Amateur Cup, away at Brentwood and Warley. 'For us to travel so far was like a struggling Third Division team reaching Wembley,' he would always say. They drew the game at Brentwood nil-nil, but lost the replay at home in front of a crowd of nearly three thousand.

It was when he was sixteen that he won a trial for the Wiltshire county youth team, which to the end of his days he described rather touchingly as 'my first break'. It was at a ground in Salisbury, and he would always look out for it from the coach when Bristol City were on their travels to the South Coast. 'I've always considered that's where it all started for me,' he would muse. He was picked at centre-half, went up to score two goals from corners and was then taken off, which he considered a slur, as all players did before the age of tactical substitutions. He was back for the next trial, however, this time with the familiar number nine on his back, and made an immediate impact when he was inevitably picked for the county team. He scored a hat-trick in each of his first two games, a seven-nil win over Dorset in Devizes and a six-three beating of Somerset at Twerton Park, Bath, and this team of largely country boys enjoyed a good run in the national county youth tournament before being knocked out by Essex at Swindon Town's ground. By this time, League club scouts were rubbing shoulders on the touchline and pretending they were watching anybody but Wiltshire's big centre-forward. One of them was Wyndham Haines from Portsmouth, but that is anticipating events.

John's next step along the road came when he was picked as a reserve in an England youth team trial against a young Spurs side at White Hart Lane: 'I packed my case, went up to London and stayed in a hotel for the first time in my life. At half time Spurs were winning one-nil and the England team looked a bit of a shambles. The manager came over to the five reserves and asked if anyone could play outside-left. I immediately stuck up my hand, though I'd never played there in my life, but I was determined to have a go at getting in the side, and would have played in goal if necessary. In those days, the fellow with number eleven on his back just stayed on the touchline waiting for the ball, but that wasn't for me. I'd been given my chance, and I decided to play the way I knew best, as a sort of inside-left-cum-centre-forward. In the first few minutes of the half I side-footed in the equaliser from a right wing centre, and then I took a return pass to crash in the winner. When the team to play Scotland at Carlisle was announced a few days later, I was in at inside-left.'

John joined the England squad at the start of the 1949-50 home nations youth tournament, the prize for the winners being a trip to Vienna for an eight-nation youth international competition. He scored twice at Brunton Park in that first international, in which Scotland were beaten seven-one, and good results against Wales and Ireland ensured that it would be England whose motor coach would be on the Channel ferry bound for Austria. It was John's first journey abroad, and it seemed a long, long way to him. England played Luxembourg in blazing heat in the first round and somehow contrived to lose to them two-one; they won their second game, against Switzerland, by the same margin after extra time on a quagmire of a pitch, but this was not good enough to send them through to the semi-finals. That was it, goodnight Vienna. Austria beat France three-two in the final, Holland put Luxembourg in their place by thrashing them six-one for the third place spot, and goal average put England fifth overall. It must be said it was not the most distinguished youth team ever to wear the Three Lions, with John going on to be the highest achiever of the bunch by quite a margin. The only other player in the team to make any kind of a name for himself was the wing-half Tony Marchi, an Italian North Londoner who was in and out of the Spurs team for years, as well as being a somewhat incongruous export to Juventus for a short while. Another Wiltshire boy in the squad was John Skull of Swindon, a Wolves junior who went on to play thirty-three games for his home town team in the late 1950s as a goalscoring right winger, while the right-back Don Campbell played a little for Liverpool in the Second Division and a lot for Crewe when they were a desperate basement team of the Football League. Goalkeeper Arthur Evans from Bury made just two first-team starts at Gigg Lane and a handful for Gillingham, forward Derek Barley was released from the Arsenal junior ranks to play hardly at all for Queen's Park Rangers and Aldershot, and no other member of the side came anywhere near to League action.

After watching the two final games, the England squad joined the other teams at a banquet and collected, if not medals, at least souvenirs of their stay. The following day they returned to England – 'we flew home by air', as goalie Evans rather charmingly reported – and a special treat as they were circling over London was the sight of a packed Lord's cricket ground below. John learned to loathe flying, but this first time, in among a dozen or more excited young boys of his age, he simply let the experience take over. He had not achieved a massive amount on his travels. The best action he had seen had come in the Luxembourg game, when he had risen to deflect a Campbell shot, and the goalkeeper had somehow changed direction in mid air and clawed it away. Along with a few other might-have-beens, this was not very much to look back on; nevertheless, it was plain that suddenly there was more than the Westbury White Horse on his horizon, even though it was to White Horse country that he would return for the rest of his days.

CHAPTER 3

POMPEY CHIMES

When Portsmouth started showing a serious interest in John Atyeo, they were at quite an advantage over other contenders. Their pre-war centre-forward Wyndham Haines ran a pub at North Bradley, near Frome, and his approach to the boy and his father Walter was more that of a friendly neighbour with very good contacts than of some anonymous stranger in a fawn mac and a trilby. 'Rub shoulders with me, and you'll play for England,' he told the lad. Better still for the Atyeos, Windy was so rustic, so bucolic that he almost (though not quite) made Walter look like Noel Coward in terms of polished sophistication. The Fratton Park crowd used to serenade him with *To be a Farmer's Boy* when he was banging in the goals that helped push Pompey to the heights of the First Division for the first time in 1927, and when he talked of the club it was from an essentially Somerset-Wiltshire borders perspective. Just before Christmas, 1949, he arranged for the lad and his dad to meet the Portsmouth manager, Bob Jackson, and an amateur contract was swiftly drawn up. Within a week of signing it, John found himself in the number nine shirt against Southampton Reserves at the Dell. The Saints ran Portsmouth ragged in a five-nil win, and the seventeen-year-old felt he never had a look-in, despite encouraging support from his seasoned inside-forwards, Duggie Reid and Cliff Parker.

Slumped in the coach back to Portsmouth he looked the picture of misery, but the chairman, James Chinneck, cheered him when he came up and said quietly: 'Never mind, lad. We'll give you another chance.' After the boss had gone back to his seat, John was joined by Windy Haines, 'and as he came and sat next to me I forgot my disappointment as we went through the match all over again, move by move. He pointed out my mistakes, and how to remedy them. When the coach reached Portsmouth I was ready to play the next match right then.' In fact he had to wait to see whether he had been

32

selected for it – but he had, and this time he hit the kind of form that had attracted Pompey in the first place. It was after he scored both goals in a two-one Combination win over Millwall in March, 1950 that he was selected to play for England Youth against Northern Ireland in Belfast.

As if signing for a Football League club was not enough for an ambitious country boy, the Portsmouth of the late Forties and early Fifties was no ordinary set-up. Nowhere better epitomised the rise of football as a spectator sport after the Second World War than Pompey; men simply wanted to get back to the old certainties, old friends, old allegiances in their everyday lives, while questioning deeper political and social issues, and if there was one town that had a surfeit of men, it was Portsmouth. The Royal Navy was still geared up and on the alert, with one devastating war out of the way but pockets of the Far East, Middle East and Africa in turmoil and the Cold War looming ever more ominously. By their tens of thousands sailors with time on their hands on weekend leave would flock through the Fratton turn-stiles, their white caps dusting the vast open terraces like snow on a hillside. Crowds like this deserved the best team in the land and for two years they got it. Their boys in blue won successive First Division championships in 1948-49 and 1949-50, all to the uproarious accompaniment of one of the greatest football anthems of them all, the *Pompey Chimes*. This was the kind of club John Atyeo was joining. It was not a case of 'Portsmouth? Well, maybe.' It was emphatically 'Portsmouth? Portsmouth?? Yes! Yes! Yesss!!'

Not that the Atyeos' attitude towards the League Champions was ever as ecstatic as that, and John made only spasmodic appearances for Portsmouth reserves, distracted as he was by school sport and exams, county and international call-ups and his loyalty to Westbury United. He liked picking up his expenses for turning out in Pompey's colours and spent them on the best sports gear he could afford, but while his parents were adoringly supportive of his footballing ambitions, that did not extend to encouraging him to go professional; anything but. Walter was *en route* to rising from signalman to railways inspector in the Westbury area, but there was not a lot of money coming in. 'It wasn't a struggle at home, but my parents worked very hard for what they'd got,' John recalled. 'They were very careful, and there was no extravagance. Neither I nor my mother has smoked or drank, and my father only smoked a little. It was a thrifty household.' It should be added that he was not averse to the odd drink as the years passed by, but always in moderation.

He explained: 'My father wasn't sold on the idea of professional football at all. When I passed my school certificate he told me to forget football and get myself a steady job that would keep me for the rest of my life. At about this time I applied to go to Loughborough Training College. I didn't think I'd have much difficulty getting in, with my sporting background. I actually received the prospectus, but these plans were shelved for about fifteen years!' He left the exact nature of this 'shelving' obscure, but it sounds very much as if Walter had intervened, and guided the boy towards quantity surveying, the sensible nine-to-five job on the doorstep which, in the final analysis, went no way to providing the job-for-life security John's father, ever-mindful of the Depression years, thought it would. Quantity surveyors deal with the financial side of construction and engineering, spending some time on site but most of their day in a collar and tie in the office, preparing plans and costings. A couple of generations ago it was the kind of post many a manual-working father would have been nudging his bright son towards, safe and understandable and home-based. It was not until John and his further-educated wife Ruth had started a family of their own that going to college became a feasible option in the Atyeo household. The irony, in his case, was that the here-today-and-gone-tomorrow trade of football gave John Atyeo a wage for years longer than the building industry did; and when he did eventually go on to study, it was not as a young prince at Loughborough, the country's pre-eminent seat of sporting learning and innovation, but as a mature student at a routine West Country teacher training college.

These were the competing pressures crowding in on the boy's life during his brief spell at Portsmouth; these and the ever-present spectre of two years away on National Service that hovered over every young man of John's generation when he reached eighteen. A myth: when Atyeo P. J. W. went before the Army medical board, he was turned down for having fallen arches, more commonly known as flat feet. A nice story, but simply not true. The real reason was psoriasis, a non-contagious, lifelong disease that generally appears as patches of raised red skin covered by a flaky white build-up of dead skin cells usually known as scale. These scale patches or lesions most commonly appear on the scalp, knees, elbows and torso, are often itchy and can be painful, as John knew all too well from an early age. Because of their genes, some people are more likely to develop it, but a trigger is usually necessary, and this can include emotional stress, injury to the skin, some types of infection and reaction to certain drugs. Could that broken leg and its aftermath have had something to do with it? Maybe. What is certain is that John had all the classic symptoms, was plagued by the disease to a greater or lesser degree all his life, and suffered from one of its most damaging complications in his later years. Incidentally, it also gave him his trademark haircut. It was psoriasis of the scalp that made him wear his hair a good length, treated regularly with Vaseline hair tonic.

Portsmouth used him very sparingly at the beginning of the following season, but they turned to him in spectacular fashion in their hour of need on November 11, 1950. 'Windy Haines called at my house one evening,' John recalled. 'Portsmouth were suffering from injuries and wanted me to play in the first team against Charlton Athletic at Fratton Park on Saturday. How about it? I was taken aback. My first thoughts were for the Wiltshire county side. I was due to play against Hampshire at Devizes and didn't want to let them down but First Division football was too good to miss, and I agreed to play. I was excited all week, and even more so when Windy drove me down to Fratton Park for the game. There were more than 30,000 people there, and those *Pompey Chimes* were deafening. When we went into the dressing room at half time I couldn't hear what the others were saying, with the sound of the crowd still echoing in my ears.' The game ended three-all, and John was satisfied with his performance: 'I didn't score, but I did provide the pass for Duggie Reid to get one of the goals.' As he noted, he was in the side that afternoon because of injuries, with seven regulars absent, so it was a weakened Portsmouth line-up; nevertheless, it still included such Fratton legends as Jimmy Scoular, Jimmy Dickinson and Peter Harris. Over in Blackfriars Road, Portsmouth, the typesetter at the Grosvenor Press felt so bombarded by late Pompey team changes that the home team's number nine appears as 'Ateyo' in the programme for the game. Big Sam Bartram in the Charlton goal was not as scared by John's shooting as the schoolboy 'keepers of Wiltshire had been a year or so previously, though the lad did hit the bar in the first half; on the other hand, if Atyeo had had just a little more experience he would surely have made hay against the Addicks' centre-half. The only other amateur on the pitch, he was the future Football Association secretary Ted Croker, who played only eight first-team games in his couple of years at the Valley and never pretended that his playing career was of any note.

Then ensued one of the strangest little interludes in John Atyeo's history; maybe even in football history. After the game, the eighteen-year-old was called into the boardroom where the always encouraging chairman, James Chinneck, was once more complimentary about his performance. Several other directors were there – the vice-chairman Alderman Privett and Messrs Cribb, Sparshatt and Hiley Jones, pillars of the local community, all – and they were equally up-beat. It would be pleasant to add that the club president, Field Marshal Lord Montgomery of Alamein, was also in the room, but there is no record that he was. The board's message, however, was simple. Next week's game would be against Sunderland at another of the great post-war arenas, Roker Park, and they would like John to be up there to lead the Portsmouth line once again; it was an irresistible offer – unless you were John Atyeo, in which case it was a matter of thanks but no thanks.

'I have never liked to break promises, and I had told Westbury United I would definitely play for them that week,' he recalled years later, still seemingly unaware that no other football-mad youth in the country would have found this a good reason to say no to the League champions of England. 'Westbury were playing a vital Amateur Cup tie against Bristol St. George, so I turned Portsmouth down.' Perhaps they did not believe what they heard, since his name appears at number nine for the visitors in the programme for that match at Roker on November 18, which was almost certainly printed on the eve of the game; in real life, however, he was battling it out not against England's emerging Bank of England team – the hard-as-nails Welsh centre-forward Trevor Ford had just signed for Sunderland for £20,000 from Aston Villa – but tangling with the tough lads of East Bristol. In truth, it was a big game for Westbury. They had fought through from the first qualifying round of the Amateur Cup to this, the fourth and final one, and 1,750 turned out to watch them that afternoon, paying £81 in gate money. Westbury thrashed their visitors five-one, all the goals coming in the first half, and John was like some Roy of the Rovers but more swashbuckling, banging in a couple, forcing an own goal, winning a penalty, hitting the woodwork three times... Portsmouth drew nil-all with Sunderland in front of 46,110 that afternoon, which did not sound nearly as much fun.

'The Portsmouth directors were very understanding, and mentioned my appearing for them again in a fortnight's time at Fratton Park,' John told the press after the boardroom meeting; but Windy Haines was by no means as convinced by the wisdom of his decision, and it must have been an uncomfortable journey back to Dilton Marsh that evening. 'I was more than pleased with John's display, especially in the first half,' he told a reporter. 'I'm sure he'll make the grade as a first-class player, but I feel he's missing a great opportunity in not playing against Sunderland next Saturday.' It was the first time Big John had confounded a close ally by making an unconventional decision that implied fierce loyalty, or lack of ambition, or steely independence, or naiveté, or whatever interpretation one might wish to put upon it; but it was certainly not the last.

The young man was disappointed two weeks later, when the team was announced for the game against Aston Villa at Fratton on November 25 and he was not to be seen in it; but he did play once more for Portsmouth's first team, at the end of their injury-hit Easter of 1951, when he was number nine in a one-all draw at home to Arsenal on Bank Holiday Monday, their third game in four days. He had just put five past Pinehurst in a seven-one Westbury win, but to leap straight up there to the First Division was still astonishing. A strange appearance: most of the Portsmouth record books show that he played just the single first team game, at home to Charlton, but contemporary newspaper reports confirm that he really was in the team that day, and it is time the statisticians caught up with the fact.

He had happy memories of the game right to the end: 'The team was stronger than when I first played. Now and again I look back through my cuttings just to see what a great side that was.' In fact the line-up that day was Ernie Butler, Jasper Youell, Harry Ferrier, Jimmy Scoular, Reg Flewin, Jimmy Dickinson, Peter Harris, Albert Mundy, John Atyeo, Terry Ryder and the Belgian Marcel Gaillard, and while there were indeed some very fine players out there, it was by no means a case of every man a star. John's finest moment came when he took a pass from Scoular and set up his team's only goal for Mundy. The Portsmouth programme for the next home game described his selection as a gamble, but one that had been justified, with the boy needing only 'training and experience to turn into a first-class centre-forward'. Atyeo recalled that it was after this game that Portsmouth first asked him to sign professional. That having been said, he did not always have the facts and figures of his early career at his fingertips as the years passed by. For instance, he recalled that by the time of the Arsenal game, Portsmouth were 'heading for the First Division championship'. In fact their two consecutive championship seasons were fast fading behind them, and they were very definitely on the slide; they finished seventh that season.

'My second game for Portsmouth was the last I ever played in the First Division, and I've often wondered how things would have turned out if I had been tempted by their offer that Easter,' he mused. 'I had then just about made up my mind to become a professional, and naturally, everyone thought I would be certain to sign for Portsmouth. I think I did, as well, but it wasn't quite as simple as that. Bob Jackson promised me I would be taken on their tour at the end of the season if I signed for them. It was a very tempting prospect for an eighteen-year-old but my father would have none of it.' Walter Atyeo's caution was to affect his son's career in two ways. In the short term, it rendered Portsmouth's terms and conditions unacceptable, and steered John into the incongruous existence of a part-time professional who should have outgrown that status as soon as it became clear that he had something very special to give the game. In the longer term, it imbued in Atyeo junior a reluctance to give a life in football his all – in contrast to being a one-hundred-per-cent trier out on the pitch – and that, surely, was to the ultimate detriment of both his career and his earning power.

The sticking points were Portsmouth's insistence that he should sign for them full-time and live in town, since they were unhappy at the thought of their young players driving cars; even new vehicles of that time were unreliable, and the club knew that most of its youngsters would have been able to afford nothing more than bangers, with all manner of missed training sessions and other irritating mishaps as a consequence. Looking back after his career had ended, John could see how Portsmouth had 'missed out', but never contemplated the fact that he might have done so, too. His stance was always that the club should have waived its policy for him, and he remained convinced that father knew best: 'He guided me during those early years, and steered me past the pitfalls that can make life difficult for youngsters in football. There were one or two big issues at stake, and Portsmouth would not relax their rules. I wanted to become a part-timer and I also wanted to drive a car. My father envisaged that within a year or two I would want to be driving up and down to Portsmouth but the more important drawback was over my part-time status. My father still had misgivings about football as a career, and he was insistent that I remained in my apprenticeship as a quantity surveyor. Portsmouth were then in a position to dictate to their players. They were such a famous club, and doing so well at that time. I would have gone to Portsmouth without a shadow of doubt if they had been agreeable to the conditions my father and I wanted. I don't think either of them was unreasonable. Windy Haines never ceased to rub it into them how they had missed me.'

Maybe so; but Farmer's Boy Haines also had enough love and esteem for Pompey to know that his young neighbour had missed out on them, too. Atyeo certainly missed out on the trip of a lifetime in May 1951, since one of the incentives the club had put his way was a place in the close season party to tour South America for three weeks. As it turned out, it proved a miserable time on the field, with three defeats and two draws, and another shadow was cast by the sending off of Jimmy Scoular in the first game. The referee was Arthur Ellis, the high-profile whistler from Halifax, who had travelled out with the team and was maybe just a little too keen to demonstrate his impartiality that afternoon. Jimmy Dickinson shuddered at memories of the previous summer, when he had been part of the England World Cup team that had lost surrealistically to the United States part-timers in Belo Horizonte, a wretchedly miserable upland mining town three hundred miles out of Rio, and decided for the second time in his career that you had to be nuts to want to play football in Brazil. Nevertheless, the sights, smells and sounds of this far-off continent left most of the players with lasting memories, and they could scarcely believe their eyes when a crowd not many short of 200,000 turned out to see their game against the Brazilians Fluminense at the Maracana.

Looking back, Portsmouth officials would ponder on how a boy just turned nineteen could possibly have turned his back on an exciting opportunity such as this; but then again, they did not know John Atyeo very well. All they were left with were riddles. As the 1950s rolled on, it became increasingly clear that their star was on the wane, but nevertheless, they stayed in the First Division until 1959, and who knows how many goals in the top flight Big John might have rattled in for them over those years? Who knows whether they would have been relegated at all, with him leading the line? Perhaps these questions also crossed John's mind, but at the time they were merely imponderables for the future. All he knew in the early summer of 1951 was that he was looking for a job in football – keenly, earnestly, but strictly on his and his father's terms.

CHAPTER 4

MR DOLMAN CALLS

It became a parade. A dozen clubs wanted to sign John Atyeo. 'I can't tell you exactly how many,' he said years later. 'I can only recall the people who actually came to the house to explain what they had to offer. Ted Drake of Reading, Louis Page (Swindon Town), Dave Magnall (Queens Park Rangers), and Bert Tann (Bristol Rovers) all spoke to me. Goodness knows how many others spoke to my father. People actually walked along the railway track, going from signal box to signal box, to seek him out for a chat. It soon became clear that signing for another club would take a lot of talking. At one stage I began to share my father's feelings that football was a dog fight between clubs. It was a constant squabble. So many people got involved in offering this and that, trying to pull a few strings to get me to sign. They were quite prepared to wear the doorstep out for my signature. They put forward all sorts of propositions, it all became confusing. No one offered any money, though.' Other clubs rumoured to be interested at the time included Arsenal, who would win the League championship in 1952-53 before plunging into nearly two decades of mediocrity; Arthur Rowe's Tottenham Hotspur, the current champions with their fluid push-and-run style; and Fulham, Second Division champions in 1949 but struggling to find their feet in their first spell in the top division. The list is a reminder of just how highly John was regarded as a prospect, and the kind of unwholesome scramble that could develop over a player of his talent; maybe today's *modus operandi*, in which footballers of this level of ability are formally linked to clubs from primary school age, has some merits in comparison. There might still be competition for an eight-year-old prodigy, but it is unlikely to be of the same intensity as for a youth who has already gone a long way towards establishing his credentials.

Bristol City were always in the frame. Harry Dolman had been chairman there for next to no time, but he meant business, as he did throughout his swash-buckling reign at Ashton Gate. Elected to the board on the eve of the Second World War, he had served impatiently under the chairmanship of the ageing Redcliffe Hill fish-and-chip shop owner George Jenkins until the 'Ides of March' boardroom coup in 1949, when Jenkins was ousted in a vote of no confidence after being the only board member to decline loaning the club £1,000 and making other financial guarantees. These measures were aimed at making a bold statement of intent to supporters who were still seething over the sale to Newcastle United for a paltry £8,000 of another young goalscoring sensation, twenty-year-old Roy Bentley, in the summer of 1945. Jenkins argued somewhat feebly that as the major shareholder he should not be expected to take on these extra liabilities, but his fellow directors did not see it that way, and off he went. Arthur Sperring served an extremely brief term as his successor, but his death later in 1949 let in Harry Dolman as acting chairman, and his status was formalised at the AGM of 1950.

So he had been at the helm for little more than a year when he went hunting John Atyeo in the summer of 1951, but he was no novice, either in football, business or life. A Wiltshire man born in Langley Burrell in 1897, Henry James Dolman had been a soccer man through-out his life, playing in any position from goalkeeper to centre-forward to a decent amateur standard, and later qualifying as a referee. When manpower was in short supply in the Second World War, he played up front for his works team until he was in his mid-forties, by which time he was already a City director. Harry Dolman made his money through engineering, having started in the trade at the lowest level, as a four-teen-year-old apprentice straight from school. The First World War broadened his perspective on life mightily, and after serving with the Wiltshire Regiment on the Somme and at Ypres he was transferred to the emerging Royal Flying Corps, a sector of the Army before the Royal Air Force was formed in 1918. Aircraft and flying remained passions for the rest of his days. Ambitious as always, he risked life and limb in one of his less successful ventures, the development of an early microlight known as the Flying Flea; after frequent mishaps, it became clear that the 'Flying' part of the name was little more than wishful thinking.

It was when the First World War ended that he moved to Bristol, first to study at the Merchant Venturers Technical College for eighteen months, and after that to join the engineering firm of Brecknell,

Munro and Rogers as a junior draughtsman. Seven years later, not long after he had turned thirty, his design flair earned him a place on the board; before long he was chairman of the re-formed Brecknell, Dolman and Rogers, and at work as well as at the football club there was no doubt about who was boss. Some saw his style as that of a benevolent dictator. Others were not too sure about the 'benevolent', but if that word implies doing one's best for an organisation, rather than necessarily doing it with kindness and kid gloves, then the cap fitted well enough.

Harry Dolman was a hard, tough, pragmatic man of the world who was no stranger to taking chances, but there was never any doubting his commitment. Neither should it be forgotten that he was more than simply a money man. A country boy from a hard-pressed family of seven children, he rose to become a money man only through his out-standing talent as a designer and innovator. His rapid rise to the top of his engineering company came about not because he was a ruthless wheeler-dealer and all the other things he became, but because his bosses recognised that here was a young man of quite extraordinary ability behind a drawing board. Brecknell, Dolman and Rogers came to flourish as producers of automated food packaging, vending machines and even one-armed bandits, and so much of it was down to him. The firm was part of a wider group of Bristol companies, headed by Mardon, Son and Hall and E.S. and A. Robinson, that raised the city to pre-eminence in the packaging industry in the middle years of the last century. These firms attracted scores of creative artists and designers to the West Country, but few could claim, as Dolman did, to be the brains behind more than a hundred various inventions.

From his earliest days in Bristol, as a student, Harry Dolman followed football in the city – but as his first home had been close to Eastville Stadium, as indeed his works were, on Pennywell Road, the Rovers were his first love. He became a season-ticket holder as he grew more settled, and his rapid rise to business success attracted the attention of the club's directors. In fact he attended a couple of board meetings at Eastville but was not impressed by what he saw, not least because the thrust of the discussion at each had concerned the sale of the stadium to the greyhound company, which he saw as a desperate backward step. One of his closest allies on the inside at Rovers was a fellow flying enthusiast, the former club manager Captain Albert Prince Cox, who none too loyally opined that Harry would be better

off turning his attention to Ashton Gate. With the unimpressive
George Jenkins at the helm there, Bristol City could in no way be
seen as an ambitious club on the rise, but Dolman took his friend's
advice, and few on the red side of the city regret his decision. Later,
heading a factory deeply entrenched in the blue side of town, he
would enjoy endless banter with his workers, especially on Monday
mornings after Derby games, when he would wear a red carnation if
City had won.

Harry had a little deal with the players every time they played
Rovers. He would say before a Derby: 'Same arrangement, lads?' and
if they delivered the goods, an envelope containing £55, a fiver for
each of them, would be handed to John Atyeo to be shared around after
the game. Such acts of casual rule-breaking were so common in football, when rich men could offer players on workers' wages meaningful
incentives without causing the bank manager to break into a sweat,
that they are scarcely to be remarked upon. A considerably more
serious issue is offering incentives to opponents to throw matches,
and suspicion persists that this line was overstepped in a brief and
unhappy period of the Dolman years.

More of that in due course; in the meantime, let us enjoy Harry
Dolman's best-remembered exchange with his Eastville workers. It
came in the days after the Bristol Aircraft Company had announced
hundreds of redundancies at Filton, and the union leaders at B.D.R.
had called a meeting to discover where their members stood at this
time of uncertainty in the industry. At a tense mass meeting, Dolman
was asked where he would start when it came to making men redundant. That was easy, he replied: the first to go would be Rovers season-
ticket holders. The meeting went on far more cheerfully after that. Say
what you liked about the boss, he was a bit of a card.

This, then, was the kind of man who made it his goal to sign the
prodigious John Atyeo in the summer of 1951; he was hardly alone in
this aim, but he had one or two advantages, not least a Wiltshire pedigree and a football club within easy reach of Dilton Marsh Halt, and
he had also seen John play more often than most of his rivals. In fact
he had sound contacts in this corner of the county, not least in two
other businessmen who had worked their way up the ladder: his friend
Graham Whittock, at that time a City shareholder and later a director,
was well known to Walter Atyeo through Frome cricket circles, while
William (later Sir William) Grant, a B.A.C. executive and chairman of

the region's engineering employers' association, did much of the early spadework before City made more formal approaches. At this stage of the game, Swindon Town was the other club that appealed to John, 'because, like Bristol, it was convenient to home – but they were pretty down-at-heel at that stage'.

This background meant that Walter had already half convinced himself that Bristol City was the place for his boy before Harry Dolman met with the family at Glenthorne on June 6, 1951. Famously, when he arrived at Dilton Marsh in his Rolls Royce, he spotted the Rovers manager Bert Tann's Austin Seven outside the house, and took a sharp detour off the main road and cruised around until the coast was clear. Happily, when his chance came, he found he was knocking on an open door – with the not inconsiderable proviso of the Atyeos' complex list of terms and conditions. A smiling Walter greeted him with: 'Well, Mr Dolman, we've weighed it all up carefully, and you've persuaded me that Bristol City is the best club for John to join.' That was the good news, but it might have turned sour if Harry had found the family's demands unacceptable.

The fact was that he was the least hidebound of football club chairmen, and unlike the Portsmouth board, he was not about to lose his man through quibbling. He agreed without demur to what John later looked back upon as 'perhaps the best contract ever signed by a player in those days; it was probably a unique document, especially for someone as unknown as I was. After all, I had only made it at amateur level, and professional football was something quite different. My father remained wary of professional football and was determined that I should have a contract that was in my favour, rather than the club's. At that time everything was loaded in favour of the clubs, and it was a long time before the players' new deal in 1961. A few days later, Mr Dolman returned with the letter that listed all the clauses my father wanted. It was signed by him on behalf of the club – so if I remained at Ashton Gate longer than Mr Dolman, the agreement would still be in force.'

John never forgot the nature of that agreement. Neither did Harry Dolman who, writing in Atyeo's testimonial brochure some fifteen years later, reflected: 'Mr Atyeo disliked professional soccer's transfer system, so I agreed that John would never be put on the transfer list. John, for the time being, at least, would only be a part-time professional, as Mr Atyeo wanted him to continue his studies. I also promised to

find John a job outside football, if necessary, and it was agreed that he
should continue to live at home with his parents.' Strangely, Dolman
omitted from this list various other conditions that were part of the
litany. From the start, John would be on the top wages allowed by the
Football League (£12 per week), he would be expected to come in to
Bristol for training twice a week – and crucially, he would be allowed
to drive, even though City, like Portsmouth and many other clubs, had
rules strictly limiting players' rights to do so. Another proviso was that
Westbury United should receive a donation (which turned out to be
£100) and benefit from a friendly game at home to a strong City team
at the end of the season. Two thousand people turned out to watch this
match in the April, which was won two-nil by the visitors, both goals
being scored by, well, who else? These were useful little bonuses for
Westbury, who knew from the start that their teenage sensation of a
number nine would not be wearing the green and white for very long,
but John always insisted that this was where the Ashton Gate largesse
stopped: 'I received a £10 signing-on fee and my wages were £12 per
week. I've heard people say since that it cost City £1,000 to sign me.
If that's the case, the cheque must still be in the post.' Despite this,
football people being what they are, speculation remained rife until the
end of John Atyeo's days and after. 'To this day, we're still not sure
what it was that Harry said to make him sign,' Graham Whittock
reflected after John's death.

More influential forces than gossipy fans, however, were wondering
just what was going on behind closed doors at Glenthorne, where
Harry Dolman and the City manager Pat Beasley signed John Atyeo as
a Bristol City player in the early evening of June 14, 1951. 'I thought
that was the end of the matter, but when the forms were sent to the
Football Association and the Football League, some awkward
questions were asked,' Harry Dolman later recalled. 'The League
wanted to know why John wanted to sign for a Third Division club
when he was already on the books of, and indeed had played for, a
First Division club in the previous season.' In fact there were three
exchanges of letters with the League that summer before, at a board
meeting on the eve of the new season on August 8, it was announced
that it had accepted the registration 'on condition that the clause relat-
ing to his subsequent transfer was deleted from his agreement'. This
was duly complied with, though it was communicated to the Atyeos
through nods and winks that the original deal still held good. There

were always plenty of nods and winks in the footballing world of Harry Dolman.

Like most old pros, Pat Beasley, who came to bless the day he signed John Atyeo, had not been a great fan of part-timers, but before the summer was out two more youngsters were signed on similar terms, Johnny Watkins and another lad who did not make the grade. 'Similar terms' solely from the aspect of part-time status, of course. Not for these other two top wages, a *carte blanche* to drive and so on. Meanwhile, in the weeks leading up to the new season, John built up his fitness and could not have been more eager. True to type, he was also keeping his nose to the grindstone in quantity surveying, and although it had not escaped Walter's notice that Harry Dolman might be an excellent contact to further his career in this field, too, Atyeo junior continued to work for the Westbury building firm T. Holdoway and Sons, whose managing director, Jack Holdoway, had also turned out for the town team. Still rooted in small-town Wiltshire, he nevertheless smelled change in the air: 'At last I was a professional and raw as I knew I was, I couldn't wait for my first match.'

CHAPTER 5

THE YOUNG PROFESSIONAL

'A taxi was waiting for me at Temple Meads when I got off the train from Westbury for my first morning's training with Bristol City,' John Atyeo recalled at the end of his career. 'I remember the occasion well, that sunny July morning in 1951, because it was the only taxi ever supplied by the club. For the first couple of years I caught the train regularly, boarded a number nine bus and reported for training. It was always a rush afterwards. I trained only on Tuesday and Thursday mornings. The rest of the time was spent working at my other job.' Naturally fit and strong in his late teens, he did not overdo the lone training at home, restricting his runs around Dilton Marsh to no more than one or two a week. Often his mother Effie would pedal along on her bicycle to keep him company, proud of her son's achievements.

While this may seem a desultory regime today, it was not much less than the work his full-time colleagues were putting in, as he was pleased to discover when he met up with them on his twice-weekly visits to South Bristol. 'I didn't find the training very difficult,' he reflected, 'but at nineteen it should be pretty easy for anyone like me, who played sport the whole year round. The long-distance runs round Ashton Court were a piece of cake for me. One or two of the older players used to ask me to slow up. Then I wondered what they were talking about, but it wasn't many years before I was saying the same thing to some of the younger ones!' Expanding on the theme in 1970, at a time when the 'Total Football' exploits of Cruyff, Neeskens and their colleagues in the Dutch national team were pushing the game to new heights of athleticism, John was happy to muse: 'I've never been sold on the idea of footballers as super-fit men. Obviously, players have to be fit, but for me, ability and experience are just as important. I was often asked whether full-time training and so-called total dedication to football would have made me a better player. I've always had my doubts about that. Security and peace of mind were far preferable to me than the strain of training every day and spending my whole time concentrating on football.'

John's recollection was always that he was made very welcome at Ashton Gate from the start. No doubt this new wonder boy's arrival had been well chewed over in the dressing room, and as Pat Beasley was still playing as well as managing, it is reasonable to imagine that the senior pros, at the very least, would be well aware of the bargain his father had driven for him – including the clause that gave him top wages before he had kicked a ball as a paid player, and a part-timer at that. Critics today say that players are obsessed by money; they were at least as obsessed by it back then, when there was next to none of it around, and John Atyeo was very much a man of his time in this respect. Another reason why the players were feeling uppish that summer – a time when the optimism of the nation generally had been boosted by the Festival of Britain – was the genuine feeling that things were beginning to look up for the old club.

The signing of Atyeo, against tremendously stiff competition and with the noses of some of the giants of the game put out of joint as a result, was one factor. Another was the return to Ashton Gate of the classy and influential inside-forward Cyril Williams, who had gone to Second Division West Bromwich Albion in the summer of 1948, helped them win promotion at the end of his first term and in all played seventy-one League games for the Baggies in three seasons, scoring nineteen goals. That was scarcely a record of failure, but there was a feeling at the Hawthorns that he was not quite up to speed in the top flight, so back to his native Bristol he came, a few months short of his thirtieth birthday. Word had it that City paid around £4,500 to bring him back, maybe slightly less than half of what he had gone to the Midlands for, and the fans were convinced they had got a bargain. They had indeed, but as we shall discover, it was not a move that reaped instant rewards.

The Ashton Gate crowd, as well as Harry Dolman and his board, were hungry for success – not least because of what was happening on the other side of the river, at Eastville. City, with a League history dating back to the earliest years of the century and seasons in the First Division and an F.A. Cup final appearance on the honours board, were traditionally the dominant Bristol club. Rovers had entered the League when the Third Division South was launched in 1920, and in the years before the war had ended the season higher than the Reds on only four occasions; in the last full season before hostilities, 1938-39, they had finished at the bottom of the heap and were forced into the humiliating ritual of applying for re-election. Recent years had seen a new spring in their step, however, and by the time John Atyeo arrived at Ashton Gate, the Blues' manager Bert Tann had inherited from his luckless predecessor Brough Fletcher – sacked, so it was rumoured, by a messenger slipping the bad news under his door at midnight – a tight-knit, never-say-die bunch of mainly local boys; really local boys, several of them, born within a whistle blast of the ground. The phrase 'all for one, one for all' might have been coined for them if the Three Musketeers had not got there first. No wonder Dolman was so keen to sign the big, coltish Wiltshire boy everyone had been talking about for the past couple of years; no wonder it was with special relish that he strode into the lad's home and landed him after he had let Bert Tann waste his time with an Atyeo senior whose mind had already been made up.

Some footballers swear, not always convincingly, that they never read the sports pages. John Atyeo was not among them, and in his early days, at least, with everything so fresh and new, he kept close tabs on what was being written about him. What intelligent young man would do otherwise? 'I had the feeling a lot was expected of me, although I was only a raw nineteen-year-old,' he said in later years. 'I suppose, after all the ballyhoo, that Pat Beasley had no alternative but to pick me for the first match of the season.' Newport County were the visitors to Ashton Gate that August afternoon, and the crowd topped 30,000 for only the fifth time since football had resumed after the Second World War. 'It was a tense moment for me, my first game in front of the Bristol public,' John recalled. 'I had played in front of bigger crowds in my two matches for Portsmouth, but this was different. I was starting a new career as a professional. It was no longer a hobby, but a job.'

As a job, it soon struck Big John that it was not such a bad one. In the first minute – or after twenty-two seconds, to be precise – he rose to nod the ball down for Arnold Rodgers to knock in the fastest goal of the season. A few minutes later he pushed the ball out to Alec Eisentrager, who scampered down the wing with it before crossing. The Newport goalkeeper, Terry Pope, came out and missed completely, 'and I only had to let the ball hit my head and go into the open goal'. City were three up in twenty-five minutes when John broke away down the right, fired in a cross-shot which the hapless Pope could not hold, and there was the other distinguished new boy, Cyril Williams, to pick up the scraps. That was the end of the scoring, but John had been involved in all three goals, and he was quite right to conclude that 'it was a wonderful start'. He was one of those players who prided himself in taking quickly to a new task, and always rather rued the day he did not go away from Fratton Park with a first-team goal under his belt. 'I believe more than ever, now, that a good start is essential in everything you do,' he reflected in 1970. 'I started well in the England youth trial, in my debut for City and for England, when I eventually achieved my life's ambition. Even now, when I'm playing golf, I can tell how well I'm going to play by my first two or three shots.'

There was no doubt in the minds of the City writers on Bristol's two sports papers. *Attaboy Atyeo!* screamed the *Evening World*'s Saturday night *Pink 'Un*, a headline so obvious that it was soon banned in local media circles, consigned to the forbidden file along with any reference to 'Shipshape and Bristol Fashion'; 'The way John Atyeo played in his first game for Bristol City against Newport County made me think I was watching another Tommy Lawton in the making,' wrote Peter Barnes... 'He is obviously a player with a big future. Besides the advantages his physique gives him, he is a player with an excellent football brain. He never allows himself to become flustered, and his actions are never impetuous. He also has first-rate ball control, and he leads the forward line unselfishly and thoughtfully.' That fleeting first impression captured all the vital Atyeo ingredients that made him the player he was. Barnes was dismissive of an oft-heard theory, even in his youngest days, that Big John was something of a lumberer: 'There are some who say he is a trifle slow, but it should be remembered that big men never appear as fast as smaller players. They are inevitably slower off the mark, but over a distance Atyeo has speed, and we should not lose sight of the fact that he is new to professional football.' John was happy enough with that snap verdict, but was irked that this sympathetic writer felt obliged to defend him against allegations of slowness, and took a dim view of the well-meaning 'over a distance' qualification. As runner-up in the English Schools hundred-yard hurdles dash just a few summers ago, he felt he had nothing to prove about his fleetness of foot.

He ended his first season with twelve goals in the League, level pegging with Arnold Rodgers, but he scored two in the F.A. Cup, to

Arnie's one, so he could rightly claim to be top scorer in his first season with fourteen goals. Jimmy Rogers was the only other City player to reach double figures in a season which, after promising so much, ended in depressing mediocrity. Atyeo was realistic about what he achieved, after that exciting debut: 'Although I was only dropped once all season, it was not before time. I was green, and I knew it. I was being carried for much of the time by the other players. I picked up a few goals, but I had a lot to learn. Players older and wiser than I was taught me things, were always tolerant and freely offered help and advice.' City were never remotely on track for promotion, particularly in those days in which only the champions of the regional Third Divisions stepped up, and a goalless draw and a one-nil defeat in the their next two games of the season, away to Bournemouth and Reading, gave them early warning that this would be a long, hard campaign. By the time the table was beginning to sort itself out in mid-September they were in tenth place, and were never again to rise higher that season. They finished in fifteenth spot – five down on their position the previous season and eight places and ten points behind Bristol Rovers. John did not score more than a single goal in any of his games other than in a two-one win at Brighton in the first round of the F.A. Cup, but he pleased the red side of town with the late equaliser he got against Rovers in the one-all draw at Ashton Gate, with more than 31,000 looking on. Rovers won the return two-nil at Eastville, when the crowd was 34,500. Even when it came to support, the boys from north of the river were far from second best.

This was the second season in charge for Pat Beasley, and his last as a player-manager; he dropped himself just before Christmas and made no more than a handful of stand-in appearances for the rest of the season. It was part of his contract that he would hang up his boots at this time, and it did not come a moment too soon. It was plain that the task of piloting this bunch of players out of the Third Division would be best achieved if he concentrated on management full-time. Stourbridge-born, really called Albert and an apprentice barber on leaving school, left-winger turned wing-half Beasley could look back over a career in which he won championship medals with Herbert Chapman's Arsenal in seasons 1933-34 and '34-35 and missed out on their F.A. Cup final victory in 1936 only through injury. He also went away from Highbury with a new name, bestowed on him in honour of the inter-war ace jockey Pat Beasley by Alex James, who as well as being the brains of the Arsenal team was an endless source of joy and funds to the bookies' runners of North London. A brief foray north saw Beasley on the left wing for Huddersfield in the 1938 Cup final against Preston, when they were sunk by George Mutch's legendary 120th-minute penalty, and he even scored for England in their two-one win over Scotland on their last pre-war visit to Hampden Park in 1939.

Distinguished service as a guest for Spurs and other London teams during the war, when he worked for the Royal Mint, kept him in trim for when League action resumed in 1946, but by now he was thirty-four and had to accept that some of his finest days had been lost to causes far beyond the influence of mere football men. Like most others whose careers had suffered a similar fate, he was philosophical about it, a phlegmatic approach perhaps strengthened by his twice in his career overcoming appalling injuries, including a broken skull and a leg fracture so complicated and severe that the doctors had considered amputation. Beasley was pleased to be given the chance to prolong his career with Fulham, in whose first post-war game he turned out as a deep-lying inside-left against Bury at Gigg Lane. Unhappily, the Bury manager Norman Bullock also had a keen tactical brain, and adopting an early version of three-three-four, his side trounced the visitors seven-two. However, the team then blissfully and innocently known as the Cottagers learned their lessons well, and Beasley was their captain when they fought their way into the top flight for the first time in their history in 1948-49.

Since regular First Division football was by this time beyond his powers, he spent his last spell at Craven Cottage as something of a national treasure, being given time out to coach in Norway and play with the sun on his back in Portugal and Spain. His transfer, when it came, was inevitably a 'free', and the offer he was made by Bristol City in the summer of 1950 was tempting in the extreme: an astonishing five-year contract, the first two doubling up as a player, plus bonuses for success that culminated in a pay rise of £1,000 a year should City be promoted. This, then, was the stature and calibre of John Atyeo's first boss at Ashton Gate – the kind of man who had seen the game from the pinnacle, but had always had to work hard and ride his luck for his rewards. For an intelligent young player of talent, he was a walking encyclopaedia of football lore and know-how.

John saw 1951-52 and '52-53 as his apprenticeship seasons in the game. He turned twenty-one in the February of the latter, and he also believed that at the end of the season he came of age as a footballer in the most unlikely of circumstances. City did better in 1952-53, ending the season fifth, scoring ninety-five goals (which made them only the division's third-highest scorers!) and avoiding defeat in thirty-seven of their forty-six games. They were five points – two wins and a draw – behind the champions, though the fact that those champions were Bristol Rovers took some of the gloss off an altogether sound and promising season, after a wretched start that saw just two points garnered from the first five games and crowds dropping to fewer than 8,000 for the midweek visit of Ipswich Town in early September. With the post-war boom in attendances now long past, the pattern had reverted to the volatility of inter-war days, with turnout dependent on immediate past performances, future prospects of success, the quality of the opposition and the weather. There was not a lot else for people to do, and when, occasionally, there was, such as on the big shopping Saturday a couple of weeks before Christmas, then the gates plunged as a result.

Two games against the neighbouring champs elect had ended in goalless stalemates, with nearly 36,000 at Ashton Gate in February, when Rovers were roaring along at the top and City still fancied their chances at fourth. The fact that they had stayed unbeaten against Bert Tann's team in its glory season offered some little comfort to Harry Dolman in his Monday morning tours of his factory, but it scarcely gave him the chance to flaunt the red carnation. The stark and surprising fact was that right through the 1950s, in the years of John Atyeo's prime, City were consistently second-best to their Eastville rivals in terms of League position; from 1948-49 to 1961-62 the tables show that the Blues were Bristol's top team. What is more, in the early and mid-1950s, there was a buzz about them, with the gasometers towering in the background and the unlikely strains of the corny American Country and Western song *Goodnight Irene* spurring them on to greater deeds. Bert Tann as manager was at the heart of all this, and at his zenith, his immaculately dapper appearance and open, honest and even-tempered manner conspired to turn him into something of a cult figure. Soon, a couple of outrageous F.A. Cup results would only add to his lustre. Tall and forever 'Mr Tann' to his workforce, he oozed authority but had just enough eccentricity to project an intriguing, likeable image. Ray Kendall, a Rovers backroom insider for more than fifty years, recalled the pre-war Austin Seven and how 'he would cram himself into this tiny car with his knees pushed up against the steering wheel, and set off at midday after training to go all sorts of distances' on football business. In contrast, Ray remembered how the boss had once asked him to pick up an overcoat in the West End of London, and 'it cost £1,000'. That was later in the 1950s, by which time the Austin Seven had been mothballed, but it is an interesting insight into a man's priorities when he will apparently drive around in a £100 car for years and then spend ten times that on a coat.

Bert Tann had gone to Rovers as coach under Brough Fletcher under bizarre circumstances. The club chairman was Con Stevens, on the strength of his being head of the greyhound company that owned the ground, as well as dog tracks at Oxford and Wimbledon, in which suburb he also had a garage aimed at the affluent end of the market. When times were hard, Rovers fans had plenty to say about that desperate deal that had delivered their club into the clutches of people who were anything but football men through-and-through – but they had to take their hats off to Con Stevens when it came to Bert going to Eastville. One day he was in his car showroom when in walked Stanley Rous, the Football Association secretary. Not surprisingly, the talk turned to soccer, and the future Sir Stanley told Con that if he was looking for a promising coach, there was an old pro at Charlton he had heard good things about. Enter Mr Tann.

Tann had been at Eastville for around eighteen months when Brough Fletcher was ushered out, and wasted little time in making his mark. He had coaching and organisational skills of a high order. Most of all he was blessed with a set of exceptionally talented players, a large number of whom he inherited from Fletcher. Bert Hoyle, Harry Bamford, Geoff Fox, Jackie Pitt, Ray Warren, Peter Sampson – and then there were forwards of the calibre of George Petherbridge, Josser Watling, Vic Lambden, Billy Roost and Geoff Bradford, who briefly, with John Atyeo, ensured that both Bristol clubs had a player in contention for a place in the England forward line. Bradford played for his country just once, scoring the final goal against Denmark in a five-one win in October 1955, and there are still Rovers fans around who argue that while Big John might have done all right with his five goals in six international games, it was only their Geoff who could look back on a hundred-per-cent goal-a-game record.

For John Atyeo, 1952-53 was a steep learning curve. When Pat Beasley dropped him this time – in early October, after scoring just three goals in the first thirteen matches – he was sidelined for a full eleven games. It was on January 10, in a one-all home draw with Reading, that he notched his fourth goal of the season, and a purple patch of six in eight unbeaten games from mid-February to early April helped move City up to second place and push John towards a reasonable though not outstanding tally for the season of eleven in thirty-three matches. It was an interesting time to be a young player at Ashton Gate. When John had first arrived in July 1951 the ground was a scene of pre-war scruffiness, wartime devastation and post-war austerity. The main grandstand, the Number One Stand, had been destroyed in an air raid just after New Year in 1941, and the only building on that side of the ground since then had been a mean little office and dressing room block. Work on the new stand was just beginning as young Atyeo was settling in, and it was quite a thrill to see the stark metal structure going up, towering above the makeshift facilities that had just about served their purpose for the best part of a decade. Even by this time, however, life was a struggle, and though building restrictions had been lifted, a shortage of both steel and money ensured that the stand was not complete until the coronation year of 1953.

The players watched its development with interest, until it was time to be introduced to their new home: in from the car park through the substantial double doors, past the main office on the left and Pat Beasley's den on the right, and then on through another set of doors into the main corridor. Then it was a case of left turn and down to the farthest end, where a red door on the left opened on to the tiled dressing room, with the communal bath and toilets on the left and ahead, the high opaque windows on to the car park from which generations of fans since then have sniffed the steam and liniment and dreamed their dreams of being one of those eleven boys in red in there. The forwards' pegs were straight ahead on entering the dressing room, along the right hand wall, and it would be there that John would find his kit neatly laid out on match days, and his eight or nine shirt hung, number outermost. The physio's room was directly next door, on the far side from the entrance, and the boot room almost opposite, on the other side of the corridor, where the seating above began to slope steeply in. Also on this more cramped side of the corridor but at the far end, up towards the away dressing room and referee's room, was the drying room, where training kit would be hung around a row of gas heaters every weekday up until Thursday, by which time it would be as stiff as a board; not a nice place to be by the end of the week.

Opposite the main stand stood the Cowshed, or the Number Two Stand, to give it its formal name. It must have crossed the minds of many who had the club's interests at heart that if Old Jerry had been really determined to have a go at Ashton Gate that night, he might have aimed his bomb to the other side of the pitch and done a demolition job on this terrible, ramshackle structure. A lot of people were surprised that the mere blast of the explosion in the main stand was not enough to bring its ugly sister down, but the creaking-gate-hanging-longest theory held good, and the Number Two Stand saw out John Atyeo's career, to be demolished in the summer of 1966 to make way for the mighty structure that bears Harry Dolman's name. John's view of the two ends of the ground, the backdrops to so many of his magic moments, did not change much over the years he was playing – open at the Ashton Road end and covered at the other. It was not until the early years of the twenty-first century that plans were revealed to replace the covered or Winterstoke Road end of the ground with a complex named in honour of Billy Wedlock; the mid-1990s John Atyeo stand that now broods over the goal at the former open end will be discussed elsewhere.

To complement the new main stand, Harry Dolman designed City's first floodlights, which were inevitably made by Brecknell, Dolman and Rogers. They were primitive, even for their time, consisting of fourteen metal pylons forty feet high, seven on each side of the pitch and each carrying a cluster of three lamps. As the lights began to spring up at grounds all over the country in the half-dozen years that followed, it became clear that the only system that mattered consisted of four tall pylons carrying massed ranks of lamps at each corner of the pitch – though now, interestingly, the emphasis is again on lower lights installed regularly along the length of the pitch, most often, as at the modern Ashton Gate, on the roofs of the stands. It might thus be argued, though not very convincingly, that in this respect Harry Dolman was fifty years ahead of his time. Be that as it may, his system cost around £3,500, a good deal of it from his own pocket, but a series of three well-attended friendly games in the early months of 1953 proved more than adequate money-spinners. Years later, as the icing on the cake, the club sold the by then modified but still quite hopelessly unsatisfactory package to Burton Albion for more than half of what it had cost.

Wolverhampton Wanderers opened the floodlights on January 27, 1953, as they did so many other clubs', and Billy Wright and his mighty men looked like beings from another planet as they took to the field in their old gold and black satin, which shimmered as if fluorescent, even under the gentle glow of Harry's lamps. It was a foul evening (though, once you were there, rain always seemed to add novelty to floodlit football in the early days) and the crowd of 23,866 would doubtless have been greater on a balmy evening in spring. Interestingly, the turnout was 26,562 when East Fife were in town on March 10, and though they were a decent team – they won the Scottish League Cup three times between 1948 and 1954 and were led by the astonishing Charlie 'Cannonball' Fleming – they had none of the glamour of the Wolves. Both teams were good enough to beat City comfortably, however, Wolves four-one and East Fife two-nil, and in between times, Cardiff City crossed the Severn to win a less high-profile floodlit friendly two-nil.

John Atyeo, still finding his feet, scored in none of these games, though from the following season onwards he enjoyed some pulsating nights under the lights. In a strange timewarp, the Reds played Wolves again for the opening of the replacement lights on December 28, 1965, this time merely by coincidence, as equals in a League game, and it need hardly be said that Atyeo was the sole City player to take part in both matches.

Clearly there were no top-scoring honours awaiting Big John as the 1952-53 season drew to a so-near-and-yet-so-far close, with the gate dropping to a rare sub-10,000 for Leyton Orient's visit in mid-April. Arnold Rodgers was top marksman with twenty-six, with Cyril Williams on seventeen and Alec Eisentrager's twelve nudging John's eleven into fourth place. No longer a prodigy, no longer a boy, Atyeo seemed to have quite enough on his plate fighting for his place in an only slightly better-than-average Third Division South team. Two years on from his last game for the League champions Portsmouth, he struck few onlookers as the lost star of the First Division. 'We all knew then what a wonderful player he was, and it's strange to think there were times when he'd be down on confidence a bit,' his captain, Jack White, recalled years later. 'I'd take him aside and talk to him and try to help get him back on track.'

Something else did that, too – Bristol City's close season visit to South Devon and Cornwall in the early May of 1953. By then, most football fans were looking forward to the F.A. Cup final in which Stanley Matthews would surely pocket his winner's medal at last, while tens of millions were excited by the thought of seeing television for the first time – in most cases, crammed into a neighbour's home – when the Queen was crowned in early June. Out in the Himalayas, leaders of Britain's Everest expedition were making the most optimistic noises ever about their chances of conquering the world's highest peak. Yes, there was plenty to excite the optimists in the early days of May that year, but City's gentle wind-down at the seaside did not strike many as the most burning of issues.

For John, however, the seven goals he got in the three games of that tour were his turning point, 'when I really blossomed out'. At Torquay, he scored once in City's two-nil win in Sammy Collins's benefit match in front of 2,684 – an apathetic gathering compared with the 7,000 who had packed Plainmoor for the League encounter back in September. That was on May Day, and on the fourth and fifth came fixtures at amateurs Penzance and Newquay in front of crowds too insignificant to be noted. Penzance were vanquished six-one, with John getting two, while he popped in four the following evening when Newquay were sunk nine-one. A sceptic might have concluded that this proved nothing – we knew Big John could pulverise below-par defences, but it looked dangerously as if it might be a different matter against the tough and worldly-wise old pros. For the player, though, it was as if everything had slotted into place. Arnold Rodgers netted four on the trip, and Jack Boxley three, but it was only John Atyeo who travelled back up the A30 with a new sense of destiny and purpose. 'As the new season opened I felt I'd arrived at last,' he later recalled. 'Everything clicked into place. I suddenly found a confidence that had not been there before. I was a fully-fledged player, and no longer felt I was being carried. Pat Beasley's patience for two years was being rewarded.' Since football is played just as much in the head as on grass, these were excellent omens for Bristol City as season 1953-54 dawned.

CHAPTER 6

THE CHAMPIONS

Bristol City finished fifth in 1952-53 with John Atyeo still finding his feet. Surely they would do better in '53-54, with him brimming with brio as part of a team that was widely regarded as a cut above this level of football? They did indeed do better, and John notched up the kind of goal tally he would be bagging for the next dozen seasons – twenty-two in the League and three in the F.A. Cup. For the team, however, 'better' was no more than a rise from fifth place to third, and there was no promotion for that kind of performance in those days. Champions were Ipswich Town with sixty-four points, the equivalent of ninety-one in today's money, so not a bad total; still, it was irksome to have been pipped by a team that had been up from the Southern League for only sixteen years, with a World War in between, and went on to prove woefully inadequate for the Second Division in the following season. Second were Brighton, a decent, always-the-brides-maid kind of Third South team who eventually rose to higher football for the first time in 1957-58, the last season of the regionalised Third Divisions. City's third place, with fifty-six points, came from twenty-five wins and six draws; that means they lost fifteen times, almost all of them away and several by quite heavy scores.

Supporters did not travel as much as they do these days, but a good number made a point of going to other West Country grounds; between October 3 and November 14 they were rewarded by a five-nil hammering at Swindon, five-two at Bournemouth (Atyeo two) and four-nil at Torquay. With those results behind them, it is astonishing to think that City were still seventh after the visit to Plainmoor – though seventh then, of course, did not have quite the ring to it that it does now. Fair results in December and January pushed them up even higher, to fourth, but after two more dismal away days, at Watford and Northampton, they slipped down to eighth and were in the kind of position that even seven wins in the remaining nine games could not put right. There was a theory that if Jack Boxley had not been injured, it might all have been different – but then again, it might not. It was even seen as a good omen, on the old 'concentrating on the League' principle, when a hot Rotherham team that ended fifth in the Second Division that season dumped City out of the F.A. Cup in the Third Round at Ashton Gate, courtesy of a Jack Grainger hat-trick. The fact that City played the game in Rovers' blue and white quarters only added to the unreality of the day. At the same time, the real Bristol Rovers were losing one-nil at home to Blackburn in their Third Round tie. The gates were 29,217 at City, 25,017 at Rovers, and the police reported nothing more worrying than an awful lot of people around at the end of the afternoon.

Twenty of John Atyeo's twenty-two League goals that season came in the first thirty-two games – he managed only two from late February onwards, in home wins against Torquay and Millwall. He scored five braces – at home and away to Aldershot, at home to Newport County on Boxing Day and away at Bournemouth and Gillingham – and there was also a hat-trick in a cheerful five-one hammering of Swindon at Ashton Gate in February, in front of 23,749. His purple patch was from January 30 to February 20, when he scored six in four games while at the same time Andy Micklewright, at centre-forward to John's inside-right, was putting in City's best scoring sequence of the season with nine in six matches. John was top scorer by some distance that season, though Rodgers, with fourteen in twenty-three games, would have been running him close but for injury, while Micklewright's sixteen in thirty-six games were all the more creditable in that while an inside-forward, he was thrown in to the team's problem right-wing spot for several games late on. There were also three F.A. Cup goals that season for Andy, who came to Ashton Gate as a youngster from Bristol Rovers, never could quite make a first team berth his own but went on to give Swindon and Exeter good service and plenty of goals. Never was he more in his pomp, though, than in the early months of 1954, playing up front for Bristol City with John Atyeo and even briefly outgunning the great man.

What Andy Micklewright did not get was a succession of big clubs showing an interest in him. Little more than two years after the great scuffle for John Atyeo's signature after his departure from Portsmouth, the offers for him, or at least rumours of offers, began flying around again, and there were times when Harry Dolman was putting out denials of a transfer almost daily. Eventually he confessed that many major clubs had made inquiries, and that 'we have received four definite big bids for John from First Division clubs this season'. These were Liverpool, Manchester City, Chelsea and Cardiff City – a line-up that might well have tempted many an ambitious young man to venture forth. In contrast, John most definitely did not want to know. We know now, of course, that he never really *did* want to know, but at this stage of his life, twenty-one coming on twenty-two, working hard for his diploma as a quantity surveyor and seriously courting the Warminster girl who would become his wife, he was less amenable to moving away than he might possibly have been a few years on.

Harry Dolman, on the other hand, would have loved to have been the man who said 'yes' – but as always in this important respect, though not necessarily in others, he deferred to the big man's wishes. Sometimes he seemed to be wavering, telling one reporter that while 'in a general way' Atyeo could not be bought, the club might have to think again: 'If anyone regards the sky as the limit, then the City would be foolish to turn them down. Only a near-record offer might tempt us to sell.' Since the British transfer record at this time was the £34,000 Aston Villa had paid Sheffield Wednesday for another goal-hungry forward, Jackie Sewell, in the spring of 1951, and Cardiff City, by Dolman's later admission, had offered more than £30,000, it is easy to imagine the dilemma the chairman faced at this time, with all the ground improvements weighing on the club's finances. Good as his word to John, however, not to mention his formidable father, Dolman chose to interpret a sum in excess of £30,000 as not tempting enough. It must have been through gritted teeth that he did it, not least because the Football League had ordered him to ignore any such agreement, but he stood by it.

The chase for Big John began early in that 1953-54 season when Don Welsh, the Liverpool manager, reportedly offered £20,000 plus two players whose joint value was placed at about £8,000. We must remember that back in 1953 the name of Liverpool did not resound through football as it does today, but though they were on the slide, they were still a mighty club. They were struggling at the foot of the First Division when they put in their bid and indeed stayed there, going down as bottom club at the end of 1953-54 and remaining confined to the Second Division until 1962. Again we are faced with a tantalising 'what if?' Six more points that season would have put them safe, and who is to say they would not have scraped them together with John up there feeding off Billy Liddell, and each of these deadly gentlemen of the game cashing in on the other's knock-downs and passes? That 1950s team would forever remain 'Liddellpool', but there was the real chance that the Kop might have been roaring 'Ee-Aye-Atyeo' a decade before they made a very similar chant their own. Back in the land of reality, the first time City played them after this, in the October of 1955, it was on equal terms in the Second Division. The West Country Reds won two-one in front of 25,496 at Ashton Gate, and readers should know John Atyeo well enough by now to be unsurprised that he got both goals.

Two further teams interested in him at this time seemed to hold out more promise. Manchester City's manager Les McDowall was at Ashton Gate to watch him score in a narrow two-one win over Northampton Town on November 7, and liked what he saw. An innovative coach, in the next couple of years he would mould Manchester City into one of the most attractive teams in the land, full of goals and almost equally capable of shipping them, despite the goal-keeping heroics of Bert Trautmann, Alec Eisentrager's rather better-known fellow ex-prisoner-of-war; in 1957-58 they finished fifth in the First Division by dint of scoring 104 goals and letting in a hundred. At the same time they were one of the most swashbuckling F.A. Cup teams of the day, reaching successive finals in 1955 and 1956 and triumphing over Birmingham City in the latter through the late switch of centre-forward Don Revie into a deep-lying role inspired by the Hungarians. Apart from Revie, a brilliant player and difficult man who would get along well enough with John Atyeo in their England days, Manchester City had goal-minded forwards in the wee schemer Bobby Johnstone, another good little 'un in Joe Hayes and speedy wingers in Paddy Fagan and Nobby Clarke. What was more, any inside-right wearing the sky blue could bank on immaculate service from Ken Barnes, a right-half who could lay claim more than most to that hackneyed honorary title of 'the best uncapped wing-half in the country'. What City did not have was a good big 'un up front, and John would have been all of that for them and more. With his deep Wiltshire brogue, he would also have added piquancy to a dressing room already known as the League of Nations through the polyglot mutterings of Trautmann, the Scots Dave Ewing and Johnstone, Welshmen Roy Paul and Clarke, and Paddy Fagan, whose first name was really Fionan; no prizes for guessing where he came from.

The other club known to have an eye on John was Chelsea, by this time run by the distinguished Arsenal old boy Ted Drake, who had wanted to take him to Reading in 1951 and still felt he could fit the bill up in the big league. Atyeo always swore that as far as all this activity was concerned, 'I was more or less in the dark except for what appeared in the press', but there was plenty of informal contact with the team then still proud to be known as the Pensioners. It came in the form of Roy Bentley, the former City star whose shock transfer in 1946 had helped stoke the discontent that led to Harry Dolman's boardroom coup. John recalled that at around this time, the autumn of 1953, Roy trained at Ashton Gate while on a visit home and 'made a special point of seeking me out quietly after training and chatting me up. He told me the opportunities I could expect, how important it would be to my future if I were with a London club, and above all, the prospects at Chelsea.' The two got on well, as they did later on representative duty together, but when it came to prising John Atyeo away from Dilton Marsh, Bentley's words fell on stony ground. It was with a sense of wry reflection, rather than of missed opportunity, that John mused that the older man's 'confidence in Chelsea's future was borne out the following season, when they won the championship'.

There was even talk of the Italian giants sniffing around. After all, the big South African Eddie Firmani was about to go off to Sampdoria after netting fifty times in ninety-nine games for Charlton Athletic, and strong, direct forwards of his phlegmatic temperament were what the Italians were seeking most of all in English football. Of the flurry of big-name departures from the mid-1950s to early 1960s, nobody did better in Serie A than the legendarily placid John Charles and Gerry Hitchens, another even-tempered hustler who had comfortably bettered a goal every two games for Cardiff City and Aston Villa. John Atyeo matched the on-field demeanour of men such as this so closely that, in retrospect, it is impossible to believe that Serie A scouts would *not* have given him serious consideration – even though, when it came to coping with life in Italy off the pitch, it is more than likely that the big man would have been more of a fraught Jimmy Greaves or Denis Law than a take-it-all-as-it-comes Charles or Hitchens.

Whatever, Bristol buzzed with all the transfer gossip for months, with endless letters in the *Green 'Un* and *Pink 'Un* and the threat of a

Little Peter's trip to the seaside: John with his mother Effie when he was three in the summer of 1935, before his parents had changed his name and moved from Berkley to Dilton Marsh

Wartime memory: John in the family orchard at Dilton Marsh, c1940, with his father Walter, elderly relatives and a makeshift air raid shelter which, thankfully, was never called upon to repel the might of the Luftwaffe

First school: The infant and primary school at Berkley, Somerset has changed little since Peter Atyeo's time, externally, at least

The family's Dilton Marsh home, Glenthorne, today, beside the small development of Atyeo Close on the old orchard

Dilton Marsh Halt: It inspired John Betjeman to write possibly his worst poem ever, but it was the gateway to the world, and his future wife, for a young John Atyeo

The last time John, second from the left in the front row, was seen in Westbury United's colours, after their game against Bristol City at the end of his first season as a League player. They are displaying the Wiltshire Senior Cup, which they had recently won

The homely face of Westbury United today. The club bought its Meadow Lane ground for a few hundred pounds in the inter-war years

Team.	Result.	Scorers.
Devizes	won 8—0	Atyeo 4, Kettlety 2, Geeves 1, Cundick 1
Headlands	won 5—3	Atyeo 2, Kettlety 2, Bush 1
Bradford	won 5—1	Atyeo 3, Kettlety 1, Cundick 1
Calne	won 5—1	Atyeo 2, Kettlety 1, Geeves 1, Cundick 1
Adcroft	lost 4—1	Atyeo 1
Bruton	won 4—0	Atyeo 2, Kettlety 1, Turtell 1
Cotham	lost 6—0	
Headlands	won 5—2	Atyeo 1, Kettlety 2, Dalton 1, Bush 1
Adcroft	won 6—0	Atyeo 3, Bush 1, Stephens 1, Geeves 1
Calne	won 8—0	Atyeo 4, Geeves 2, Dalton 1, Bush 1
Old Boys	won 5—2	Atyeo 2, Kettlety 1, Dalton 1, Bush 1
Bradford	won 6—1	Atyeo 2, Kettlety 2, Bush 1, Dalton 1

P. J. ATYEO.

On reading these notes it will be obvious from glancing down the list of goal scorers that Atyeo was the inspiration of the School XI. His scheming, ball control and leadership were of tremendous value to the team, but his most outstanding asset was his powerful shooting which brought him many goals and scared quite a few goalkeepers. The success of the 1st XI was due, to a large extent, to Atyeo's capabilities as a player, his keen captaincy and loyalty to his team.

EDITOR.

Above
Twenty-six goals in twelve games, John's prolific record for Trowbridge High in the spring of 1949. Before 1950 was out, while still at school, he would be leading the line for League champions Portsmouth

Left
Some of Trowbridge High's rugby first XV in the autumn of 1949, with John top left. Although already around six feet tall, he does not stand out physically in this group of players.
Teacher and coach Mr F. W. King could have walked straight out of a schoolboy adventure story

The England Youth team of 1950, with John Atyeo cutting a dominant figure in the middle of the front row. Several went on to taste League action, but John enjoyed by far the most successful career. Tony Marchi, the player far right on the back row, was highly regarded at Spurs, but found first-team chances scarce in the Glory, Glory years. He did, however, have some rewarding years in Italy with Lanerossi and Juventus

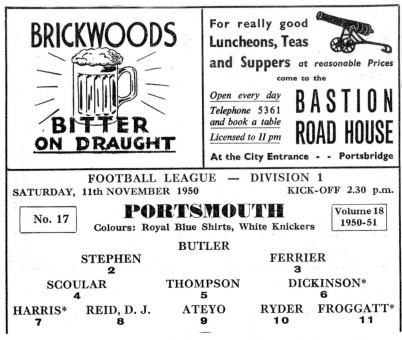

FOOTBALL LEAGUE — DIVISION 1

SATURDAY, 11th NOVEMBER 1950   KICK-OFF 2.30 p.m.

No. 17   **PORTSMOUTH**   Volume 18 1950-51

Colours: Royal Blue Shirts, White Knickers

BUTLER

STEPHEN   FERRIER
2   3

SCOULAR   THOMPSON   DICKINSON*
4   5   6

HARRIS*   REID, D. J.   ATEYO   RYDER   FROGGATT*
7   8   9   10   11

John's League debut, for Portsmouth at home to Charlton Athletic in November 1950. So many team changes were phoned over to the printer at the last minute that he could hardly be blamed for getting the hardest name wrong...

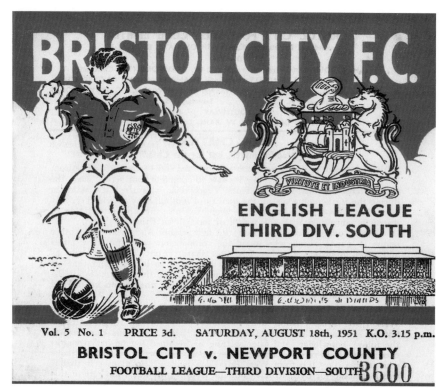

Vol. 5 No. 1   PRICE 3d.   SATURDAY, AUGUST 18th, 1951 K.O. 3.15 p.m.

BRISTOL CITY v. NEWPORT COUNTY
FOOTBALL LEAGUE—THIRD DIVISION—SOUTH 3600

The programme for John's League debut for Bristol City, against Newport County in the first game of 1951-52. He scored the opening goal in City's three-one win

John Atyeo with his first team-mates at Bristol City, 1951-52: Back row: Stone, Rodgers, Roberts, Sullivan, Atyeo, Presley, Bailey, Guy. Front row: Eisentrager, Peacock, Beasley, C. Williams, Boxley

Man on the terraces: John poses in front of the new main stand at Ashton Gate, which was opened in 1953

Bristol City, 1954-55, coming together into a winning team.
Back row: Guy, Regan, Cook, Peacock, Atyeo, Watkins.
Front row: Rogers, Rodgers, White, Boxley, Bailey

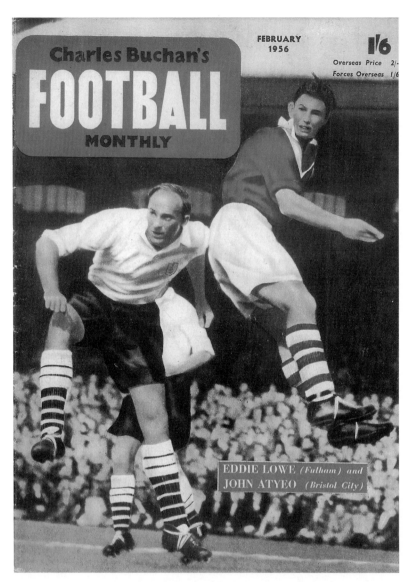

Man on the up: Colour illustrations in early *Football Monthlies* gave players a strange other-worldliness, making the stars seem even more like the gods they appeared to be to little boys on the terraces. Come the mid-1950s, John Atyeo was coming in for the full treatment

Much sought-after young man is John Atyeo, whom Bristol City value at £30,000. Well built and powerful in finishing he made his mark last season with Young England and seems destined to capture the game's highest honours. He played a notable part in his club's promotion to the Second Division.

The England squad in training at Molineux before John's first full international v Spain, November 1955. From left: Clayton, Perry, Baynham, Finney, Atyeo, R. Matthews, Hall, Wright, P. Sillett, Jezzard, Byrne, Dickinson, Haynes and Edwards

November 30, 1955, and it is 'Atyeo of England'. John's centre-forward partner was Bedford Jezzard, in for the injured Nat Lofthouse

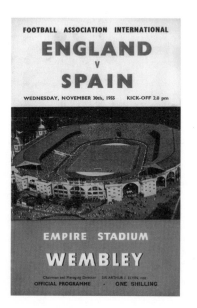

FOOTBALL ASSOCIATION INTERNATIONAL

ENGLAND
v
SPAIN

WEDNESDAY, NOVEMBER 30th, 1955   KICK-OFF 2.0 pm

EMPIRE STADIUM

WEMBLEY

Chairman and Managing Director   SIR ARTHUR J. ELVIN, MBE
OFFICIAL PROGRAMME   •   ONE SHILLING

PLAN OF THE FIELD OF PLAY

ENGLAND
(White Shirts, Dark Blue Shorts)

Goal
R. BAYNHAM
(Luton Town)

2
Right Back
J. HALL
(Birmingham City)

3
Left Back
R. BYRNE
(Manchester United)

4
Right Half
R. CLAYTON
(Blackburn Rovers)

5
Centre Half
W. WRIGHT (Capt.)
(Wolverhampton Wanderers)

6
Left Half
J. DICKINSON
(Portsmouth)

8
Inside Right
J. ATYEO
(Bristol City)

10
Inside Left
J. HAYNES
(Fulham)

7
Outside Right
T. FINNEY
(Preston North End)

9
Centre Forward
N. LOFTHOUSE or B. JEZZARD
(Bolton Wanderers)   (Fulham)

11
Outside Left
W. PERRY
(Blackpool)

11
Outside Left
E. COLLAR
(Madrid Athletic)

9
Centre Forward
PAHINO
(Corunna)

7
Outside Right
G. MIGUEL
(Madrid Athletic)

10
Inside Left
J. MAGUREGUI
(Bilbao Athletic)

8
Inside Right
M. DOMENECH
(Seville)

6
Left Half
J. SEGARRA
(Barcelona)

5
Centre Half
J. GARAY
(Bilbao Athletic)

4
Right Half
I. MAURI
(Bilbao Athletic)

3
Left Back
M. CAMPANAL
(Seville)

2
Right Back
F. GUILLAMON
(Seville)

Goal
S. CARMELO
(Bilbao Athletic)

Referee :
M. GUIGUE
(France)

SPAIN
(Red Shirts, Black Shorts)

Linesmen :
R. SAUTEL
(France)
Flame Flag
M. LEQUESNE
(France)
Orange Flag

9

Goal For Atyeo: England Beat Spain In Floodlight Finish

JOHN ATYEO

Atyeo in Football League Team

John Atyeo, of Bristol City, who was in the England team against Spain at Wembley today, has been selected to play for the Football League against the League of Ireland at Goodison Park, Liverpool, next Wednesday. The Football League team is the same as that which met Spain.

Half-time:
England 2
Spain 0

Final:
ENGLAND 4
SPAIN 1

JOHN ATYEO, of Bristol City, scored his first goal in a full international match when he opened England's account against Spain at Wembley this afternoon. England proved the superior side and won comfortably.

The fog which at one time threatened to cause the cancellation of the match, fortunately lifted by the time of the kick-off, but 17 minutes from the end the light became so poor that the floodlights were switched on.

The light was fairly good, with all parts of the ground visible, when the teams came out together. The Spaniards kicked off, and three free kicks came in the first minutes—one to Spain, followed by two to England. Tackling infringements seemed the reason. Obviously the referee was determined to show he intended to be firm.

PENALTY SAVED

The left half Maguregui played

Baynham tumbled, but the goalkeeper recovered as the Spanish inside forwards bore down on him. Ten minutes before half-time, Pava brought the ball back from the line and squared it to the front of the goal. Arieta flung himself forward, made contact with his head, but the ball flashed outside the post.

HARD FOOTBALL

Hall soon recovered after a collision. The football was hard, but generally fair. There had been no shirt-tugging or other deliberately doubtful tactics.

Five minutes before the interval, England should have scored again. Haynes sent Perry

fourth goal for England from a pass by the untiring Clayton.

LIGHTS ON

Midway through the second half the light became poor for spectators without being a handicap to the players.

Then, 17 minutes from the finish the floodlights were called into use to be as strong as any in the world. The lights said by the referee. The lights said to be as strong as any in the world. The improvement in visibility was marked and the numbers could once more be picked out on the players' shirts.

With 11 minutes left, Spain scored. Gonzalez centred and, ARIETA, leaping high, headed past Baynham to make the score 4—1.

The attendance was approximately 100,000.

A little piece of history: John's scoring international debut against Spain was the first time England had played under floodlights

In the thick of it: John in action against the Republic of Ireland in the World Cup qualifier at Wembley in May 1957, when he scored twice in a five-one win. Picture: Colorsport

Above
John shakes hands with Earl Mountbatten
before the World Cup qualifier against the
Republic of Ireland in May 1957. Billy
Wright is introducing him, Tommy Taylor
and Johnny Haynes are to his left on the
picture and Stanley Matthews and Jeff
Hall to the right

Left
Cap, Three Lions shirt, a dream come true;
a pity the football could not have
smartened itself up a bit for this formal
picture

On the mark: John bags the fourth goal against the Republic of Ireland in the World Cup qualifier at Wembley in May 1957. In the return game he headed a late equaliser which saw his team through to the finals in Sweden – and never touched a ball for England again. Picture: Colorsport

Some of the England party in West Germany in May, 1956, an unhappy tour for John, despite the broad smile. Back row: Ray Wood, Grainger, Lofthouse, Atyeo, Cummings, Wright. Front row: Edwards, trainer Jimmy Trotter, Byrne, Haynes and Berry

Top hat and tails: John's wedding to Ruth at the Minster in Warminster in October 1956, with Jack Boxley an immaculate best man

Favour returned: The new Mrs Pat Boxley shapes up for what promises to be a shy and awkward kiss from Jack's best man

Frome Cricketer Weds

Mr. JOHN ATYEO MARRIED AT WARMINSTER

The Minster Church at Warminster, on Monday was packed long before the start of the ceremony for the wedding of England and Bristol City footballer and Frome cricketer, Peter John Walter Atyeo, only son of Mr. and Mrs. W. Atyeo, Glenthorn, Dilton, Westbury, Wilts., to Miss Ruth Harraway, youngest daughter of Mr. and Mrs. A. H. Harraway, The Cedars, Warminster.

Bristol City were represented by directors Mr. H. J. Dolman (chairman), Mr. C. Crawford (vice-chairman), the Rev. F. C. Vyvyan Jones, Mr. George Jones, Mr. W. Garland, Mr. J. Saywell, manager Mr. Pat Beasley and members of the club's playing staff.

Local civic representatives at the church included Mr. W. Parker, chairman of Westbury U.D.C., and Mrs. Parker.

The service was conducted by the Vicar of Christchurch, Warminster, the Rev. H. Green.

The bride, given away by her father, wore a dress of ivory brocade with boat shaped neckline and carried a bouquet of red roses, white heather, lilies-of-the-valley, and stephanotis.

Bridesmaid was Miss Ann Morgan, friend of the bride who wore a pale yellow lace dress and the best man was Mr. Jack Boxley, Bristol City outside-left.

A reception was held at Byne House Hotel, and when the bride left for the honeymoon in London she wore a fawn suit with cherry accessories.

Bathtime with the boys: John, third from left, enjoys a steamy session with Jack White, Cyril Williams and Jack Boxley

It was in another county, after all: The *Somerset Standard* keeps its feet on the ground about the Atyeo wedding

Bristol City, 1955-56, Third Division South champions.
Back row: Trainer Wilf Coppin, Milton, Guy, Anderson, Atyeo, C. Williams, Thresher.
Front row: Peacock, Rogers, White, Burden and Boxley

Portrait of power: Another of those strange *Football Monthly* images that used to give impressionable little boys the creeps

mass boycott if City sold. In the end, John reflected, 'the whole thing died a natural death', drawing a line under all talk of a step forward in his career that to most players of his talent would have seemed a good deal more 'natural' than wanting to keep on rubbing shoulders with the Colchesters and Aldershots of the Third Division South.

By 1954-55 his footballing life beyond the League basement was taking off in a way that would whisk him off on exciting journeys away from home over the next two or three seasons, though they always ended up back at Dilton Marsh Halt. More important for Bristol City, the season at last brought long-promised promotion, and League football played through the length and breadth of England and Wales for the first time since 1932. For John, however, that was only half the story of the season.

'While I was furthering my personal career, Bristol City were becoming one of the outstanding Third Division teams of all time,' Atyeo recalled. 'The statistics of that season tell their own story. Our seventy points equalled the (then) record and the second team, Leyton Orient, were nine points behind us. I scored thirty goals (the record books say twenty-eight) and we had the look of champions from the way we started the season, unbeaten for the first thirteen matches, to our run-in of eighteen games without defeat.'

He did not exaggerate. City were never out of the top two from the time the League table began to settle down after five games, and stayed in the top spot from early March onwards. The only time they wobbled, as is so often the case with good footballing sides in the lower divisions, was when they had mud on their boots. Four of their six defeats came between December 18 and January 22, including a disastrous start to 1955 when they lost away to their two main rivals, Leyton Orient and Southampton, and between the two were sunk at home for the only time that season, nil-one against Norwich. That reverse sent them back to second in the table, and all the dire terrace murmurings about a team that flattered only to deceive bubbled to the surface once more. This time the knockers were silenced in spectacular style.

John scored consistently right through the season, from the opening day's one-all draw at Gillingham to four games from the end, when his Easter Tuesday double helped sink Crystal Palace at Ashton Gate. Newport County, from deep down the table, slipped in through the Severn Tunnel the following Saturday and tried to spoil the party by grinding out a nil-all draw, but by this time another 27,000-plus crowd was in no mood to be subdued, and they said you could hear the Red, red robin bob-bob-bobbin' right back into the city centre. A win would have been nice, of course, and two goals to take the season's tally up to a hundred would have been nicer, but all such thoughts disappeared after the final whistle – and besides, three goals in the last two games, both away, solved the latter of those problems. Arthur Oakley, senior vice-president of the Football League, presented the championship shield to Jack White as the crowd formed a great semi-circle in front of the main stand, and Harry Dolman declared it 'the happiest day of my life'. Jack, addressing the hordes in his broad South Yorkshire accent, ventured to take issue with his boss. 'The chairman has said he's the happiest man in Bristol tonight,' he said, 'but I don't think he is, because I am.' Another great roar went up, as it did for each of the players in turn. One that threatened to raise the roof was reserved for John Atyeo, not for the last time in his life.

The brace at home to Palace was John's sixth of the season, the others coming away at Coventry and Walsall and at home to those good old whipping boys Aldershot, as well as Milwall and Bournemouth. He was far from alone in grabbing the Saturday night headlines, however. When a team scores one hundred and one goals and the top scorer grabs twenty-eight of them, it gives plenty of others a chance to get in on the act. Chief among these was Jimmy Rogers, who moved to centre-forward after Arnold Rodgers lost form in late January. In his early thirties by now and a City player since 1949, Arnie left for a brief spell with Shrewsbury Town that told him his playing days really were through. His contribution to the championship push before all went awry for him was thirteen goals in twenty-six games. As for Jimmy, his spell at centre-forward during the Reds' unbeaten last eighteen games saw him score fifteen, in addition to the ten he had already grabbed from the wing, and even John Atyeo had no answer to his purple patch in February and March, when he lashed in eleven in nine games. Like Andy Micklewright the season before, he could not believe how easy bagging goals could be when Big John was laying the ball off, flicking it on and generally putting the opponents' defence on the rack.

The defensive heroes who won Bristol City their only post-war championship to date were goalkeepers Tony Cook, who injured his arm in November, and Bob Anderson a hasty signing from Bristol Rovers reserves; right-back Ivor Guy; left-backs Jack Bailey, another broken arm victim, and his replacement Mike Thresher; right-halves Jimmy Regan and skipper Jack White, who started the season at left-half, before Cyril Williams dropped back and made that position his own; and centre-half Ernie Peacock.

When Jimmy Rogers switched to centre-forward, the number seven shirt went to Arthur Milton, an inspired stop-gap signing from Arsenal in the February who played in fourteen of the last fifteen games. Bristol-born, a glamour boy at Arsenal, and England's last double international at football and cricket, he did not kick another ball in League football after that, retiring at the age of twenty-seven to concentrate on the summer game, but this was a brief and happy swansong. The Gunners asked £3,000 for his services, a reminder that the sentimental nature of his homecoming did not wash with their money men. The significance of this brief sojourn was not lost on Pat Beasley, however, who had a special commemorative medal made for Arthur when he fell one game short of qualifying for an official championship gong.

John Atyeo, of course, was at inside-right, with Rodgers and Rogers taking turns at number nine, Tommy Burden taking over at inside-left from Cyril Williams and Jack Boxley whizzing down the left flank. Inevitably, one or two faces changed. Time was all but up for Jimmy Regan and Alec Eisentrager, though the latter played in a smattering of Second Division games over the next couple of seasons.

The most significant newcomer apart from the transient Arthur Milton was Tommy Burden, whose arrival in October 1954 was hailed by Atyeo as the finding of the last piece of the jigsaw: 'He'd had a dis-agreement with Leeds United, walked out on them and took a job at Clark's in Street. I suppose Leeds had no real alternative but to accept City's offer of £3,000 – and what a great signing he turned out to be. He was outstanding, and showed class in everything he did. We had a good team before he came. His arrival made it special.' Burden, a part-timer and thinker, was a man very much after Atyeo's heart, as later events would prove. Almost an honorary West Countryman, born in Andover, he was admired by his new team-mates not just for his experience – he had carried enough authority to be captain at Elland Road – but for the smooth passing from wing-half that had helped bring out the best in a developing John Charles and would now serve Atyeo and Williams handsomely. He was a natural leader who liked responsibility and dictating tactics on his feet, but Raich Carter, his

boss at Leeds, mistrusted part-timers as much as Peter Doherty
would in a few years' time, and now, at the age of thirty, he saw a
job in management at a West Country shoe factory as his best step
forward. He later took charge of works at Plymouth and Barnstaple.
Harry Dolman was straight on the case, and that £3,000 fee was
made up of £1,500 on the nail and another £1,500 depending on
appearances. Since Tommy went on to turn out for City a further two
hundred-plus times, Harry Dolman presumably found the top-up fee
well worth paying for a man seen by many beyond John Atyeo as the
missing link, the one who made things happen.

   Though this was a team in the true sense of the word – the best City
line-up since the war, according to some diehards, though others deem
this harsh on the boys of the late 1970s – it had undoubted stars in John
Atyeo, Tommy Burden and Cyril Williams. Atyeo himself put the
magic down to the blend Pat Beasley had put together – 'a bit of everything in the team. Tom Burden and Cyril Williams had a lot of craft
and experience, Jack Boxley and Jimmy Rogers had tremendous pen-
etration on the wings, scoring plenty of goals as well, and the defence
was dominated by Ernie Peacock, Jack White and Ivor Guy. We were
like a very good First Division side playing in the Third.' Atyeo was
particularly proud of the way the team bounced back from those two
serious arm injuries: 'In two successive matches we suffered cruel
blows. Jack Bailey broke his arm at Northampton Town and didn't play
again that season, and in the following match at home to Watford, Tony
Cook broke his arm and Ivor Guy went in goal for about an hour. That
was an incredible match, and one people still talk about. The pitch was
heavy and we only had ten men, because there were no substitutes in
those days. Ivor Guy didn't play badly, but he had all the luck in the
world. We held out until the last minute, when Jimmy Rogers broke
away on the right and from his cross Jack Boxley crashed one of his
many stunning drives in to give us a one-nil win.' The fact that it did
not happen quite as John recalled it does not detract from that heroic
performance. In fact Cook was deemed fit to turn out against
Southend United in the F.A. Cup the following weekend. All was not
well with him, however, and after a four-one home defeat by
Gillingham just before Christmas he gave way to Anderson for the rest
of the season. None of this alters the fact that on that heroic afternoon
against Watford, Bristol City battled with ten men and a full-back for

a goalie for eighty-six minutes and then pinched the game at the last gasp.

Ivor Guy, a home-grown wartime signing who was still just under thirty but seemed years older with his huge bald pate, intrigued and amused John Atyeo, a player whose career was about to soar. 'He was one of the greatest characters I came across in football.' John recalled. 'He always reminded me of the old-time amateurs who couldn't care less. Money didn't seem to matter very much to him. I've heard Syd Hawkins, the secretary in those days, call to Ivor and say "come in and get your wages, I've got six pay packets here for you". When the team sheet went up, Ivor would say to me "now then, Johnny, if you're round Ashton Gate at two o'clock tomorrow, drop in, because we might be busy".' What might have escaped John's notice here was the distinct possibility that it was Ivor Guy, the ultimate old pro, who was slyly and jokily treating the young part-timer to whom everything seemed to be coming so easily as one of 'the old-time amateurs' who might or might not deign to call in at the ground on a matchday afternoon. He was sparing enough with his attendance during the week, after all.

At the end of his career, John looked back with affection on several other team-mates from that championship year: 'Ernie Peacock was always full of life, and loved every minute of the game. He was a Jekyll and Hyde character. When he pulled on a football shirt he would tear your heart out, but off the field he was one of the nicest fellows you could wish to meet. Jack White was a very good signing from Aldershot. I thought Jack was a bit slow, but he had lots of ability and was one of the best volleyers I've ever seen. Then again, Mike Thresher's long association with the club started this season. He took over when Jack Bailey was injured and became a good pal of mine over the years. You didn't have to worry about right-wingers when Thresh was playing. He was so quick, was tremendously fit and tackled like a ton of bricks.

'Arnold Rodgers used to take all the knocks and sort defences out. He was one of the best actors in the game. He could get a penalty better than anyone I've seen. He fell over legs that weren't even there.' Moving on, John commented: 'I learned a lot from Cyril Williams, a most accomplished player. In my earlier days he couldn't understand why I couldn't play the ball back to him. I always wanted to go forward, but he taught me to play the ball back and then go forward. Jimmy Rogers had a lot of pace, lots of fire and was very brave for a slightly-built chap. His humour and prowess as a practical joker kept the team in fits all the time he was at the club.' Finally, John reached the outside-left position: 'During my time with the club we had three different left-wingers with fantastic left feet. Jack Boxley, as good as any you'd find that season, had the most cultured left foot of all. He could drop the ball anywhere, at any height and any pace. Johnny Watkins, who came later, could do anything with his left, but Peter Hooper had the most powerful left foot of the three. Some of the goals he blasted in were amazing.'

City rounded off their celebrations with a continental tour that took in a dreary succession of five meaningless games in ten days, four in Germany and one in the grey North Austrian steel town of Linz. The top crowd was 7,000 to see the Reds whip Hamborn 07 five-one in the opening match, and there followed a nil-all draw at Augsburg, defeat at Linz and narrow wins at Stuttgart Kickers and Singen. By the time they got home it was early June, and wonderful though the beautiful game had been for them that season, they had seen enough of it for a couple of months. Even John Atyeo was losing his appetite for it, not least because he always saw being away from home as a trial, but an incident late on in the trip never ceased to amuse him.

He was always fascinated by the contrast between the manager Pat Beasley 'quiet, unassuming and a bit of a worrier' and trainer Wilf Copping, a tough sergeant-major type who looked as if he would explode if anyone gave less than 100 per cent, with the proviso that 'as long as you were winning, he didn't give a damn. You could please yourself what you did'. Wilf's party piece was to head-butt the heavy treatment room door growling: 'There, hardest part of the body, you see.' There was a rule on this tour that the players had to be in the hotel by eleven at night, which all of them, including Atyeo, thought was too early. They said as much to Wilf Copping, who replied: 'Don't worry, lads, stay out a bit longer, I'll get Pat drunk.' There was a perverse inevitability about the upshot, as recalled by John: 'When we rolled in about midnight, there was Pat waiting for us in the lobby, as fresh as a daisy. Wilf was slouched out in a chair.'

CHAPTER 7

HERE BE DRAGONS

Promotion to the Second Division meant more than a step up in the world. It put players who had plied their trade in one part of the country on the national stage for the first time, and the Wessex Coaches drivers out at Brislington suddenly found far-away places with such strange sounding names as Grimsby, Doncaster and Bury on their itinerary; knowing the routes in those pre-motorway days, the petrol stations and the refreshment and toilet stops, took research, experience and skill, and though it was up to the club to book hotels for meals and overnight stays, it was down to the driver to find these often tucked-away hidey-holes, in the middle of winter and almost invariably in the dark. They were all right on the West side of the country as far as the Potteries, through Port Vale's long, incongruous and reluctant membership of the Third Division South: A38 to Worcester, A440 to Stafford, A34 to Newcastle-under-Lyne, and then off for Burslem on the A53. It was a mantra they could chant off by heart, but anything north or east of that was strictly Here Be Dragons territory. For longer journeys, particularly in the Peter Doherty era, the team often travelled first class by train, arriving back at Temple Meads in the early hours of the morning in sleeper cars after particularly long trips. The railway was also the only choice for games in South Wales before the first Severn Bridge opened in the autumn of 1966, too late for John Atyeo as a player.

If the travelling was a bugbear to the men who wore the proud livery of Wessex Coaches, it was even more so to John. He disliked it intensely, both the being away from home and the physical experience of it. Just as he could never seriously see football as an occupation to demand a man's full-time attention, he felt a deep pointlessness in trailing the length and breadth of the country to play it every other Saturday afternoon, spending Friday night away from Dilton Marsh more often than not. Every time the coach was grinding endlessly back

71

home from a trip to Carlisle, John would grumble that it would suit him just fine if that club thought of joining the Scottish League. He held this belief into his retirement, arguing that 'their own travelling would be greatly decreased, and I know many teams in the South of England would be delighted'. Doubtless the lads at Brunton Park would have been just as happy to see Bristol City consigned to the Welsh League. That was the trouble with England, in John's view; on Saturdays, it was just too darned big.

As a travelling companion, John Atyeo was quiet and easy-going, a popular lad rather than one of the lads. Tommy Burden was very much the same, in a world of his own with his novel. John would very occasionally join the likes of Tony Cook, Bobby Etheridge, Ivor Guy, Ernie Peacock, Wally Hinshelwood, Ron Nicholls, Alan Williams and the *Evening Post* man Peter Godsiff in their card school, usually brag or hearts, but more often than not he was happier reading the paper or a book, or chatting for a while with anybody or everybody. No intellectual snob – he was too unworldly and unpretentious ever to run the risk of being accused of that – he nevertheless knew that he was coming from a different direction from several of his team mates, with their smutty jokes and banter about birds and booze and dog results at Eastville. The City director Graham Whittock was both a neighbour and a friend, and he would happily while away an hour or so chatting with him on the coach. When he had been a young engineer working in Frome after leaving school at thirteen, Whittock had played cricket with John's father Walter. He was a flamboyant character, renowned for his spats and jazzy ties on match days and a devil-may-care attitude to life, but he took great pride in his friendship with the Atyeo family and what he saw as his duty of care to Walter's talented son, for whom he would often act as a chauffeur.

The lads would occasionally see the Atyeo entrepreneurial skills at work. 'We were up at Bradford one time, and for some reason none of us could understand, the chairman presented John with half a dozen suit lengths,' Brian Clark recalls. 'We wondered what he was going to do with those, but we soon found out. He was up and down the aisle trying to sell them to us.' John would also talk to reporters aboard the coach from time to time, and liked to pick up insights into their slant on the game and life in general – especially in his later playing days, when he was seriously considering a career in journalism. Prime among these was David Foot, at first the *Evening World*'s reporter at

Ashton Gate and later a versatile freelance, and the two would discuss cricket at least as often as football. The summer game was Foot's first sporting love, and there were times he could almost imagine it was Atyeo's, too. David prized his independence, as he still does, and never felt altogether at ease travelling with the team. Sometimes, however, somewhere up in the West Riding and with no prospect of a train until eight o'clock, he would swallow his pride and gratefully hitch a ride on the coach. This was not always a fruitful exercise. Once, Pat Beasley, discovering David was aboard and still seething over a piece he had written about a hushed-up injury to Thresher in a preview to the match, ordered him off the bus in the blowy Pennines between Huddersfield and Sheffield with the mercifully brief command of: 'Out!' Happily, warmer relations were soon restored.

John would fall quiet for the radio for the latecomers' reading of the classified results on *Sports Report* and later for *Transatlantic Quiz*, a show that soared above the heads of most of the others aboard. He was one of those people who could hear the results just once and know them by heart, whether it was Wolves against Manchester United in the First or Brechin-Cowdenbeath in the Scottish B. It is not an attribute that necessarily denotes academic intelligence, but you still have to be bright and extremely interested in the subject to do it, and have the kind of way with numbers that makes quantity surveying and teaching maths less of a burden than they would be to most people. The lads called him Rosie at times like this, after Bristol Zoo's celebrated elephant.

As for *Transatlantic Quiz*, it stretched his brain and extended his knowledge in a way that always pleased him. The British panel consisted of (Lord) John Julius Norwich and the 'Brain of Brains' Irene Thomas, who pitted their wits against two equally intellectual heavyweights in New York under the chairmanship of Anthony Quinton, a former Principal of New College, Oxford; the show was not known to be the radio programme of choice for many Football League teams returning home on a Saturday evening, and the fact that the other players humoured John and let him have it on is a sign of their respect for him and his 'differentness'. He also loved playing around with obscure hypothetical football situations, along the lines of 'if a forward shot and the ball was going wide but hit the ref's backside and went up in the air and bounced off a seagull and came down off a policeman's helmet into the net, would it be a goal?'. The ears of his team mates would be deaf to such conundrums, however, and it was not until he joined up with the England party and encountered Reg Matthews that he finally found someone to join him in these flights of tortured fantasy.

Goalkeeper Matthews was the same age as John and had a very similar pedigree, rising to international status from the Third Division South. The difference was that Coventry City, his home town team, stayed down there while City went up, and unlike Atyeo he had the nerve and ambition to move on to Chelsea just before Christmas 1956. He used to drive the teenage Jimmy Greaves crackers on the coach. Once, Greavsie recalled, Reg and a team mate rode half the length of the country arguing the toss over whether a level pitch was the same thing as an even pitch. John, on the other hand, remembered the goalie as: 'A great character. I had the privilege of playing with him and getting to know him really well. No tour could be a flop with this humorous man included.' Tell that to Jimmy Greaves.

Big John soon tired of the card school, and not only because he was too careful with his money to put very much of it at risk. When he did join in, he could sometimes surprise some of his more worldly-wise colleagues. 'In my record of playing poker, you're the only player who won every time he sat down for a game,' Bert Tindill told him after he had moved back north, 'but then, not everyone has a poker face!' Tony Cook remembered him to the end not for playing cards, but for telling him where he was going wrong. More often than not, though, John would lean on the backs of his team-mates' seats and watch them play with amused interest, and get some kind of vicarious pleasure from seeing what seemed to him to be big money changing hands. He could also see how card games, if they stayed friendly, could cement team spirit. On a trip to Northampton as a youngster he had got involved in a hand of solo, which he had never played before, and came unstuck when one of the other lads went *misère*, declaring that no tricks would be taken: 'I'd got rid of one suit, except the four. I didn't think there was much danger, but I got caught, and the others cursed me.' Hours later, after battling it out at the County Ground for eighty minutes or more, City had a free kick awarded against them on the edge of the penalty area. Tony Cook was waving his arms and screaming at his wall to firm up and move a yard left, the Northampton lads were moaning 'Ten yards, ref, they're never ten yards', and behind the net the home fans were baying for the goal that would give them the points. John Atyeo was pulled back into the wall between Ernie Peacock and Ivor Guy as they tugged and jostled each other in response to Twink Cook's roars; then the referee raised his arm to signal that he was about to blow, a sudden hush fell over the terraces, and there was Ivor growling: 'Hey, Johnny, you should have thrown that bloody four away, you know.'

It was always Bobby Etheridge who came up with these fancy card games. When they were travelling north he would hop on the coach or train at Gloucester, and as he made his way down the aisle to the reprobates' corner towards the back he would be chirping 'Got a new one for you this week, lads'. They would be up towards Worcester before he had finished explaining it, with John listening in as intently as any of the gamblers. Bobby was certainly up to all the tricks. One day they were in the middle of a game when they got to the ground and agreed to put their cards in their pockets and take it up where they left off on the way home. Ethers and Alan Williams quietly compared what they had got, cobbled together a winning hand between them and split the money. For them, at least, it was a good start to the return trip.

As time went on, John's special mate in the team was Mike Thresher, another young West Countryman; but he liked Etheridge, who was streetwise and quick-witted in ways he was not – 'the original Alfie', according to Peter Godsiff – and the big man found himself rooming with him for a time. This could have its tricky moments. One Saturday morning in a Plymouth hotel Atyeo was making for his bedroom door when David Foot intercepted him in the corridor.

'I wouldn't go in there at the moment, John.' 'Why not?' 'Well,' said Foot, with that air of diffidence that has never quite left him after sixty years in journalism, 'Bobby's in there showing the chambermaid how you're going to beat Argyle this afternoon.'

One morning, at the start of a three-day stay at a hotel in Derby, John and Bobby were served tea in their room by a pretty young maid. 'She's nice,' said Etheridge, 'I'm going to take a chance with her tomorrow.' 'You can't,' John protested. 'You're going to get us into trouble.' Bobby would have none of it, though, and next morning, when they heard the clinking of cups in the corridor, he threw aside the bedclothes to reveal himself in all his glory. Not daring to look, John flung his blanket over his head, only to hear a woman of very mature years saying: 'If that's all you've got, I'd keep it covered up.'

Sometimes it seemed that Bobby was just intent on shocking his more strait-laced friend. One midsummer night at Dilton Marsh, at one in the morning, John was roused from his sleep by the telephone. 'I've achieved my lifelong ambition,' a familiar Gloucester voice was slurring. 'I've just had a black piece.' Then clunk, the phone slammed down, and he was gone.

Adventures with women were never part of John Atyeo's routine, but in other ways he went with the flow when he was on the road with the team, to the extent that Alan Williams, centre-half in the late 1950s and early '60s, felt he would have been a good pal off the pitch as well as on if only he had not disappeared back to Dilton Marsh as soon as he could. Even for the full-timers, the training schedule was hardly arduous, rarely going on much after mid-day from Monday to Thursday, with perhaps a Sunday afternoon 'soap massage' after a hard Saturday afternoon. Many of the players would uphold a long tradition and drift along to the Robins café on the corner of the Ashton Road entrance to the ground after they had showered and dressed, drink tea in the little back room and eat the kind of lunch that will not be found in any modern sports nutrition manual. John would be in there with them, but only for a quick cuppa before getting on with his life. He was not alone in this, but others might sit around for hours; it was easy to see who saw training as the first phase in a busy day and the ones for whom the afternoon and evening stretched ahead inconsequentially, maybe interspersed by a frame or two of snooker here, a round of golf there, a picture or a night out with the lads chasing the birds.

Alan Williams, a dedicated night owl in those far-off days, has happy memories of trips to the Glen at Durdham Down, a Mecca ballroom set in old-fashioned pleasure grounds, the Town's Talk on the A38 south of town and the Lamb and Lark near Keynsham, a traditional coaching inn that was demolished to make way for a Somerfield supermarket. One of those great rambling places with a yard and outbuildings, it ran regular Tuesday evening ballroom dances in a hall at the back, and the smartly suited Williams, Jim Terris and Jimmy Rogers would often be seen there. 'It was good that it was on Tuesdays, because that was the last night of the week we were allowed out,' says 'Will', with a face so poker that it is easy to see why he won so many hands of cards on the coach. All Alan Williams will say about the activity at the Lamb and Lark today is that the lads used to play 'grab a grot', a version of 'grab a granny', in which one of them would ask the plainest girl in the room to dance and the others would take it in turns and do an 'excuse me' and whisk her off for a few more circuits of the floor; except, sometimes, they stayed put at the bar, and left their mate to battle it out unaided. The merriment of their evening presumably did not always begin and end there, but 'Will's' straight face deters further probing.

Bobby Etheridge never ceased to make good-natured fun of John Atyeo, especially his reluctance to put his hand in his pocket. One day as they were queuing at a coach stop there was much whispering and shuffling around behind the big man and somehow Bobby had manoeuvred the situation so that John felt obliged to pay for the whole order, something like fourteen cups of tea at threepence a cup. It was widely rumoured to be the only time he bought a round of drinks in his life, and his team mates, at least, liked to think he never quite got over it. There were other rituals. If City had won, Ernie Peacock would serenade the coach with a heartfelt 'Thank you for the points today, Lord'. Then there would be the ceremonial dropping-off of Bobby Etheridge at Gloucester – or John Atyeo at Standerwick, his true native patch, just where the lane to Dilton Marsh met the A36, if the game had been down in Bournemouth or Southampton. The sight of him standing waiting for the coach on the outward journey was a timeless little vignette. Sometimes he would have Graham Whittock with him but always, it seemed, he would be wrapped up in that old fawn mac of his, buttoned and belted against the elements. Men's mackintoshes of the 1950s are often thought of as trenchcoats these days, but the latter were very different, lighter in colour and texture and with reinforced shoulder panels. Humphrey Bogart wore trenchcoats. Big John and conventional men of his generation wore fawn macs, identical in design to blue or dark green gabardines worn by school-children since the 1930s. There was nothing remotely Humphrey Bogart about John Atyeo's fawn mac; more a grown-up Just William.

Away trips also gave John's team-mates the chance to view his prodigious appetite at close quarters. 'He'd eat up first, and then ask if he could have our scraps,' Johnny Watkins recalls. There were plenty of big eaters at Bristol City at that time, and John's physique and call-ing gave him every excuse and reason to keep well stoked up, but there were occasions when he shocked even his closest companions. One was the night before the fourth round F.A. Cup tie against Sunderland

in January 1964, no time to be travelling to that part of the country
with memories of the previous year's Big Freeze still vivid. John was
out of sorts with it from the start – to paraphrase the Humphrey Bogart
he was not, he wondered 'of all the football grounds in all the world in
the middle of winter, why did it have to be Roker Park?'– and by the
time he was sitting down to dinner on the Friday evening, he had lost
the plot completely. As the waiting staff buzzed around, he heaped
food on to his plate until he looked like Desperate Dan behind his cow
pie in the *Dandy*.

'Crikey, John, you're going it a bit tonight.'

'Might as well,' Atyeo replied. 'It's all we're going to get out of this
trip.'

At the time, City were a very decent Third Division outfit,
Sunderland a Second Division team heading for promotion behind
Leeds at the end of the season. Of course they might have been expected to win at home, but the Robins had their full-strength team out, and
there was the prospect of playing on a wintry pitch that might prove to
be a great leveller. Some of the lads quite fancied themselves for a
draw and another big night at Ashton Gate. The following afternoon
Sunderland won six-one in front of more than forty-six thousand, and
nobody in the visiting party was very proud as they slunk back to
Bristol that night. John Atyeo had more reason to reflect on the day
than most. It was one of those rare times when he let down both himself and the club he loved.

City had let themselves in for another tricky January journey five
years earlier, in 1959, when, dressed in the borrowed blue of Cardiff
City, they had drawn at home one-all to the away-strip whites of
Blackpool in the Cup. They travelled north by air for the replay four
days later; it was the first time the team had flown to an away match,
a decision reached because of treacherous and wintry road conditions
and the fact that Squires Gate airport was all but on the doorstep of
Bloomfield Road. John had flown before on international duty, and
had hated the experience. On the Blackpool trip he was desperately
nervous, more so than anyone else in the aircraft, a mixed party of
players, management, directors and journalists; maybe he looked
around him and thought of another such group at a snowy Munich
airport twelve months previously, and pondered the horrific fate of a
Manchester United party whose dead included four players he had
fleetingly learned to admire and respect as England team-mates.

Of course, his fears were unfounded, and not long after touchdown the team was safely ensconced at the Norbreck Hydro, a health spa hotel much favoured at that time by Northern football clubs for winter breaks, with its gyms, brine baths and bracing runs along the sands. 'I was on the first floor, and we'd hardly arrived when a familiar Wiltshire voice came booming down from two floors up,' the journalist David Foot recalls. 'John was shouting: "Hello Ruth. Got here safe." He was on the phone home to his wife, but to me he sounded more like a boy reassuring his mother that he was safe and well. He was an emotional man, and he was fraught on that journey. We were all relieved for him when we touched down.' Blackpool won an undistinguished replay in the fog one-nil without Stanley Matthews, who, as will be explained, was John's reluctant flying partner of earlier days. More than 42,000 had seen Stan played out of the game at Ashton Gate by Mike Thresher, and Blackpool were not going to risk that happening again. In defence of the old maestro, he was a few days short of his forty-fourth birthday at the time, while Thresh was twenty-seven. No matter, Blackpool at home in the Cup was a game the strong lad from Cullompton remembered for the rest of his life, and deservedly so. The Atyeo nerves were further jangled after the Wednesday night game, when the thickening fog ruled out an early return home, and come Thursday morning, still stranded at the Norbreck Hydro, he was not the only one fretting and thinking that this was far from ideal preparation for Saturday's game at Ashton Gate.

CHAPTER 8

ATYEO OF ENGLAND

Life was never more exciting for John Atyeo than in that champion-ship season of 1954-55. Still in his very early twenties, he was grow-ing into a hero at home and a player whose feats were becoming increasingly admired elsewhere. The first he knew of important out-side interest – 'my big break', as he always looked back upon it – came early in the season, in the October, when he was picked for the F.A. XI to play the Royal Air Force at Highbury. He scored twice and hit a screamer against a post, while Stanley Matthews was also on the score sheet, having been selected to add lustre to a game against the armed service of his war-time years. It was a great night for John, and there was icing on the cake the following morning when the newspapers reckoned that only he and Ron Flowers, even younger at barely twen-ty, were the only two players who had enhanced their reputation. Flowers, too, was making his debut at this level, and impressed because, although picked at left-half, he found his feet instantly when he was switched to centre-half after Derek Ufton of Charlton had cried off injured.

Flowers looked glamorous with his blond curls and was a rising star in one of the most high-profile teams in the country in Wolves, but off the field he was just a down-to-earth lad from Doncaster, and John got to know and like him when, before very long, they found themselves in the full England squad. In the event, they were lining up together again a few nights after the R.A.F. game when they were kept in the F.A. side to play the Army at Hillsborough. John played in four more of these games over the years, including a nine-nil rout of the R.A.F. at Ashton Gate in front of 23,396 in October 1955 in which he scored four; it is sad to think that his last appearance in an F.A. XI was just four years after the Highbury win, in October 1958, when he turned out in a weak team against the R.A.F. to help boost an indifferent crowd at Ashton Gate to above 14,000. He scored his side's only goal in a four-one defeat that night, and when he left the field he could not but have thought back to Highbury, 1954, and reflected on how different life had looked to him then.

As a reminder of the extent to which he regarded football as simply a part of life, rather than the be-all and end-all, he also looked back on the heady season of 1954-55 as the time he was awarded his diploma as a quantity surveyor. This should have been a happy occasion, but it was not, since his employers were growing increasingly concerned about the time he was spending away from them. It has been suggested that this was a short-sighted attitude on their part, and that there would have been kudos and sense in keeping the big man on their books for publicity value, but this is surely debatable. The duties of a small-town quantity surveyor are not for public consumption, and besides, John Atyeo was scarcely Bruce Forsyth or Hughie Greene in terms of 1950s showmanship. They asked him to give up either football or working for them, which was a pretty silly question, even given John's balanced view of the world. He handed in his notice, but soon found another post with Syd Bate, a smaller builder in Westbury. It was the kind of job that offered no chance of promotion, but Syd knew enough about Atyeo as both a man and a footballer to allow him to have as much time off as he needed. 'For the next two or three years, that was quite a lot,' Big John recalled laconically.

In a classic build-up to full international honours, his next milestone was selection for the England under-23 side, or Young England as it was called in those days, to play Italy at Stamford Bridge in January 1955. He was the first City player to be honoured by England at so senior a level since Billy Wedlock in 1914, and his sense of history and tradition was strong enough for this to mean something to him. England won the game five-one, he headed one of the goals and felt quite at home in a team that boasted such class acts as Duncan Edwards and Johnny Haynes. Another team-mate was Stan Anderson of Sunderland, who talked his English in a very different way from John, but kept him amused by tales of the antics of Len Shackleton, the 'Clown Prince of Soccer' whose biography famously featured a chapter headed 'The Average Director's Knowledge of Football', followed by a blank page. Shackleton's days at the top were over, but experiences such as this steeped Atyeo more and more in football lore, and gave him stepping stones to be part of a wider picture.

Most of the team that played Italy stayed together to beat Young
Scotland six-nil at Clyde's Firhill Park in Glasgow the following
month, and again John was on the scoresheet. The next call-up letter
was for the Third Division South team to play the Third North at
Reading's cramped old Elm Park on March 16, 1955 – but there was
obviously not a lot of liaison between the various selection committees
at the Football League's odd little backstreet headquarters at Starkie
Street, Preston, and just a couple of days later another letter came
through, inviting him to represent the Football League against the
Scottish League at Hampden Park. That was obviously the one he went
for, but though he played well enough, the Scots won through three-
two. Their goals came from Bobby Collins and Harry Haddock and
through an o.g. by the England centre-half Joe Marston, a big
Australian who played for Preston North End and was within a month
or so from retiring from League football after a not particularly distinguished career; since it was taken as read at that time that the Football
League team was made up very largely of England squad players, his
selection was something of a mystery.

The League's goals came from John Evans, who enjoyed a brief but
goal-laden stint with Liverpool, and the Bristol boy made good at
Chelsea Roy Bentley. There is an astonishing photograph of Bentley
scoring for England at Hampden Park in which the vast, packed terraces behind him seem to soar half a mile high, an intimidating sight.
There was no such atmosphere that night, with just under 20,000 on
the ground, about a sixth of its capacity. John Atyeo had mixed feelings about the evening. On the one hand, he played well in a team that
included England giants of the stature of the Busby Babes Ray Wood,
Bill Foulkes and Duncan Edwards and two wingers who could put a
ball across, West Ham's Harry Hooper and Chelsea's Frank
Bluntstone. On the other hand, he did not end up on the scoresheet. He
thought the crowd looked nothing on such a vast ground, and was
struck by features of the Hampden pitch that reminded him more of
parks football – the square goal posts and a playing surface so poor
that it was a reminder that it was used week-in, week-out as the
amateurs Queen's Park's home ground.

Meanwhile, down in Reading, the two Third Divisions were battling
it out in front of 10,000 people who very definitely did not make Elm
Park look deserted. It was the first of these floodlit South-North
games, six of which were played before regionalised League football

ended in 1957, and like most of the rest of them it was a rip-roaring affair. The South won two-nil, the first goal coming from John's replacement at inside-right, John Rainford of Brentford; but this was news scarcely likely to send shivers down the big man's spine as he headed south from Glasgow the following morning. Come the end of the season, Bristol City would not be concerned with Third Division matters any more, and as for him, he was still on target for the ultimate prize, a full England cap.

John played two more representative games that season. On March 23, 1955 he was in the England B side that fought out a one-all draw against West Germany at Hillsborough, while on the eve of the Newcastle United-Manchester City F.A. Cup final in May he played in a Young England exhibition game, not a recognised international, at Highbury. He remembered it chiefly as the only time he played centre-forward in a representative match, all the others being at inside-right. His old Westbury United team-mate, Ernie Barber, still remembers being John's guest at the Cup final the following afternoon, and trying to appear nonchalant in the stand as he watched the game with Atyeo on one side of him and Haynes on the other. So ended a season that saw him a stranger to the international stage at its start, and ended with a string of honours to his name. He could not wait for 1955-56, Second Division football with Bristol City and more opportunities to make a name for himself on a wider stage. 'Pre-season training couldn't come soon enough for me in July 1955,' he recalled. 'That summer I was as excited as a schoolboy, knowing that the coming year promised so much for me and Bristol City. I was on the verge of my life's ambition of playing for England, and City were in their first season back in the Second Division after our wonderful promotion year. I had trained as hard as I had ever done, when we started we were playing with confidence and after a dozen games we were top of the division.' He was scoring as regularly as he had done in the Third Division, and, never one to be unhappy to see his name in the headlines, he now had the satisfaction of knowing that the England selectors would be seeing them, too.

In October, he was pleased and relieved to find himself selected for the England B team to play Yugoslavia at Maine Road, Manchester. 'This was more than just another round of international preliminaries for me,' he reflected at the end of his career. 'This was virtually the final trial. That was certainly how it looked to me at the time, and the sportswriters thought the same.' John scored the first of England's five goals and impressed generally, as the papers made plain the following morning. Many of the commentators, in the North just as much as the South, were sitting up and taking notice of this West Country part-timer, not just because his elevation to full England honours would make a good story, but also for the very sound professional reason that they wanted to be on the case when he made his seemingly inevitable move to one of the moneybag clubs. The next full international was at Wembley against Spain on November 30, and sure enough, P.J.W. Atyeo was named in the squad of seventeen selected for special training for the game. 'I wasn't actually in the team then,' he recalled, 'but everyone seemed to think I was a certainty.' For once, everyone was right.

'Dear Atyeo', the letter telling him to report with his boots began, but John was not quibbling about common courtesies or the lack of them. He was about to step out into unknown territory, and this was one adventure he was not shy of facing up to. Even so, it was not until he was walking out on to the Wembley turf in the famous Three Lions shirt that he could believe that he had made it: 'I had played in dozens of representative matches at all levels leading up to the England team itself. Mine was a comprehensive apprenticeship, and I had been kept going all the time by the faith and advice of my parents. They always impressed upon me that each game I played was a trial for England. I used to gear myself up for these different matches and without boasting, I played some remarkably good games. My consistency probably earned me my chance.'

The game was on a Wednesday afternoon. John had been training with the England squad at Molineux, the Wolves ground, during the previous week, but he was never one to count his chickens. He heard the news of his selection at 3.30 p.m. on the Sunday, when the City manager Pat Beasley phoned him at home at Glenthorne. Tom Lyons, the *Daily Mirror*'s man on the West Country sports scene, went through life thinking he was the one who broke the news, but he was not.

'Well, how do you feel about it?' Tom asked when he called Dilton Marsh a couple of hours later.

'About what?' asked a cagey John. He could be very cagey at times.

'Well, you're in the England side. Didn't you know?'

'Crikey!'

It gave Tom a good story, anyway, in the following day's paper and for the rest of his days.

John caught the London train from Bath the next morning to link up with the party at the Hendon Hall Hotel. City were top of the League at the time, but had come unstuck three-two at struggling Doncaster at the weekend, when he had failed to score. Nevertheless, he had more exciting thoughts on his mind now. A huge challenge lay ahead for him, but he drew some comfort from the fact that the recent Molineux get-together was not the first special training session he had attended, and he already felt he knew most of the players fairly well. Hendon Hall, with its sweeping lawns and sports facilities, was and is one of the great football retreats, and a wonderful setting in which to train, rest and relax. On the Tuesday evening, however, as was usual on the night before the game at that time, the players were bundled aboard a coach and driven down into the busy West End to see a variety show at the London Palladium.

It was a distracting, disorienting episode. Crowds jostled around them in the foyer, begging for autographs and asking in vain where Stanley Matthews was, and the Palladium was abuzz with self-importance. Commercial television had been launched in the London area a couple of months earlier, and one of its most talked-about shows was ATV's *Sunday Night at the London Palladium*, hosted by Fulham's comedian chairman Tommy Trinder. In the weeks after that, some people had gone along just to gaze at the Palladium, such was the magical power of television in those days, and for them suddenly to find themselves mingling with a dozen or so athletic-looking young men wearing the blue Three Lions blazers of England must have made them feel that they were at the centre of the universe. There was an irony about all this glitz and glamour, since television – the medium that helped make the atmosphere at the Palladium so electric that night – was already well on its way to destroying variety in provincial theatres.

Not that this conundrum was occupying too much of John Atyeo's attention that night; in fact, as he glanced around him, and to the left and right of him along the England team's row of the best seats in the house, all he could wonder was 'what am I doing here?' It was a two-pronged question. The only place he really wanted to be was back in the hotel, thinking about the game, perhaps strolling around the grounds and taking in the evening air before an early night; kick-off was two o'clock the following afternoon, so Wednesday morning would soon slip by. He would laugh at the odd joke, grin when a team-mate made a saucy crack about the dancing girls, but really, what was going on up there on stage could have been a million miles away. The other reason he had to pinch himself was the company he found himself in: for Ernie Peacock, Alec Eisentrager and Jimmy Rogers, read Billy Wright, Tom Finney and Nat Lofthouse. He simply sat there pondering on the next day, and better than anything on stage was the spectacle that met his eye on either side of him, the household names who were suddenly accepting him as a colleague and an equal.

John was up early the next morning, and went for a walk in the grounds. It was foggy, visibility was down to a few yards, and he began to worry that the match might be cancelled and he would never be called on again, some hapless footnote in football's litany of quirky hard-luck stories. By the time the squad was getting together for breakfast, however, the thought did not seem to be in anyone else's mind as the manager Walter Winterbottom and captain Billy Wright bustled around to make sure all the lads would be ready in the foyer for the coach just before noon. One man who needed no second bidding was their inside-right. At last, even John was beginning to accept that nothing was going to get in the way of that first cap. As he boarded the bus his thoughts inevitably turned to his father, and the heartening words he had given him not long before: 'Once you walk out in that England shirt, you've made it. From then on it's "Atyeo of England".'

'Perhaps that was one of the reasons why I played so well in that first match,' John later reflected. 'It was a weight off my mind. I'd achieved what I'd intended from the first moment I signed as a professional. I bought about twenty-five tickets for the match, and once it became pretty obvious that my chance was about to come, I made a mental list of all the people who had helped my career from my very early days. I gave them each a ticket for the game. Most of the £50 match fee was spent on tickets, but the money didn't matter a bit that day. I was an England player, and that was all that counted.' A good number of his City colleagues were in the stands, and it need hardly be said that his parents were among his special guests, as was his girl-friend Ruth Harraway, his engagement to whom was announced two days after the game. Walter and Effie had hoped to snatch a word with him before kick-off, but after a slow and frustrating train ride in the fog, they were not even in their seats by the time John set the stadium alight. The team that afternoon was Ron Baynham (Luton), Jeff Hall (Birmingham), Roger Byrne (Manchester United), Ronnie Clayton (Blackburn Rovers), Billy Wright (Wolves), Jimmy Dickinson (Portsmouth), Tom Finney (Preston North End), Atyeo, Nat Lofthouse (Bolton Wanderers), Johnny Haynes (Fulham) and Bill Perry (Blackpool). The reserves were Reg Matthews, still at Coventry, Peter Sillett (Chelsea), National Serviceman Private Duncan Edwards, Bedford Jezzard (Fulham) and Dennis Wilshaw (Wolves), an inside-forward who, like Big John in later years, combined his football with teaching. The game was televised, and for the first time at Wembley the floodlights were switched on in the second half as the evening mist flowed in.

John made a great start. The game was only five minutes old when he and Haynes combined to put Finney through; he was brought down ten yards from goal, but had his spot kick saved by Carmelo, who was at full stretch again a minute later to save from Atyeo. Better was to come. In the eleventh minute, Lofthouse, Finney and Clayton – not a bad trio of accomplices – combined for the Blackburn man to chip a ball across to Atyeo from the right-half position; he caught it on his thigh, and as it dropped he hit it on the turn and it flew into the top corner of the net for the opening goal. A minute later he linked up with Lofthouse to pave the way for Perry to get the second, and England were home and dry. His marker was Jose Maguregui, a quick and attacking-minded half-back from Bilbao, younger than John by a year, but he was also seeing plenty of the left-back, Campanal, a notorious tough guy from Seville whose main task that afternoon was to try to stop Tom Finney by fair means or foul. It gave Atyeo huge satisfaction and confidence to see the two Spaniards exchanging heated words about him, pointing and gesticulating to empty space where each thought the other should have been after he had broken through once again. For years he had prompted this kind of bickering among Third Division South defenders. Now here he was doing it on the international stage, in a language he could not begin to understand. It was a new experience for him, and it felt tremendous. In the second half Tom Finney made amends for his penalty miss, and Perry grabbed his second to give England a four-nil lead before Spain were allowed a late consolation goal under the lights. John might have had another, too, but the referee pulled up play for a foul on him when advantage would have left him with only the goalkeeper to beat. The ref. was more popular seventeen minutes from the end, when he called for the floodlights. There was a huge cheer as they lit up, and even the players glanced at one another in surprise at the transformation. They were well used to playing in the semi-dark in the depths of winter, and saw it as no great hindrance; but yes, this was better, this was good.

The match ended at 3.40 p.m. and there were tears in John's eyes as the massed band of the Grenadier and Welsh Guards brought proceedings to an end with the National Anthem. Back in the spacious but spartan home dressing room, he was elated, and bursting with joy and pride when Billy Wright began ceremoniously handing around the caps. He was horrified to see how some of the experienced players just slung them into their bags: 'This was something I'd strived so hard to achieve, and when Billy handed me mine, I fondled it carefully and packed it neatly away.' Wright had a soft spot for the big lad from Bristol City. By this time he was nearing his hundredth cap for England and about to marry the lead singer of the Beverley Sisters, who by some stretch of the imagination might be looked back on as the Spice Girls of their day, but here any parallels between Billy Wright's lifestyle and that of a later England captain come to an abrupt halt. Deep down he was still an unassuming lad from the Ironbridge of the Depression years, and he was well equipped to recognise what made young Atyeo tick. As he handed him his cap he shook him formally by the hand and said: 'You'll never forget this moment.' John never did. In fact he never forgot the whole week, since his engagement to Ruth on the Friday was followed at the weekend by his second hat-trick of the season, in a five-one home drubbing of Lincoln City. More than 26,000 sang his praises to the rafters at Ashton Gate that afternoon, and life had never seemed sweeter for him. Before the end of the following week, Westbury Urban District Council announced that it planned to host a civic reception for him, at which he would be presented with an illuminated address. At the age of twenty-three, he was already well on his way to being one of his adopted county's national treasures.

There was another goal for him on the following Wednesday, when the England team that beat Spain was brought together again as the Football League line-up to face the League of Ireland at Goodison Park. There were times when the League team was seen as a way of honouring the not-quites of English football, or good Scots players who seemed to be discriminated against by their home country for being 'Anglos'; a Football League jersey was the sum total of the sublime Bert Trautmann's representative honours, for while the West German authorities were well aware of his abilities and liked and respected him, they felt unable to cap him as an exile playing in England. At this stage, however, the League squad was seen very much as a bonding exercise for the full international team, even when it was up against the two line-ups of part-timers from over the water, the League of Ireland from the South and the Irish League from the North. On this occasion, in front of 25,000 on Merseyside, the Football League ran out five-one winners, with John getting the third of the goals. He had played in more meaningful games in front of bigger crowds, but as he set out for home through the rush-hour crowds of football-mad Liverpudlians the following morning he felt that extra fraction more comfortable in his role as one of England's leading footballers. Hurrying for his train down the platform at Lime Street, he knew one or two heads were turning as he passed. He was no longer that obscure and distant chap from the Third South who might have gone to Anfield for a heap of money a couple of seasons back.

Back home at Ashton Gate, John kept on banging in goals for Bristol City on their return to the Second Division; but they did not set the League table alight, and it was with huge delight and relief that he learned at the end of the season that he was in the England team to play Brazil at Wembley three days after F.A. Cup final day. There was also, before then, that extraordinary civic reception and dinner at the end of February at the Laverton Institute at Westbury, at which the council presented him with an illuminated address in honour of his sporting achievements. John told friends he had first been in the hall eight years earlier, to go to his first big dance, and he did not know which was the more nerve-racking. 'I feel more nervous now than when I played in front of thousands at Wembley,' he told the gathering in his acceptance speech. He was never at ease on formal occasions, and to the end ran the risk of looking like the country boy dressed up when he had to wear a suit, but he had no need to worry that night, since he was truly among, if not friends, then well-meaning admirers. 'John Atyeo is the only subject the council is in full agreement on,' said the councillor proposing the toast.

Presenting John with the document, bearing the council's seal, the chairman, Councillor N. T. Parker, said that while its economic value might not have been very high, 'it is the highest honour a civic authority can grant. I speak for the majority of the town when I say that although only a little has been done by Westbury, we would all like to think that we did play some small part in your fantastic rise to fame.' In reply, Atyeo came over as every inch the modest local-boy-made-good he truly was and would remain. 'This is a wonderful and memorable occasion for me, and I will treasure this gift for the rest of my life,' he said. 'The little fame I have achieved I owe to the people who helped me. It is my desire to be a member of the team that will one day bring First Division football to Bristol.' Among the guests, besides Walter, Effie and Ruth, were Harry Dolman and representatives of Westbury United, the Wiltshire Football Association, Warminster and Westbury Rural District Councils and John's old school. Perhaps oddly, on such a night, Councillor Parker sounded a solitary note of caution. He was sure that John would agree with him when he said that it would be a lot easier to fall from his position than remain there, because there were always hundreds of young players fighting for a place in the England team. Home truths, indeed.

The end-of-season game at Wembley was billed as 'The Old World meets the New', and even inward-looking England had had prior notice of the exciting new players being drafted into Brazil's team after their drab showing in the 1954 World Cup in Switzerland. Brazil had played Austria in Vienna a few days earlier, and while Walter Winterbottom's visit to the game was dismissed as 'just another holi-day for him' in some quarters, he saw enough of the South Americans to draw up a plan of campaign. At that time, for instance, it tended to be the wing-halves' job to take throw-ins, and Austria found it hard to cope with the Brazilians' tactic of having the full-back take them, leav-ing the halves free to roam. 'Every throw, pick up Dequina and Zozimo,' he instructed his inside-forwards, John Atyeo and Johnny Haynes. Meanwhile, at the back, Billy Wright was frantically school-ing Jeff Hall in the subtleties of the offside trap in the short time he was allowed away from Birmingham City's Cup final preparations. Arthur Turner, the Birmingham manager, had a great down on the off-side game and did not use it, which left poor Jeff with a steep learning curve. Such was the rudimentary level of tactical awareness of some – by no means all – aspects of football fifty years ago. The game was three days after the Cup final.

Just four men who would help Brazil win the World Cup 1958 were on duty that night – Gylmer in goal, Djalma Santos and Nilton Santos at full-back and Didi up front – but there were other tremendous players in a team which English fans, to their great credit, always will to be exciting and artistic. There seems to be something amiss with the natural laws of the game if Brazil turns out a set of mediocre cloggers; we need to believe in our Brazils and our Real Madrids, god-like idols from afar who can always open our eyes to fresh aspects of the Beautiful Game. That was certainly the spirit of the 97,000 who (almost) packed Wembley that late spring evening, each paying, on average, 48p in decimal money to do so. They gave the visitors a tremendous cheer before the kick-off, making it plain that they were there to be entertained and to admire, and nobody was under greater scrutiny than Didi, whose 'banana kicks' had already been the sensation of one World Cup and would be of another. Much acreage of newsprint was devoted to how he did it, an almost unbelievable scenario, given how footballs swing around today. Just as unbelievable was the incomprehension of Didi's technique displayed by even our most skilful forwards; maybe they, too, prized the tradition that the Latins had that little bit of extra magic. The England team sent out to counter their menace that day was Reg Matthews, Hall and Byrne, Clayton, Wright and Edwards, Stanley Matthews, Atyeo, Taylor, Haynes and debutant Colin Grainger of Sheffield United.

Whatever the expectations, it quickly became clear that England had not read the script. Tommy Taylor tore through the field in the opening seconds, 'like a fire engine', according to Billy Wright, and only just missed with a scorcher. A minute later he went one better by putting the home side ahead, and within five minutes they were two up through Grainger. England were playing tremendous football at this stage, with the newly recalled Stanley Matthews, aged forty-one, asking searching questions of Nilton Santos. More goals looked a certainty, but when they came they were for Brazil, through Paulhino on the right wing and Didi, who equalised with the kind of bewildering banana for which most in the crowd had been secretly longing.

In between times, however, the Brazilians were showing their tougher side. Central defender Billy Wright received – almost unbelievably, by today's standards – the worst 'knock' of his career to date, a gash over his left eye that called for three stitches. There was also an infamous display of Latin temperament in the second half, much to

John Atyeo's chagrin. England had gone ahead again through Taylor, and then there was a farcical hold-up following a quickly-taken free kick by Haynes. Nilton Santos jumped up and caught the ball, knowing his defence was not ready and believing that the referee, in the light of such blatant handball in a friendly game, would agree that it was all a bit too quick and order the kick to be retaken. Instead, Monsieur Guige, a gendarme back home in France, made an expressive Gallic gesture towards the penalty spot, and Atyeo knew his moment had come. It had been agreed before the game: if it was a penalty, he was the man. Not everyone could understand why that decision had been taken, but it had.

Unfortunately, for a maturing player who was beginning to feel he had seen a lot in football, he was not prepared for what came next. One of the Brazilians grabbed the ball and made towards the touchline with it in protest, and the rest trooped off after him; minutes later, after peace had been restored, John could only muster a poorly placed spot-kick which Gylmer saved without too much difficulty. Not long afterwards England won another penalty, and this time it was Roger Byrne's turn to give Gylmer a further moment of glory. Billy Wright had never seen the likes: a cut head and England missing two penalties. Afterwards he mused on what he would have done if there had been a third: 'Maybe I'd have had a crack myself, though I've never yet taken a penalty. With nearly 100,000 pairs of eyes fixed on you, that goal can seem a very, very small thing into which to crack a football.'

It was a strange game in many ways, not least through the new lease of life it seemed to give Stanley Matthews. Johnny Haynes asked him for his autograph in the dressing room before the match, and his hands were shaking so much that he asked him to wait until after it. The Brazilians had been trumpeting in the pre-match build-up that no winger in the world could outwit Nilton Santos, but that evening he could not get near the Maestro. 'Mister Matthews, you are the king,' he told him after the game, and maybe the English selectors should have borne that in mind. Two years later it was Nilton Santos who was running around Stockholm with the World Cup, Stanley Matthews having relinquished his international career more than a year previously. John Atyeo always looked back on this as the most exciting and spectacular match he played in. He certainly cited Matthews, Atyeo, Lofthouse, Haynes and Finney as the best forward line in which he had ever been a part, and it is hard to quarrel with that. When it came to the Matthews or Finney controversy, his vote, as did that of almost every player of his generation, went to Tom: 'I thought an awful lot of him. He was quiet, unassuming and a charming fellow, very talented in everything he did.' Finney has equally affectionate memories of John: 'I mean, there were Nat Lofthouse and Stan Mortensen who couldn't get a game because of this lad from the lower divisions. We were all very, very proud of him.' On tour, John liked the way Tom was just one of the lads, while Stan was always out somewhere, being feted or doing some kind of business or another. He also never forgot the tactical talk he got from Walter Winterbottom before the Brazil game: 'Don't go too far out towards the touchline. Stanley doesn't like it.' That was it. What we must remember, however, is that by judging Matthews and Finney from a 1950s perspective, John and the rest were not comparing like with like, since Tom was more than seven years Stan's junior. By all normal footballing criteria, Matthews's career should have been over by 1950.

John Atyeo accepted all the well-meaning backslaps for his part in England's morale-boosting win over Brazil, though the penalty miss cast something of a cloud over the evening; more of that much, much later in this book. No matter; the powers that were – Winterbottom, the selectors, Billy Wright – saw this, above all, as a victory for England's emerging new talent, in whose number, at this stage, they most definitely counted the big West Countryman. Looking back on the Brazil game, Wright reflected that 'all the young players who had been drafted into the side were familiar with each others' style because of games they had played together either in Service teams or the Young England XI. Outstanding youngsters such as Reg Matthews, Duncan Edwards, Ron Clayton, John Atyeo and Johnny Haynes have all starred at some time or another for Young England, and the Football Association, at long last, appear to be receiving the praise they deserved all the time for their splendid approach to the problem of giving youthful starlets big-match experience together. What's more, the big pay-off is now taking place, and I'm especially honoured to think I've had the opportunity of skippering such bonny young foot-ballers who have dedicated themselves to putting England back on top.'

No doubt Billy did not breathe a word of any such sentiments to this fivesome at the time, at least in so many words, but none of them could have doubted that they were basking in the warm glow of approval a week after the Brazil win, when they were all in the sixteen-man squad for a brief close-season tour of Sweden, Finland and Germany. The choice of the first venue in particular was a reminder, if any was needed, that this was an exercise with World Cup '58 very much in mind. 'The tour was not the success I had hoped it would be,' said John, looking back. 'I kept my place for the first match in Stockholm against Sweden, but failed to score again, and the game ended without a goal. I was dropped, and the selectors were justified when England beat Finland in Helsinki and then went on to Berlin for a big prestige match against West Germany, who were then the World Cup holders. England won to complete a highly satisfactory tour – but the high-lights were achieved without me getting back into the team.'

In fact, if it was a frustrating and fruitless game for John at the Rasunda Stadium, it was a poor day on which to make judgments about his performance. The match was played in blinding sunlight and a gale so fierce that even the most subtly nudged ball up towards the forwards would swirl away for a goal kick, and on a ground that just a few weeks earlier was a tundra of snow and ice. Poor, bumpy pitches came to characterise World Cup '58 – Scotland's Tommy Docherty likened conditions there to the junior football grounds of his youth – and there was a further note of unreality in that the amateur Swedish team did not get together until the eve of the game. Nevertheless, that afternoon, the King and Queen of Sweden were there to shake the players' hands, 50,000 of their countrymen were in the stadium with them and the referee was Holland's legendary Leo Horn; all served as a reminder that freak weather and ground conditions aside, this was a real grown-up football match with national honour at stake.

With the sun low in the West but due to fade by the second half, Billy Wright knew he had to win the toss. Six years previously, in 1949, poor old Ted Ditchburn of Spurs had faced that sun in goal in Stockholm, and England had lost three-one. Billy duly lost the toss once more, but this time Reg Matthews played a blinder, and could not have done more. Up front, John Atyeo was sandwiched between the Manchester United pairing of Johnny Berry and Tommy Taylor, with Johnny Haynes and Colin Grainger on the other flank; but even an attack as crafty and forceful as this could make no impression on such a day. Afterward, Billy Wright was able to reflect: 'That match did us a great deal of good. It put everyone still more on their toes for the hard match we knew we had ahead in Berlin.' By 'everyone', of course, he meant everyone who played in that West Germany game, and John was not of one of them; competitively, his tour ended when he walked off the pitch in Stockholm.

Before the Berlin showdown there was the game at the Olympic Stadium in Helsinki, where Manchester United's Ray Wood took over from a battered and bruised Reg Matthews in goal and the forward line was reshuffled at the expense of both the right-sided players in Stockholm, Berry and Atyeo. Birmingham's Gordon Astall was brought in at outside-right, Haynes was switched from inside-left to inside-right, Taylor and Grainger kept their places at numbers nine and eleven and Dennis Wilshaw was given another outing at inside-left. England won five-one in an eerily three-quarters-empty ground, and there were goals from Astall, both inside-forwards – plus two from Nat Lofthouse, who had come on for Tommy Taylor after the Manchester United man had been injured in a collision with the Finnish goalkeeper Hurri. For Nat, it was a game of high emotion. He needed two goals to overtake Steve Bloomer's overall total of twenty-eight for England, had all but given up on the chase because of Taylor's consistently brilliant form – and now, given the sniff of an opportunity, he seized it with both hands.

The dressing room was abuzz after the game, and it left John Atyeo in pensive mood, pondering the fates that can leave sportsmen in the depths of despair one day and as high as kites the next. There was further food for thought for him in the evening, when the Finnish football association threw a banquet that Wright looked back on as the greatest team party he had ever seen. The life and soul of it was Colin Grainger, an even more recent addition to the England squad than John, and a modest and seemingly anonymous Yorkshireman who had spoken very little in the few weeks he had been part of the set-up. This was the night the England team discovered what was soon to be a very well known fact about him – that he was a night club singer quite able enough to go professional, and with a personality that shone like rhinestones as soon as he was under the spotlight. Up on stage he was the voice of them all – Johnnie Ray, Frankie Laine, Al Jolson, Dickie Valentine – in a bravura performance which at first startled and then excited his team-mates.

In the great scheme of things it made zero impact on his career as an England player – he won seven caps to Atyeo's six – but there must have been a part of Big John that was wishing, on this night of all nights, that he could make a little more off-field impact on his fellow players. He was not sorry when it was time to turn in, with a five-thirty alarm call for the flight to Hamburg the following morning. There were a few quiet younger lads like him in the squad, but there was one fewer after that night.

Next day, the team had a long coach journey from the airport at Hamburg to the England training camp at the Barsinghausen Sportschule, near Hanover. It was one of several set up by the German football association on money from pools companies, and there was nothing remotely like them in the rest of Western Europe. Billy Wright had been there before, and was looking forward to the reaction of the players who had not. He was not disappointed. They had been travelling since six in the morning and by now it was six at night, but as soon as they saw the huge gymnasium, some sixty metres by twenty-five, they demanded an eight-a-side game after dinner was over. It started off in slapstick fashion; the two jokers of the team, Nat Lofthouse and Reg Matthews, were chosen as captains, and before the kick-off the teams were formally presented to the 'guests of honour', Walter Winterbottom and trainer Jimmy Trotter. Then the players rolled their sleeves up and slogged away at as fierce a practice kickaround as could be imagined and John was in his element again, in the thick of it and getting among the goals. He also pleased the lads when it was his turn to make them their morning tea, only to discover that Tommy Taylor had taken all their keys and hidden them. Big John put all his Dilton Marsh tree-climbing skills to good use by clambering through the window of his room and ensuring that they had their cuppa on time.

The West Germany game was at the Olympic Stadium in Berlin, a city starkly divided in those pre-Wall but still bitterly Cold War years. Even so comparatively soon after the Second World War there were already few in the squad who had fought against Germany, and the older hands mused on how quickly the conflict was passing into history. The flight from Hanover landed at an airfield in the heart of the city, where England found a large crowd awaiting them. There was sightseeing to be done from their base at the Gurhas Hotel, not least to the still heavily bomb-damaged Eastern Sector, where they saw the Reichstag, Hitler's bunker and the great new Russian war memorial, but they were all glad to retreat back into the incomparably more prosperous West; more a different world than another part of the city, Billy Wright concluded. On the eve of the match the squad went down to the stadium to look around, and it was there that the team was announced. The surprise, for those who had not seen that vigorous eight-a-side game, was that the two Finland casualties, Jeff Hall and Tommy Taylor, were both fit and raring to go, which meant that Nat Lofthouse, for all his record-breaking heroics, was back on the bench. As for John Atyeo, he was expecting nothing from the team sheet, and he was not disappointed; the forward line was the same as the one that started in Helsinki. All he could do, next day, was sit in the stand, along with the tens of thousands of British Servicemen who made up nearly half the 100,000 crowd, as England went about demolishing a transitional German side that contained only five of the World Cup winners of two summers previously.

This is the match remembered as the finest international ever played by Duncan Edwards, who like Byrne and Taylor was fresh from helping Manchester United win the League. He scored a scorcher from twenty yards in the twentieth minute, dominated the midfield and defence and created the platform from which Johnny Haynes and Colin Grainger netted in the second half, sparking a cheerful pitch invasion each time. Fritz Walter, the classy German captain, hit back with a fine individual goal, but the day belonged to England and to Duncan Edwards, at this time exactly half-way through his two years' National Service in the Army. At the final whistle the squaddies surrounded him and carried him off as one of their own, even though in real life he spent most of his military career not in Berlin but at R.A.O.C. Shrewsbury, where, far from bashing squares, he found himself playing around ninety games a season for England, Manchester United and the Army; a team-mate for at least one of these last matches was Alfie Biggs of Bristol Rovers.

The next day it was back to England, and the heroes of Berlin were still bubbling with excitement. Rather more quiet were the five who sat the game out – Ray Wood, Tommy Cummings of Burnley and Bolton's Johnny Wheeler, neither of whom got a kick all tour, Nat Lofthouse and John Atyeo. For him, on the final leg of his journey back to Dilton Marsh Halt, it suddenly seemed a long time since late November, and that glorious night in the floodlit Wembley mist against Spain. He had had more big nights since then, and he doubted whether any of his contemporaries had been feted and honoured by their local community in the way that he had. Nevertheless, there was a good deal more work to be done. It was marvellous to be the 'Atyeo of England' he had always longed to be, but was it really the state of true bliss about which he had dreamed? Now that was a different question.

Not that he let the disappointments of the tour throw him off his goalscoring stride as Bristol City began their 1956-57 Second Division campaign. The first England match of the season was the Home International against Northern Ireland at Windsor Park, Belfast on October 6, and it was hard to see how John could have staked a more convincing claim for a call-up, having scored ten goals in eleven matches before the selectors met; City were not tearing up any trees, but their most valuable asset certainly was, and he was quietly optimistic on the Sunday the team was announced. Sadly, it was not to be, and Don Revie, playing a more conventional game than the deep-lying role that was winning him rave reviews at Manchester City, filled Atyeo's number eight berth. It turned out to be a dreary game; a rare goal from Stanley Matthews, his eleventh and last in international football, gave England a dream start, but Jimmy McIlroy equalised after ten minutes, when Reg Matthews patted a long throw from Packie McParland into his path, and that was the end of the scoring. Stan's previous international goal for England had been eight years earlier, also against Northern Ireland at Windsor Park, and after the game, Danny Blanchflower told him that he had been watching in short trousers when he got that one. 'You'll have a long beard by the time I get the next,' smiled Matthews. In the November it was Wales's turn to play England, at Wembley, and though Revie did not keep his place at inside-right, Big John was again overlooked. Johnny Brooks of Spurs was chosen for the first of his three games in the national colours, and he made it a scoring debut in a routine three-one win. That was enough to keep him his place in the friendly against Yugoslavia at Wembley a fortnight later, and he was again on target with the first goal in a three-nil win.

The next game, on December 5, 1956, was the first in England's 1958 World Cup campaign. They had been drawn in a winner-takes-all group of three against Denmark and the Irish Republic, home and away, and they were kicking off with a home leg against the Danes. It seems odd, now, to reflect that the game was not at Wembley, which in the previous month had hosted more or less meaningless matches against Wales and Yugoslavia, but at the ageing Molineux ground in Wolverhampton; it somehow spoke volumes about the Football Association's attitude to both the Jules Rimet trophy and their visitors.

Maybe they were not so far off the mark on the latter count, since England ran out easy five-two winners; Tommy Taylor scored a hat-trick and there were two for Duncan Edwards, pushed up front in place of the injured Johnny Haynes and revelling in his role of a goal-hungry forward. Both were booming long-range shots, he had another spectacularly saved and nearly cracked a post in half with a thundrous free kick. It seemed that half the population of his native Dudley were in the ground, and there were more tumultuous scenes around him at the final whistle. Johnny Brooks at inside-right simply slipped quietly down the tunnel and out of the England shirt.

There was then no more international football before spring, when the last of the Home Internationals, the big one against Scotland at Wembley, was followed by the remaining three World Cup preliminaries. At City, John was not having the easiest of seasons, but he still got twenty-three in thirty-seven League games plus five in three F.A. Cup ties, including the goal of all goals at Villa Park in mid-February, and there were plenty of commentators who felt he should come back at the expense of Brooks against the Scots on April 6. It was not to be. The man at number eight this time was Tommy Thompson, astonished to be back for his second and last international cap six years after the first one, and completely marked out of the game by his Preston team-mate Tommy Docherty. At inside-left was debutant Derek Kevan, who equalised after Scotland had gone ahead in the first minute through Clyde's flying winger Tommy Ring, while the winner was set up for Duncan Edwards by Stanley Matthews.

So came the three games in twelve days that would decide whether or not England would be travelling to Sweden in the following year – and would reap John Atyeo half his international caps, and four of his five goals in the Three Lions shirt. The Republic of Ireland were played home and away, at Wembley on May 8 and Dalymount Park, Dublin, on the nineteenth, while sandwiched between them was the return fixture against Denmark in Copenhagen on May 15. Almost miraculously, after all the chopping and changing of the previous year, the England team suddenly began to have a settled look about it. The goalkeeping place was still completely up for grabs, though Sheffield United's Alan Hodgkinson was in favour for all three of these games; the full-back partnership of Hall and Byrne was coming to be seen as one of the classiest in international football; half-backs Clayton, Wright and Edwards looked as sure on their feet as Freeman, Hardy and Willis; and those who liked to think in terms of youth blending with experience took greatly to the prospect of a forward line reading Matthews, Atyeo, Taylor, Haynes and Finney.

Yes, Big John was back, after missing seven games in which four different players had been tried at inside-right. He never counted his chickens or discussed his chances much with outsiders, but he liked a lot of what he saw here. The fact that these were Word Cup qualifiers, with the finals just over twelve months away, counted for something special in his eyes. In those games he had missed, nobody else had come along to make the inside-right slot their own, and it was hard to see that any of them would; Revie's club role was so at odds with England's style as to make him a rank outsider, Brooks and Thompson had clearly been discarded and as for Johnny Haynes, who had taken over from him in the two continental tour games, his natural position for England would always be inside-left. There was a chance going here, and John was going to grab it with both hands.

So he did. England overwhelmed the Irish five-one at Wembley, with a swashbuckling hat-trick from Taylor and two from Atyeo, who felt and played as if he was among old friends. He loved the company of the legends, Wright, Matthews and Finney, all of them quiet and dignified men who were happy to let their feet do the talking; modest men, too, as much as it was possible for sportsmen of their pre-eminence to be, since each was well aware of his worth to his club and country, and expected a degree of deference. John could understand that, and relate to it, in a way he could not always be on the same wavelength as players of his own age. The Irish centre-forward that day was Dermot Curtis, who had joined Bristol City from Shelbourne the previous December and was very briefly a prolific goalscorer at Ashton Gate. Apart from the excellent result, John looked back on the day as the only time Bristol City had two players in a full international at Wembley.

A few days later, he and Stanley Matthews sat together and fretted on the flight to Copenhagen, willing the aircraft to land with its undercarriage safely down and without catching a wing on the ground as it hit the runway, those perennial preoccupations of the terrified flier. In fact this turned out to be Stan's last game, at the age of forty-two and twenty-two years after the first of his fifty-four caps, and it was a memorable swansong as he helped England to an accomplished four-one win. Denmark took the lead in the twenty-fifth minute, but Johnny

Haynes equalised just before half time, and three goals in the last fifteen minutes sealed the victory. Tommy Taylor got two of them, and in between times, in the seventy-fifth minute, John Atyeo was there again, rising at the far post to head in a centre from Haynes. He felt happy and relaxed in the hotel that night, and as convinced as he could be that he would be in the team for Dublin at the end of the World Cup qualifiers. Oddly, after winning all three games to date handsomely, with a goal aggregate of fourteen goals for and four against, England still needed a point to be sure of going to Sweden; a win for Ireland would open the way for a play-off meeting of the two of them on a neutral ground, when anything could happen.

Dalymount Park on May 19, 1957, was no place for faint hearts; not that there were any in an England line-up that remained the same defensively for the fourth consecutive game, and with a forward line of Finney, Atyeo, Taylor, Haynes and David Pegg, the young Manchester United winger who would never add to this single international cap. On this day, however, they found that the Irish were no respecters of reputation. Never the best of starters at this stage in their history, England were rocked as early as the third minute by a goal from Alf Ringstead, who crashed a loose ball wide of his Sheffield United team-mate Alan Hodgkinson to roars of ecstasy. From then on England laboured to make any impact at all against an inspired Irish defence in which the Bournemouth goalkeeper Tommy Godwin and Millwall's young centre-half Charlie Hurley were outstanding. John grew to dislike playing against Hurley intensely in the years that followed, though the big man was up against Tommy Taylor that day, and making a mockery of the kind of form that had seen the Manchester United star knock in two or three goals for England in almost every recent game. There was nothing for him that day, and as the game entered its final minute, the huge Irish crowd knew that a victory as famous as any in the country's history was so nearly in their grasp.

Then enter Nemesis, in the form of John Atyeo, and a moment that lives on in Irish football folklore for all the wrong reasons. Tom Finney was allowed to slip free on the right flank, over came an inch-perfect cross to John Atyeo's head at the far post and – bang! – it was England for the World Cup finals. Seconds afterwards, the whistle blew. His last act in the match had been to send the ball crashing into the net. It seemed absurd to imagine that this would also be his last deed in an England shirt, at the age of twenty-five, but so it proved to be. 'The place was packed out with enthusiastic Irishmen,' John recalled years later. 'They are among the most fanatical supporters in the world, and many sides with far more talented players have fallen unceremoniously at Dalymount, so it was something of an ordeal for us. Our fears were fully justified as the game went on. Nothing we could do could shake their packed defence as the 47,000 fans roared every time we lost possession or the ball was booted into the stands. The minutes ticked by and the church clock overlooking the ground told us that the ninety were up. The crowd, waving orange and green flags and lighting their programmes to wave as flaring torches, yelled to the Scottish referee to end the game and allow the celebrations to begin. We were in injury time when Tom Finney, a late replacement for Stanley Matthews, who was unfit, picked up a ball along the right that had been kicked upfield hopefully by Jeff Hall. It was our last chance. Tom beat Pat Saward on the inside, sent Noel Cantwell the wrong way and beat Saward a second time as he reached the dead ball line. He crossed the most perfect centre you could wish to see. I was coming in, in the inside-left position, and just nodded it down into the net. As soon as the kick-off was taken the match came to an end. That was the last time I played for England, so I must hold a unique distinction of scoring a goal with my last touch in international football. I scored five goals in six matches and was never on a losing side.'

A phrase has echoed through Irish football from that day to this, describing the scene at Dalymount Park as the full enormity of Atyeo's goal struck home. It was coined by Philip Greene, a leading sportswriter and broadcaster in that country, and it was as bizarre as the moment itself: 'The silence was so deafening, it could be heard in O'Connell Street.' It is recalled to this day by Irishmen who were not even born at that time, including the Dublin-based football poet Peter Goulding, whose ballad *Atyeo 1957* concludes with the stirring lines:

The obese lady cleared her throat,
And Finney motored down the flank,
Picked out Atyeo remote,
And Ireland's brave resistance sank.
No silence such had e'er been heard
As that which fell on Dalymount.
No curse, no groan, no single word
Could anybody, stunned, recount.

Thus Atyeo saved England's pride
And spared his country grievous pain.
No more, though, did he make the side,
For he was never picked again.

It was not just the wordsmiths who saw and heard it that way. Paying tribute after John had died, Tom Finney said: 'With about two minutes to go, the crowd were wild with excitement. They were about to put England out of the World Cup [sic] when I crossed the ball from the wing and impossibly, somehow, John got on the end of it and nearly burst the net. Well, you could have heard a pin drop. It killed them, that goal did, and I'll never forget the silence that followed. It was like finishing the game in a cathedral.' Peter Goulding, in the verse above, is spot-on with his reflection that Atyeo's goal saved England a lot of embarrassment and a hammering from the press, while for the Irish it has made any subsequent victory over the old enemy all the more sweet.

'What a Glorious Twelfth! What joy! What euphoria!' one of their reporters proclaimed when a Ray Houghton goal sent England tumbling to the bottom of their group in the 1988 European Championships in Germany (though Ireland also failed to progress). 'We finally laid the ghost of John Atyeo! Vengeance, be-Jeasus.' John's goal really was as important as that, yet when it came to the next international, against Wales at Ninian Park in December 1957, West Bromwich Albion's Derek Kevan was in the number eight shirt, and the Atyeo era was at an end. Characteristically, and endearingly, Big John recalled that he made just one further representative appearance in his career, 'for the Football Combination against the Dutch (reserve league) in Rotterdam'. He was an unlikely member of that touring party, as was a youthful Jimmy Greaves, since neither of them saw much reserve team football in their long careers; in fact it was a forlorn, unwanted fixture generally, and if the silence could be heard at Churchill Plein that night, it was simply because hardly anyone was at the ground.

So where did it all go wrong? Any striker who can deliver five goals in his first six internationals might well be seen, in football talk, as being 'a little bit special'. Wayne Rooney was at an almost identical stage of his career when the England manager was talking about him in the same breath as Pele; back in 1957, the England selectors were talking about Big John in the same breath as Johnny Brooks. It was not even that England had an otherwise settled team. Of the Matthews, Lofthouse, Finney triumvirate, only the last was on the plane to Sweden, while the Munich air disaster in February 1958 deprived the squad of Tommy Taylor, Duncan Edwards, Roger Byrne and very possibly David Pegg. Also left at home was the ill and dying Jeff Hall, while the goalkeeping position was up for grabs between Hodgkinson, Bolton's Eddie Hopkinson and Burnley's Colin McDonald, who in the event played in all England's games in the finals.

The loss of Taylor in particular should have had the F.A. looking in Atyeo's direction. The two young men had a lot in common, on the pitch, at least. Both were strong, mobile, positionally astute, good on the ball and unselfish with their knock-downs and flick-ons, providers as well as natural-born target men and strikers. It is hard to believe that in the build-up to the finals, somebody at Lancaster Gate did not say: 'Now look, with Taylor gone, what about moving that Atyeo chappie to centre-forward?' Not that he was the only striker to feel aggrieved. Brian Clough had just rattled in forty-two League and F.A. Cup goals for Second Division Middlesbrough over the season, and made no secret of his displeasure at missing the cut. There was also surprise that Nat Lofthouse was rejected; he was a veteran, of course, but one who had just smashed Manchester United out of the F.A. Cup at Wembley, by fair means or foul, and was still in raging form. Perhaps even Chelsea's teenage whizzkid Jimmy Greaves deserved a blooding, while Stanley Matthews, quite surreally fit for a man of his age, had played superbly for England in recent games.

The end result was that Atyeo, Clough, Lofthouse, Greaves and Matthews stayed at home, while England went to Sweden with only twenty players when they were allowed twenty-two. Maybe the F.A. deemed the likes of Edwards and Taylor irreplaceable, so as a consequence simply did not try to replace them. Not that there was much time to think about it, as the national team arrived at its base in Gothenburg just two days before the tournament kicked off, and stayed in a city-centre hotel with no sports facilities; the top brass then sent Winterbottom out to look for somewhere where the squad could train. It really was as haphazard as that.

In England's four games at World Cup '58, Bobby Robson wore the number eight shirt against the USSR, Brazil and Austria in the group stage, only to be dropped in favour of the debutant Peter Broadbent of

Wolves in the vital play-off against the Soviet Union, which was lost one-nil. On the right flank outside Broadbent was twenty-year-old Peter Brabrook of West Ham United, also making his debut, at the expense of Blackburn's Bryan Douglas. The right wing pairing that had got England to the finals was Finney and Atyeo; did the selectors really expect the two rookies they fielded at Gothenburg that day to be an improvement on those two? Not that the press, outside Bristol, was asking any serious questions on Big John's behalf. The Fleet Street papers pressed the claims of Haynes and Brabrook, the Northern editions of the national press sang the praises of the boys from Lancashire and Yorkshire, but nobody was saying 'We could have done with someone like Atyeo out there this afternoon', and the fact that England's loss was West Country amateur cricket's gain that summer was of comfort to few outside a tiny sporting circle: on June 8, while his former England colleagues were scrapping out a two-all draw against Russia in Gothenburg, John was knocking thirty-six for Frome at Corsham, including a six and three fours, and getting three for seven; the following weekend, when a far more disappointing two-two draw with Austria consigned Billy Wright and Co. to an ultimately fruitless play-off, the height of John's sporting endeavours was an afternoon with Bristol City's cricket XI at Cheddar, strawberries and cream for tea and all.

The real England controversy at World Cup '58 was over the non-appearance of Bobby Charlton in the tournament, after he had scored three in his first two England matches earlier that year. He was in the twenty and there was a huge clamour for his inclusion in the team, and conspiracy theories abounded after the tournament ended. Tom Finney was among the senior England men who insisted that there was really no mystery at all, and Charlton was left out simply because of his lack of experience. There was also, of course, the question of his state of mind as a survivor of Munich only a few months before, but the 'inexperience' argument hardly holds water in the light of the selection of the even less tried and tested Brabrook and Broadbent – and if experience really was so much of an issue, what were Lofthouse and Atyeo doing back home? Conspiracy or not, the first question put to Walter Winterbottom when he was met at London Airport by his little son Alan was: 'Daddy, why didn't you play Bobby Charlton?' That was it. Jackie Charlton's 'Our Kid' was an England regular from that day on.

John Atyeo would ponder on his fate as an international cut off in his prime: 'I remember Walter Winterbottom writing in my testimonial brochure in 1966, saying he could not understand why I was overlooked when my record stood up to any scrutiny. Many said I had been treated unfairly, but Winterbottom had the final say.' The England coach's exact words in the brochure were not quite as John recalled them: 'He gave England great service in his six full international appearances. Unfortunately, there was some concern among the selectors that he was a part-time professional footballer; perhaps it was a mistake to drop him at a time when we were badly in need of a prolific goal scorer. He was one of the most unselfish footballers who ever played for me, and he was known as "Big-hearted John" among the England party.'

Some Atyeo fans see this as a very disingenuous piece of writing on Winterbottom's part. By the time in his managerial career that John was on the scene, the selectors held sway in name only, since the manager had long tired of the endless kicking around of names by a group of men who knew little of the professional game and whose preferences usually ran along purely geographical lines. Come the mid-1950s, Winterbottom had groomed the F.A. into accepting that he would place a team sheet before them, and that this would be the team they chose. There was still scope for a few minutes' discussion about each position, but it was strictly of the Brian Clough-Peter Taylor school of debate: they would talk it over, and then agree that Walter was right all along.

On the other hand, maybe the selectors did have deeper reservations about Atyeo's semi-detached status than the manager, making him feel justified, in John's brochure, to nudge the blame in their direction; after all, if he knew that to put the Bristol City man's name forward would only set off half an hour's tedious bickering about the pros and cons of part-timers, it is perhaps understandable that he would be tempted to turn to some other promising youngster to try in the number eight shirt. When he says in the tribute 'perhaps it was a mistake to drop him', he is not specifically excluding himself from being party to this mistake. As for the exact nature of the selectors' concern over John as a part-timer, we might not be far off the mark in surmising that this could be a diplomatic shorthand way of admitting that really, nobody at Lancaster Gate could make head nor tail of where this big West Country part-timer was coming from. As a contribution to a well-loved player's testimonial brochure, Walter Winterbottom's words were probably just about as frank and revealing as he felt they could be.

Set against all this, being part-time did no harm to the half-back Bill Slater's chances of playing in Sweden in a career that saw him win twelve full England caps and become Footballer of the Year in 1960 (even though the Burnley chairman Bob Lord, when presenting the statuette, told the football writers in no uncertain terms that they were wrong, and it should have gone to his man Jimmy McIlroy). Slater was very much a Walter Winterbottom type, a graduate amateur who played for England in the 1952 Olympics in Helsinki and a future director of physical education at Liverpool and Birmingham Universities. In other words, he was not a quantity surveyor for a little firm of builders in Westbury, Wiltshire. Winterbottom did not write a lot in John's testimonial brochure, but the other paragraph read: 'I am particularly pleased that John Atyeo has taken up teaching at a soccer school. A teacher of his calibre will check the drift towards rugger at some schools, and spread the gospel of Association Football.' Three thoughts are prompted here: first, that if John had followed an early instinct and studied at Loughborough College, then his career choice outside football might have been more to the England manager and selectors' liking; second, that Winterbottom little knew that Atyeo the teacher, as a lover and encourager of so many sports, was doing anything but striving to 'check the drift towards rugger'; and third, that the sight of his small-town secondary modern being marked down as 'a soccer school', rather as blazered buffers might describe Shrewsbury or Charterhouse, must have given John cause for one of his wry smiles.

Atyeo rightly saw Bristol City's mediocre form in the Second Division as another reason why he was overlooked. 'My England career coincided with City's two great seasons, but in the following two seasons things started to go downhill at Ashton Gate,' he reflected. 'That was the time I should probably have been thinking about moving to a bigger club, but I didn't think too much about leaving Bristol City.' Alan Williams is one of Atyeo's City colleagues at the time who remembers his constant insistence that if he or any of the lads wanted to be in the frame for an England call-up, the team had to be right up at the top of the table challenging for promotion. There was no bar against Second Division players representing their country in those days in which Sheffield United's £20 a week was just as good as Manchester United's. Ronnie Clayton and Bryan Douglas of Blackburn, Peter Brabrook of West Ham, Johnny Haynes of Fulham and Alan A'Court of Liverpool were all players from the second grade who were in the England squad in the World Cup finals in 1958, but West Ham and Blackburn had just gone up as champions and runners-up at the end of the previous season, Fulham succeeded in 1958-59 and Liverpool, while having to wait until 1961, quickly made up for lost time when they did so. Bristol City, on the other hand, were languishing at seventeenth in the season before Sweden '58, and that was a long way off the pace. Nevertheless, John Atyeo was still banging in the goals for this struggling team, and besides, the selectors should have known enough about him by then to have been able to judge him on his own merits.

Maybe they did – both on the field and off; and maybe that was the problem. Of course, as an England squad member and tourist, he was the least troublesome of charges, but it is plain that something died in his international career on that England tour of Sweden, Finland and West Germany, despite his later brief reprieve. He really was an outsider in his ways, brighter than most of the rest of the lads at one level but naive and unsophisticated and with the kind of accent none of them had heard before except in comic sketches on radio and TV. The likes of Duncan Edwards and Tommy Taylor were scarcely sophisticates, but they were bright, self-confident young men with bustle and street cred. Johnny Haynes, with whom John never hit it off, was another, quick enough on his feet to manoeuvre the sharp-as-a-tack Tommy Trinder into making him Britain's first hundred-pounds a week footballer in 1961 (even though, as he still protests, he never saw another pay rise in the rest of his long career). Atyeo shared a room with Billy Wright, and it is hard to believe that this was for any reason other than to allow the considerate and morale-minded captain to take the young West Countryman under his wing. The chairman of selectors, who had led the continental tour party, was the Chelsea boss Joe Mears; he had been baffled by John's negativity when he declined to go to London a couple of years previously, and saw nothing in this trip to cast light on what made this big, rustic-sounding fellow tick.

Winterbottom was doubtless trying to sound complimentary when he wrote that Atyeo was always thought of in the England camp as 'Big-hearted John', but even if that were true – and it hardly sounds the kind of nickname a group of young sportsmen would bestow on one of their number – it does not speak of a very close and inclusive relationship with him. There would have been far more intimacy implied by 'Atts', or 'Bongo', or 'Stonky', or any other silly nickname that spoke of him as one of the lads, rather than a big inside-forward from the distant West who was just passing through; but just passing through he most surely and unhappily was, and his son Philip vouches for the fact that the sense of hurt stayed with him until the end.

'No-one should believe that my father took the abrupt ending of his England career lightly,' he says. 'He was quite affected by it, and became more vocal about it as the years went by. He was in no doubt about the reason for it – his staying semi-professional with Bristol City – and if he regretted not moving at all it was for this reason, the curtailing of his international career. It was a big disappointment to him.'

CHAPTER 9

WHERE THEY BELONGED

The four seasons between 1955-56 and 1958-59 saw Bristol City establish themselves as a solid, average Second Division team. In April 1956, at the end of their return season to this grade of football, they were eleventh in the table; in 1957 they were thirteenth, in '58 seventeenth, in '59 tenth. Obviously there were shades of difference in these campaigns, but these were the years Jackie Charlton had in mind when he told a 1980s Bristol sportsmen's dinner, to not universal acclaim, that he would not be happy until he saw City back where they belonged – 'twelfth in the Second Division'. For the first two of these seasons, John Atyeo's profile as a footballer was at its zenith; he only had to open the colourful Charles Buchan's *Football Monthly* or the inky and disreputable looking *Soccer Star* for confirmation that he really was the 'Atyeo of England' his father had always told him he would be after he had got that first international cap under his belt. Towards the end of those four seasons, as the careers of Charlton, Clough and Greaves began to blossom gloriously, he began to accept that when international selection day came around, his name was not even mooted, less still chosen, despite the fact that he was in his physical prime. His goal tally was never less than impressive: thirty in the League and one in the F.A. Cup in 1955-56; twenty-three and five in '56-57; twenty-three and two in '57-58; and twenty-five in '58-59. These four seasons came in a run of nine in which he was his team's top scorer, as he was in twelve of the fifteen seasons he played at Ashton Gate.

City took the Second Division by storm in the first half of 1955-56, and were top of the league from mid-November to Christmas Eve, playing in front of the biggest regular crowds ever seen at Ashton Gate. December, however, showed that they were not the same with mud on their boots, and they went into the new year in fifth place, with a return for the month of five defeats and just two wins. That was clearly anything but promotion form, and they were rarely in the hunt for honours from that time on. A poll of various experts and pundits in the *Daily Herald* just before Christmas revealed them as clear promotion favourites, with forty-eight votes to Sheffield Wednesday's thirty-six, Liverpool's twenty-six and Leeds United's ten; as it turned out, it was the two Yorkshire teams that prevailed, with Wednesday champions, Liverpool in third place and City nowhere. The Robins team was still studded with the championship heroes of the previous year, but Ivor Guy, Jack White, Ernie Peacock, Cyril Williams and Alec Eisentrager were all past or passing their peak, and by the end of the season the side that had looked like a First Division squad playing in the Third began to wear the distinct air of a team that would need strengthening merely to stay afloat in the Second. A bonus had been a late blossoming of Eisentrager's talents on the right wing, in his last significant season in the team. This allowed Jimmy Rogers to stay at centre-forward, and he and Atyeo accounted for fifty-five of the team's eighty goals that season, with Jimmy getting twenty-five of them. John also scored City's sole goal in the F.A. Cup, in a routine third round three-one defeat by Everton at Goodison Park.

Midlander Jimmy, a couple of years older than John, had already been at Ashton Gate for twelve months or more when the big man arrived in 1951, but his first team opportunities had been strictly limited until the start of 1954-55. Those fifty goals in seventy-eight games over two seasons were by a long way the greatest achievement of his career; he was quick and gritty and benefited not only from Atyeo's flicks and lay-offs but from anything that might bounce his way from Big John's cannonball shooting. Woe betide the goalkeeper who fumbled a shot when Jimmy Rogers was sniffing around the penalty area. With pin-up boy good looks and a ready line in patter – he used to go out selling paint brushes in the afternoon – Jimmy had little to do with John off the field, but their professional relationship could hardly have been more close and profitable. Rogers used to joke that he was lethal in front of goal – from six inches – and there is no doubting that John played his full part in giving him those close-range chances. On the other hand, Atyeo, like most strikers, loved to hunt in pairs, and for a couple of seasons, his partnership with Jimmy was as fruitful and exciting as any he was to experience. Sadly, it could not last. Before Christmas in the following season both Jimmy and Jack Boxley had taken a step down to Coventry City, then a decidedly mediocre makeweight team in the Third Division South. Harry

Dolman's close ties with the Coventry chairman Derrick Robbins led to much coming and going between the clubs over the years, most notably in the arrival of Alan Dicks as manager in the late 1960s, but at this stage City were very much the dominant force.

Some highlights of the 1955-56 season were games against the glamour teams of the division, the kind of clubs it had been worth battling out of the Third Division South to earn the right to play. Against Leeds United and the majestic John Charles at home in early September, City stumbled to their first defeat of the season, one-nil in front of 31,060; but they had the chance to make amends three days later, when West Ham came to town and were soundly whipped three-nil, with goals from Atyeo, Arnold Rodgers and an obliging Hammers defender. Middlesbrough and Liverpool were sent away pointless in quick succession, with John reminding the Anfield board of what they had missed with both goals in a two-one win, and then, on October 22, came the game all Bristol had looked for when the fixture list came out in the summer – the first ever Second Division Bristol derby. At Ashton Gate, it drew 39,583 noisy spectators, the red half of whom went wild when Jimmy Rogers equalised in the last ten minutes.

It was a heady time for Bristol football, with both teams tilting for the top division, Geoff Bradford challenging his friend John Atyeo's right to be seen as the city's footballing top dog, and crowds of 25,000-plus turning out on both sides of the river to cheer on their favourites. City won the return in March by a comprehensive three-nil (Atyeo two, Rogers), with 35,324 crammed in under the shadow of the gasometers; but it was Rovers who had the last laugh for the season when, in the final scuffle for honours, they ended three points and five places above the Reds in sixth spot. There was a no-buy, no-sell policy at Rovers, whose fans later swore that if they had splashed out on a centre-forward they would have waltzed into the First Division. They were still in with a chance until Leeds beat them two-one in the second-last game of the season at Elland Road, and four train-loads of supporters spent the long journey home pondering on what might have been. What they did have from that season, and have clung on to for evermore, were memories of that astonishing four-nil thrashing of Manchester United in the F.A. Cup. City's fans have had more highs than Rovers', over the years, but that is an achievement they can only look upon in awe and envy.

It was the week after the Bristol derby that City first began believing they could rise to the top flight, when they beat Blackburn Rovers six-four at Ewood Park. At the end of their careers, some players looked back on this as their most memorable game. With Ron Clayton, Bill Eckersley, Bryan Douglas and Eddie Quigley in their ranks, Blackburn were First Division-bound, and though they had to wait two more seasons to achieve it, they were still a classy team. Another reason why the win was important for City was the fact that it was their first visit to Lancashire since promotion, and the Manchester-based national press – more or less Fleet Street's equal, on the football front, at least – was given a first-hand opportunity to run the rule over these West Country upstarts with their star forward with the funny name. John Atyeo would make his England debut against Spain at Wembley just a month later, and after that afternoon at Ewood Park, when he scored twice, none of the Soccer's Mr Footballs from the Northern editions could find it in his heart to challenge his right to be there. City were a goal down in thirty seconds, four-two up at half time, pegged back to four-four after seventy minutes but then strong enough to punish Blackburn with another two with nine minutes still to go.

The win pushed the Reds up to second place, and after two more famous victories – five-two at home to Hull City and two-nil at Nottingham Forest – they went into the home match against Sheffield Wednesday on November 19 knowing that two points could put them on the top of the table. A win was indeed what they got, three-two, in front of a crowd of 32,731, but the real entertainment came when Cyril Williams, who had been having his ankles tapped by Wednesday's emerging Golden Boy of Football Albert Quixall all afternoon, twice laid the lad low with haymaker punches. The ref saw the second one, and Cyril did not wait to be told to take an early bath. Back to boring old football, it was the Atyeo-Rogers combination that saw off Wednesday, with Jimmy getting two. City went top until Christmas Eve, when relegation-haunted Notts County dispelled festive cheer at Ashton Gate with a coupon-busting three-one win.

Worse was to come on Boxing Day, when City were whipped five-nil by Plymouth Argyle at Home Park. Tony Cook had an unhappy time in goal, to the extent that some blamed him for years afterwards, completely without foundation, for being drunk on duty. There were lurid tales of his drinking heavily on the team coach; in fact they had gone by rail, and he had not touched a drop. Tony could take a joke as well as dishing one out – his nervy habit of disappearing into the toilets before a game for a crafty smoke was the cause of much ribbing – but he could understandably never see the funny side of this slur on his professionalism. Neither was he happy when the Plymouth result saw Bob Anderson back between the sticks for the return game twenty-four hours later. This time it was City's turn to run riot, six-nil, with the old firm of Atyeo (two) and Rogers (three) accounting for five of the goals, and Tommy Burden chipping in with the other.

It must be said that with teams playing one another home and away over twenty-four hours at Christmas at that time, peculiar results were far from uncommon. A year after City's games with Plymouth, Bristol Rovers played Bury, losing seven-two to them at Gigg Lane on Christmas Day and taking a six-one revenge at Eastville on Boxing Day. Since Bury were bound for relegation and scored only sixty goals all season, Rovers' shipping of seven of them in one go seems especially odd. Speaking generally, it is hard to believe that alcohol or other unprofessional behaviour did not play a part in results such as these, over the years; what is hard to take is the unfair branding of individual players for collective shortcomings.

Season 1955-56 was a double challenge for John – his big breakthrough in the England team and the graduation to a higher grade of League football. His thirty goals answered any lingering doubts about his ability to step up a division, and he scored regularly until well into the new year, when City suddenly began to lose their way and make nonsense of those Christmas promotion predictions. Atyeo's ten goals in the second half of the season did not compare well with his twenty in the first half, which had set him dreaming of a massive tally. The Robins failed to find the net in six of their last ten games, a most un-Bristol City state of affairs at that time, and a three-nil defeat by West Ham at Upton Park on the last day of the season saw them plunge to eleventh place, the lowest they had been all season. On the other hand, it was a tight division, and just two more wins would have seen them pip Liverpool to third place.

John tried to draw comfort from that fact. He was also satisfied that the only significant newcomer to the club, Wally Hinshelwood, was a clever little Cockney right-winger – signed from Reading – who looked as if he would give him good service over the next few seasons; he did indeed, but the bigger question was whether John should have stayed around long enough to benefit from Wally's wizardry. A detached view, had he been able to take one, would have told him that Bristol City were about to enter a period of transition that would not be good for his wider interests, and this was most definitely the optimum time for him to move on; but then again, when did John Atyeo ever take a detached view of his life in Dilton Marsh and Ashton Gate?

The 1956-57 campaign was a sad one for City in the League, with spirits lifted only by a run into the fifth round of the F.A. Cup. A dreadful start to the season saw them down to twentieth place by early September, and their final ranking of thirteenth was achieved only on the strength of a five-game winning run late on. Some ultimately impressive performers were drafted in as the season drifted away – local teenager Alan Williams at left-half, Dermot Curtis from Shelbourne at centre-forward, Gloucester City's £3,500 striker Bobby Etheridge at inside-left and Johnny Watkins, after long schooling in the reserves, on the left wing – but none of them found it easy to click in a team that seemed to have lost belief in itself. John Atyeo was not a happy man; England continued to ignore him, and he was alarmed to see a waning interest in City's fortunes reflected in distressingly low gates. Now only the most attractive and best-supported teams drew 20,000-plus to Ashton Gate, and it was pitiful to see fewer than 13,000 cheer on the Robins' five-one thrashing of Lincoln City on the notorious shopping Saturday just before Christmas. Big 30,000-plus crowds still turned out for the Bristol derbies, which ended five-three for the Reds at home (Atyeo two, Cyril Williams two and Hinshelwood) and nil-all at Eastville; but despite this, Rovers were again Bristol's top dogs at the end of the season, ninth in the table compared with City's thirteenth.

John's twenty-three goals in thirty-seven League outings were fairly evenly spread throughout the season, with a couple of braces and a very satisfying hat-trick in a five-one demolition of a star-studded Sheffield United at home. The only other City player to reach double figures was Dermot Curtis, who popped in thirteen in just sixteen games and of course shared the distinction, with Atyeo, of being one of the only two Ashton Gate men to appear together on the international stage at Wembley, in England's World Cup victory over the Irish Republic. The Reds were not short of goals that season, scoring seventy-four, but they conceded seventy-nine to end the campaign with a deficit for the first time in five years; it would not be the last time that decade.

The F.A. Cup was such an exhilarating relief. In the third round, Rotherham United were despatched four-one (Atyeo two, Curtis and Hinshelwood), as City wiped out memories of the Millers' victory three years earlier; in the fourth round, non-League Rhyl had the thrill of their lives playing in front of 29,438 at Ashton Gate and gave a decent account of themselves by losing by just three goals (Atyeo two, Etheridge). Came the fifth round draw on the following Monday morning, and the Robins got a tough one. Not only had their luck in landing home ties run out, but they found themselves away to an Aston Villa side which (rightly, as it turned out) already had a vision of itself running round Wembley with the Cup. This was one of City's biggest games of the decade. Saturday, February 16, 1957 was a filthy day, but fifteen packed trains left Temple Meads station, helping to swell the Villa Park crowd to 63,099, some 15,000 of whom wore the red and white. What they saw, on a pitch with ankle-deep mud down the middle, was a blood-and-thunder, old-fashioned ding-dong of a Cup tie; they also saw John Atyeo's finest goal of them all. In his own words: 'The pitch was a gluepot. We were losing to a Peter McParland goal and were not really in the game. Then a ball was driven out from defence and I latched on to it. I went past Jimmy Dugdale and then Stan Lynn as I advanced down the left hand side of the pitch. I hit the ball with my left foot from about 25 yards. It popped up a fraction as I connected and was like a golf ball on a tee before it sped like a bullet past goalkeeper Nigel Sims. It was certainly a spectacular goal, but to no avail, as Jackie Sewell got the winner. Ernie Peacock might have become our hero. He was injured and limping in the forward line. In the last minute or two I got the ball over from the right but Ernie just failed to get his foot to it in front of goal.'

The way he outwitted both Dugdale and Lynn, two of the toughest defenders of their day, told the football world everything it needed to know about John's credentials at the highest level of the game, and Dugdale's spot summary after the match is one that still stands today: 'It was one of the best goals I've ever seen.' As far as City fans are concerned it is *the* best, as confirmed in a competition held by the club's programme editors at Christmas 2004. The winner, Dave Robbins, wrote: 'I have been watching City since 1945 and have seen many wonderful goals from the likes of Don Clark, Jimmy Rogers, Arnold

Rodgers, Tom Ritchie, Paul Cheesley, Bob Taylor and Alan Walsh. Brian Tinnion's goal at Liverpool (Liverpool nil, Bristol City one, F.A. Cup fourth round, 1993-94) was another to remember – but for the best, I have to go for Big John's against Aston Villa.'

The season was a big one for John off the pitch. His engagement to his schooldays sweetheart Ruth Harraway had been announced on December 3, 1955 – he presented her with a diamond ring hours after scoring a hat-trick in that home demolition of Lincoln City – and the wedding, at the fourteenth-century St Lawrence's Minster Church in Warminster, took place on Monday October 22, 1956. Ruth's father Arthur was a pillar of local society, a successful horticulturalist well known in Conservative circles. The firm of T. H. Harraway and Son, nurserymen of Sambourne Road, had been founded in 1876, and by this time it put some twenty acres in and around the town to good use producing rose and fruit trees, hedging plants and cut flowers, as well as running a popular shop in the Market Place. It had been Thomas H. Harraway, chairman of Warminster Urban District Council, who had signed peace celebration certificates in 1918 to thank each young ex-serviceman of the town 'for the patriotism he displayed in the Great War'. It was that kind of family.

The town was abuzz on wedding day morning, not least because of the posse of press photographers who prowled a Church Street packed with cars as Ruth and her father completed the short journey from their home, The Cedars, in Silver Street. Her best friend Ann Morgan was her bridesmaid, while among the three ushers were her brothers Harold and Jack. This was an occasion quite important enough for civic representatives of Warminster Urban District Council to be present, led by their chairman and his lady. On the groom's side, a coachload of wellwishers from Dilton Marsh helped swell the happy throng. Six Bristol City directors headed by Harry Dolman led the club contingent, which included Pat Beasley and most of the players, who formed a guard of honour as the couple left the church; Jack Boxley was John's best man. Otherwise, the occasion was not over-burdened with football lore, since as we have noted, the Harraways were quite prominent enough locally to have a wide social circle of their own, but there were smiles in the congregation when it was seen that Ruth's bouquet consisted of red roses and white heather, lilies of the valley and stephanotis, and she upheld the theme with cherry-coloured accessories to her fawn going-away outfit.

The reception was at Byne House, an imposing eighteenth-century town house turned hotel right on the spot in Church Street, which sprouted a big marquee on the lawn for the occasion. From here the happy couple set off for a brief honeymoon in London, but the following Saturday John was back at Ashton Gate amid a big, joshing crowd that made a special fuss of him when he whacked in the first goal in a tight two-one win over Huddersfield Town. The *Warminster Journal* found events surrounding the wedding so unusual that it put the story on the front page, though unillustrated and half-way down. 'Footballers Honour Colleague' was its somewhat enigmatic headline. The *Somerset Standard* was rather more dismissive of an event which, after all, had taken place not only outside the Frome boundaries but in a different county altogether. 'Frome Cricketer Weds', was its headline on a short single-column, inside-page report, presumably the work of the sub-editor who had written 'North-East Man Dies In Atlantic Tragedy' when he was handling the *Titanic* story early in his career in Aberdeen.

Three weeks before the wedding there had been another off-field development. Early in the close season in 1956 Atyeo had bought a little grocery business in Westbury Leigh, a villagey part of Westbury on the road to Dilton Marsh, for a fit person, within easy walking distance of both communities. It had been a village shop since the turn of the century so was very well established in a low-key kind of way, and he and Ruth took it over early in the October before their marriage, with John's father Walter also lending a hand. Today it seems a strange move. Both John and Ruth were aged twenty-three, and she, the daughter of a successful local businessman, had already made more of a career for herself than many women of her age had done at that time. After school she went to the City of Bath Training College of Domestic Science, where she gained an Institute of Management Association certificate, and then worked on the cooking staff of one of the big London hospitals for two years before taking charge of catering at Trowbridge and District Hospital. This background led the local paper to conclude that being a village shopkeeper would be 'an ideal arrangement for Ruth', who gave up the hospital job on the strength of it, but it is hard to believe that she did not go into it with some misgivings. Heaven knows what they thought of it down at Warminster Young Conservatives.

As for John, this was the beginning of the end of his days as a quantity surveyor, the supposed good, safe job that had set him on course for a lifetime of ambivalence towards full-time football and a lifestyle that almost certainly cut short the international career that meant so much to him. Now, but briefly, he would be a grocer – a 'master grocer', according to the Wiltshire press, in a headline that must have caused paroxysms of rage among genuine claimants to that proud title – and he simply did not take to it. He had problems with a light-fingered shop assistant he employed, and being the worrier he was, he fretted if perishables he had bought were showing signs of not selling; according to affectionate family folklore, he would harangue customers to take goods nearing their sell-by date off his hands. The plain truth was that all John Atyeo was really cut out to be professionally was a footballer, and, after his retirement from the game, a wonderfully caring school teacher. As soon as Walter Atyeo died in 1958, John got a good offer for the shop at 79 Westbury Leigh and sold it, and he and Ruth moved back to Dilton Marsh until 1970. Their first plan was to build a house in the orchard, but Effie – 'strong-minded' is one description of her that springs to the mind of her grandson Philip – would have none of it, so it was a case of moving back into Glenthorne with her. Her, and as the years passed by, a regularly updated supply of little girls.

CHAPTER 10

THE SUMMER GAME

Summer meant cricket for John. In local league action as a high-order batsman and dangerous seam bowler, he turned out for Berkley from his schooldays in 1948 but was best known locally for his years with Frome, for whom he played regularly through most of the 1950s. He was also a mainstay of a Bristol City side which at various times in the 1950s and early '60s included eventual Test cricketers in Arthur Milton and Ken Palmer, Gloucestershire county players in David Smith and Barry Meyer and good club performers in the likes of Bobby Etheridge, Peter Wilshire, Johnny Watkins, Cliff Morris and Tony Cook. A bizarre postscript to this was that years later, Palmer and Meyer stood together as Test umpires. In his physical prime, John was a very good club cricketer, but to make any more exalted a claim for him than that is to take a quantum leap. Of course, he might have played for Somerset 'if he had set his mind to it', but then again, many middle-aged and elderly men of his ability with the bat and ball can ponder similar unfulfilled dreams. The fact is that, in those less pressurised times, he had every opportunity to set that very determined mind of his to a second career in county cricket if the ability had truly been there; after all, he was in a job that kept him as fit as a fiddle, he played regularly to a very good standard with a well regarded team, and he had been a known quantity to the men in the know at Taunton since his days in the Wiltshire schools XI. What is more, the amateurish Somerset set-up of those days would not have seen him battling for his place against the likes of the Ian Botham, Viv Richards, Joel Garner triumvirate of later glories. As a schoolboy he went to winter nets at the county ground, which is probably the basis of the rumour that he 'had trials' with Somerset County Cricket Club. Maybe there was even something a little more formal than that, since the Frome club had high-level links with the county, but detailed archives at Taunton show no record of P.J.W. Atyeo playing for any Somerset team.

For Bristol City's cricket XI, though, yes, he certainly did. 'Harry Dolman would arrange a cricket match every year against Gloucestershire,' the reserve team trainer Bill Harvey recalled of these meetings, for which Les Bardsley, as physio at both Ashton Gate and Nevil Road, acted as the catalyst. 'We used to have a coach take us to the Grand Spa Hotel [overlooking Clifton Suspension Bridge] for lunch, and then on to the county ground for the match. Peter Doherty and Les Bardsley always went by car, leaving me in charge of the players. One time we had a young goalkeeper on trial – plus three jokers in Jimmy Rogers, Ernie Peacock and Jack Boxley. When it was time to board the coach after lunch, the keeper came to the bus with his coat bulging as if he was expecting. I asked him what he had under it. He said those three had told him to help himself from the drinks trolley, and he had two bottles of Scotch and a bottle of sherry. I duly left him standing outside the hotel.' The City players would play a number of games around Somerset over the summer, and always proved good company. John, Mike Thresher and the rest played at Cheddar Cricket Club several times in the 1950s, including that visit at the height of England football's World Cup '58 campaign, and sat down with the local lads at tea to enjoy strawberries and cream. 'In the evening they were welcomed to the homes of several Cheddar players for supper, drinks and a chat,' one of the home team, Tony Dyer, recalled a few years ago.

John was still in his teens when he first began to make a mark in the Frome team, where he batted at four or five and for several seasons linked up with Philip Fussell in a devastating 'speed twin' partnership. It is all very well now to sit back and pronounce that really, the two of them were no more than medium-fast, but that goes no way towards explaining the havoc they wreaked among opposition batsmen over the years. Of course it was by no means a winner every time for the two of them, either with bat or ball, but when both were on song they could make quick work of their opponents. To take just one random example, in a couple of weeks in the high summer of 1951 they made mincemeat of two teams that had beaten Frome early in the season. Fussell ended with four for twenty-two and Atyeo three for ten when Midsomer Norton came to Fromefield, while at Keynsham a couple of weeks later the home team were reduced to twenty-five all out, their second-lowest total of all time, after Phil had claimed four for eleven and John five for ten. Keynsham won the toss and chose to bat on an over-watered pitch, after which they found Fussell and Atyeo 'practically unplayable', according to the *Somerset Standard*. 'The two bowled unchanged, and Keynsham were back in the pavilion in three-quarters of an hour...' At one stage, John's figures showed three wickets for no runs. Since the game was over so quickly, the two teams decided to have a knockaround for ninety minutes each, and this proved a far more even contest. Top scorer for Frome was John Atyeo with fifty-eight.

As the decade progressed, another excellent bowler emerged at the club in K. P. Jones, who took ninety-five wickets at a cost of twelve runs each in 1956; Phil Fussell bagged seventy-five and two other bowlers got more wickets than John's twenty-one, but his was the best average for the season at 7.81 runs per wicket. The headline in the *Bath Evening Chronicle*? 'Atyeo Heads The Bowling'. Mr Jones was well versed in the mysteries of cricket, in which his ninety-five wickets apparently counted for less than John's twenty-one, but it is safe to assume that his mum had a thing or two to say about the *Chron*'s version of events.

There must have been times when Atyeo and Fussell thought there really might be a future for them in county cricket; in fact Phil did play for Somerset twice, in 1953 and 1956, as well as for the second XI on occasions, and has a solitary championship wicket to his name. He also turned out for the prestigious Lansdown club at Combe Park, Bath, revelling in the summer game from April to September. That, of course, was where John could not compete, never being available for Frome's Saturday games until early May and tied up with pre-season football from mid-July onwards. Occasionally, however, even in club cricket, he and Phil had close encounters with some memorable names. Frome played Yeovil at South Petherton and found that rumours of the Pakistani fast bowler Khan Mohammed's declining powers had been greatly exaggerated. For a few years after the Second World War, Khan and his comrade-in-arms Fazal had formed that most unlikely of partnerships, a Pakistan new ball pairing of genuine ferocity. Once, Khan, piqued by an Indian batsman's challenge to him in a Test at Dacca, had bowled the next ball at such a fearsome speed that it broke the bat in two. There were not quite those kind of histrionics at South Petherton that afternoon, but his five wickets for thirty-three included that of Big John, who top-scored for Frome with eighteen. Atyeo and Fussell both watched him carefully, and decided that perhaps they had some way to go, after all.

On the other hand, according to Ken Palmer, they were quite dangerous enough to book him a successful trial at Somerset – and so, by logical progression, open the road to his years in county cricket, England honours and a distinguished career as an umpire at Test and county level. 'I was on a good run of form with the bat with Devizes when we met Frome, where John and Phil were firing on all cylinders,' he recalls. 'I did well against them, getting sixty or so, and the Frome captain (and Westbury United chairman) Jack Pearce arranged for me to go to Somerset for a trial. It all went on from there, so you could say that John Atyeo and Phil Fussell helped me on my way – even though all they really wanted to do was get me out.'

CHAPTER 11

SEND FOR THE DOC

As the summer of 1957 sped by, John had every reason to look forward to the new season with relish. He had no good reason to think that the stirring goal he had headed in for England at Dalymount Park would be his last touch in international football, and that stunning F.A. Cup strike at Villa Park had been a reminder to him and everyone in football that he could perform spectacularly at the highest level. The team was entering its third season back in the Second Division, and the hopes were that after two years of mid-table respectability, it now had the know-how and experience to do better than that. A lingering doubt was over the flip-side of 'experience' – the almost inevitable dip in a player's form when he enters his early thirties. Atyeo, of course, was still at the peak of his powers, but he knew that that did not apply to a good number of his colleagues, and there had been no major close season signings to bolster them.

As John reflected on the 1957-58 season in his newspaper memoirs in 1970: 'The disasters started from the first match, when Liverpool beat us at Ashton Gate (after City had led at half time through a goal from Johnny Watkins). We had practically the same team as when we gained promotion – and that was quite an old, experienced side. This was our third season in the Second Division, and some of the old bones were beginning to creak a bit. We were near the bottom of the table for a long time, but in January we were paired with Accrington Stanley in the third round of the Cup. We drew the first match, won the replay three-one in front of 32,000 – and at the same time, Pat Beasley was sacked. This was my first experience of this happening. Pat was player-manager during my first year at the club, and he had been a great player. He was even a good player when he finished. I got on well with him and found him a level-headed person, although he often gave people the wrong impression of his capabilities. He didn't have the smooth-talking approach of some managers, but with the players he knew what he wanted, and got his points over. His record was certainly not a bad one. He had bought pretty wisely, and after all, he did take the team into the Second Division.'

As John reflected, he liked Pat Beasley. Indeed, it was often said that he and Tommy Burden, who was also a part-timer, had an undue influence on team selection in Pat's time, and that was seen as a bit odd by some of the old pros. Beasley's contract expired at the end of the season, in any event, and Harry Dolman was not alone in feeling that there was no great imperative for the club to renew it. To draw two-all with Accrington Stanley at Peel Park had not been the worst result of all time, since Stanley were a power in the Third North in the years before its demise in 1958, finishing second twice and third twice in the league's last four seasons. City, however, came back south that night feeling lucky to have scraped a replay, when even a relatively routine win at Ashton Gate failed to save Beasley's skin. By this time, their Second Division status was under serious threat, and when Liverpool followed up their opening day win with a four-three victory at Anfield four days before Christmas, City were in one of the two relegation places for the first time since their return from the Third South. In the three weeks between Beasley's departure and the appointment of his successor Peter Doherty on January 28, 1958 the team was first run jointly by Dolman and trainer Les Bardsley and then, for nine days as a caretaker before he took the reins as manager of Millwall, by Jimmy Seed. He was an interesting type just to be passing through, a former Durham miner best remembered as the coach behind Charlton Athletic's rise from obscurity in the late 1930s and '40s. He was also an England inside-forward who had helped Tottenham win the F.A. Cup in 1921 and Sheffield Wednesday (or strictly speaking, The Wednesday on the first occasion) to their back-to-back League championships in 1929 and 1930. Seed and Atyeo treated one another with mutual respect, and John briefly enjoyed the input of a football man of such a rich pedigree; but of course it was all over almost before it began, and he and his team mates found their playing fate in the hands of Peter Doherty.

If one man was delighted by the arrival of the Irishman it was Harry Dolman, who had wanted to sign him as manager nine years earlier, in 1949, after he had left Huddersfield Town. Instead, the legendary inside-forward, some say the finest ever produced by Northern Ireland, went on to Doncaster Rovers, first as player-manager but for the most part simply as boss, and it was from there that he came south to Ashton Gate. Dolman's fellow directors, thinking they were merely meeting to discuss who might be invited to take on the vacant post, were aghast when the chairman revealed him with a flourish from the room next door, and more than one wondered what might lie ahead as he signed his three-year contract. Skipper Jack White had more reason than most to be taken by surprise. 'Harry Dolman told me around two years before I left in 1958 that if I looked after myself, I could well become the next manager, and I was thrilled,' he told David Foot, years later. When Doherty arrived and let it be known that he was going to bank on youth, 'I knew, like a lot of players, that I'd be on my way at the end of the season.'

Although Doherty had enjoyed a peerless reputation as a player, he was widely seen as a difficult and discontented man, a fact reflected in his mere sixteen international appearances; his admirers, very possibly correctly, viewed his spikiness as a sign that he was a person and a footballer well ahead of his time, with firm opinions on players' rights and the on-field speed of thought and vision that could make other talented colleagues look dim-witted and lumpen in comparison. At Fulham at much this time, the mercurial Johnny Haynes was putting poor Jimmy Hill through the agonies suffered by so many of Doherty's colleagues (though in the long years since then, Jim has been able to argue that with dozens of goals scored in nearly three hundred League games at Craven Cottage, he must have been doing something right, somewhere).

The problem the Bristol City players were to discover soon enough was that Doherty the manager was equally out of touch with exactly what could and could not be done by a footballer at this level of the game. 'Who does he think I am – Puskas?' 'I'd have liked to have seen Billy Wright cut that one out.' It was not long before the rumbles of discontent began to roll around the dressing room. As a player at his peak, he had been an inside-forward about whom John Atyeo had heard from childhood. He was a tall and gifted ball player with a tremendous body swerve and most of his shooting power in his left foot, while his speed off the mark won him valuable time and space for a telling pass or shot. A natural dribbler with a legendary passion for hard work, he had endless on-the-field qualities that Big John could admire; as we shall discover, it was rather different on the other side of the touchline.

Doherty had started his career with Coleraine, working as a bus conductor until the passengers got fed up of waiting for him to stop kicking a ball around in the park, and then he stepped up to Glentoran, with whom he won the Irish F.A. Cup before joining Blackpool for £2,000 late in 1933. When he went to Manchester City two years later, the £10,000 they paid for him was only £1,000 short of the British record. He was a star of City's League Championship side of 1936-37, scoring thirty times with head and feet alike, but his admirers said he could also tackle like a defender and dribble like a winger. He was one of the generation that lost their best years to the Second World War, but after it, now almost thirty-three, he was still good enough to join Derby County and team up with another legend, Raich Carter, to help them win the 1946 F.A. Cup and lift the Victorian gypsies' notorious curse on the Baseball Ground and its team. Within weeks, however, he was at odds with the board over his wish to take over a pub, and he was on his way again, this time to Huddersfield Town.

Three years later he celebrated his thirty-sixth birthday by moving on to be player-manager of Doncaster Rovers, who won the Third North in his first season. He hung up his boots shortly before his fortieth birthday, but though he then kept Rovers afloat in the lower reaches of the Second Division for the rest of his time at Belle Vue, they were in desperate straits when he jumped ship to Ashton Gate and went to the bottom at the end of that 1957-58 season. Perhaps his greatest triumph at the club was the discovery (by his assistant Cliff Duffin, who followed him to City) of Alick Jeffrey, the teenage wonder boy whose career as a high-flier ended in serious injury in an Under-23 international against France at Ashton Gate in 1956 (though it is often forgotten that he returned as a free-scoring lower division journeyman in the 1960s). Peter Doherty, however, had a coaching career beyond South Yorkshire, and when he arrived at Ashton Gate it was as manager of a Northern Ireland team about to contest the World Cup finals for the first time. Doherty had taken on the part-time role in 1951, and his achievement in guiding the team to the quarter-finals in Sweden was the highlight of his eleven years in charge.

The record books show that Peter Doherty helped inch City clear of the very depths of the Second Division that 1957-58 season, and their eventual seventeenth place was familiar territory to him from his Doncaster days; seven wins and two draws in the final third of the season was no mean feat, drawing a veil over the fact that in his first game in charge, three days after signing, he took City up to his old stamping ground at Belle Vue and they lost two-one; the Doncaster crowd, not given to spontaneous mirth, fell about in laughter at that. He earned the Robins some kind of respectability in the weeks that followed, but he knew that Harry Dolman wanted more from him than that. Still, his new boss had clearly taken a shine to him, his ready Irish charm and his close links with the horse racing world; that Doherty missed Doncaster Racecourse more than the Belle Vue soccer ground went entirely without saying, and soon the chairman and manager would be seen out and about in the Dolman Rolls-Royce, with Harry enjoying basking in the Doc's reflected glory.

From the start, Peter Doherty did not expect very much from John Atyeo, which was not the way to get the best out of the big man. When Doherty arrived John's father Walter was dying of cancer, and there were times when his worries clearly affected his form, despite his final tally of twenty-three goals. Apart from that, he was genuinely upset and shocked by Pat Beasley's departure, and his replacement by a man with whom he had already crossed swords. A couple of years earlier City had beaten Doncaster four-one, one of the goals coming when John shoulder-charged Harry Gregg into the back of the net, giving him a taste of what Nat Lofthouse was to do to him in the 1958 Cup final. Doherty and Atyeo had debated the matter in the tunnel afterwards in a way that served as a reminder that when push came to shove, John was no shrinking violet – 'Call yourself an international?' said Doc. 'Piss off,' replied John – and the incident was still fresh in both men's minds. The fact was that the new manager would have been happy enough to see that fighting spirit from John, and a good many of his team mates, out on the pitch on a Saturday afternoon, but he found most West Countrymen infuriatingly and bafflingly unco-operative and passive.

Atyeo was twenty-six by now, in his absolute prime, but apart from anything else, Doherty felt he was a spoilt player because of his long-standing part-time status. The two men talked over the issue and John, ill at ease through the death of his father, no longer a shop-keeper and with a new sense of responsibility as head of the family, was persuaded to sign full-time from the start of the 1958-59 season; this lasted until 1962-63, a fleeting state of affairs that only served to uphold his long-held belief that part-time football was by far the preferable option for him. Doherty was a great talker and would-be motivator in the dressing room, but much of what he said brought a cynical reaction from the players, expressed by the looks on their faces and head-bowed silence. 'All pull together and we'll win the boat race,' he'd urge, but he felt this lot could not row from one side of the Floating Harbour to the other. They would not take him on, and this was a manager who craved a fiery reaction from his players. 'If I had a team of Ernie Peacocks, we'd do all right,' he would grumble to the press, fully aware that he would not have even one Ernie Peacock for much longer. Big John was far and away the star of the Bristol City side the manager had inherited, but he was never heard fantasising about a team of eleven John Atyeos. It is facile to conclude that this was the time that Atyeo should have moved on; after all, in terms of a conventional football career, he should never have been at Ashton Gate in the first place. It must be said, however, that had he made the leap in the summer of 1958, he would have saved himself a good deal of unhappiness over the next couple of seasons.

In hindsight, we now know that it was Peter Doherty's penchant for former South Yorkshire players that poisoned his relationship with the club and sent it crashing into the Third Division in 1960; but in February 1958, just a few days after his arrival, his signing of Bert Tindill for £6,400 was the master stroke that saved City from relegation, as he rattled in ten goals in fourteen games. Tindill, at Doncaster since the Second World War, was thirty-two before 1958 was out; the press said he was thirty, but City fans would not have minded if he had been eighty, as long as he was playing as he did. In a dozen years at the same club, most of them with Doherty as boss, he had fallen into a content-ed and well-looked-after way of life, sharing the Doc's love of the turf at Doncaster and Thirsk and always dapper in his dress. John Atyeo, unsure of what to make of his signing, was at first sceptical about his ability and disturbed by the rumour that Bert was a better player out-side the penalty area than he was. A top-of-the-range club house up on Bedminster Down was quickly found for him and his family, and John soon latched on to mutterings that the new man was enjoying a privi-leged existence. Tindill was having heat treatment one day when the trainer Les Bardsley growled: 'What's the matter with him? He's not the king of the castle.' The mere suggestion of anyone other than John Atyeo being king of this particular castle was a culture shock.

Nevertheless, the advent of Doherty had put John on his toes, and even before he went full-time he took to reporting for an extra day's training, making it three in the week. He made it clear to 'The Wanderer', his long-time contact on the *Bath Evening Chronicle*, that nothing should be read into the decision: '"It is not a step towards my becoming a full-time professional," he assured me. There was no question of that. When I said that full-time training might make all the difference (towards his regaining his England place), John said that he did not think that that mattered at all. He quite rightly pointed out to me that he reached the top when he was a part-timer. I was pleased to hear him add that if he could do it once, he could very well do it again.' It was a strange interview John gave 'The Wanderer' that day. For a start, it is hard to believe that it had not filtered through to him that at least part of England's turning against him had been precisely *because* of his part-time status. Second, his attitude in other ways seemed honest to the point of negativity. When the reporter asked him, in the immediate aftermath of Tommy Taylor's death in the Munich air disaster, whether he felt he had a chance of returning to international colours, 'he said there were quite a few players in front of him yet'; and greatly more bafflingly, when he was put the stock question about the following day's big F.A. Cup tie against Bristol Rovers at Ashton Gate, the one to which the only possible answer is: 'Of course we'll get through, but it's going to be tough', he said: 'I think they (Rovers) will win.' This really does seem extraordinary (if ultimately correct), and even the faithful 'Wanderer' could not take it lying down: 'For once I told him: "I think you are wrong, John. It's up to you..." '

John Atyeo and Bert Tindill quickly learned to respect and even like one another. They would sit together on the coach doing crosswords and the radio *Transatlantic Quiz*, or John would be happy to listen to Bert's appraisal of the day's runners and riders, intrigued, as he always was, by insights into his team-mates' passions and interests. Best of all, he found the new man the best of comrades-in-arms on the field. At this stage, City were playing John at centre-forward, rather than inside-right, and with Tindill and Atyeo at eight and nine, opponents knew that they would have their work cut out if both were on song. The fact was that John was not on song in the final months of the season, with his father's terminal illness hanging over him. Only five of his twenty-three goals were scored after Boxing Day, while in the fourteen games he played with Tindill in 1957-58 he netted just four to Bert's ten. It was one of those fleeting spells in his career, as with Jimmy Rogers in 1955-56, Dermot Curtis in the previous season and Brian

Clark to come, when Big John's name was not necessarily the one that would jump out on the score sheet.

Tindill's first goal came in his third game, in a narrow three-two defeat by champions-elect West Ham at Upton Park, but the crowd quickly warmed to him when he won City both points on successive Saturdays in March, with one-nil wins over Notts County away and Ipswich Town at home. The best-remembered game of that season was late on at Craven Cottage against a high-flying Fulham that still harboured promotion hopes. City ripped them apart and were four-nil up at half-time, thanks to a Tindill hat-trick and one from Atyeo. In fact Tindill had also scored three in the previous game, a five-nil thrashing of Barnsley, and suddenly nobody was talking about the dreaded drop any more. 'Bert was a true professional who scored a goal with the minimum amount of flamboyancy,' John Atyeo recalled later. 'He was a crafty player. A little nudge from Bert, unseen by the referee, was sufficient to put himself on the ball and send his opponent off balance. He was a very good fellow to play with, and completely unselfish.' After Tindill had gone back north, this time to Barnsley, at the end of 1958-59 – 'on the very top wages, but the transfer was straight and above-board', he told Atyeo – the two men corresponded for a while, with real stamps and envelopes in those pre-text days. 'Thank you for your most welcome letter,' Bert wrote to John in July 1959. 'Sorry I haven't answered sooner, but my wife and I have just returned from a touring holiday in North Wales.' The Yorkshireman was in his early thirties at the time; a different world, indeed.

Bert Tindill was Cup-tied for that home draw against Bristol Rovers in the fifth round of the F.A. Cup; after the ups and downs of Accrington Stanley they had seen off Notts County two-one at Meadow Lane in the fourth round, and there was high excitement when the men with the velvet bags delivered Bristol's ultimate derby game. John Atyeo was always amused, looking back, that City's three Cup ties that season were under three different managers – Beasley, Seed and Doherty: 'The only time in football history that happened', he would say, and it is hard to disbelieve him. There was the usual great build-up in the local press the week before, with City going to Weston-super-Mare to train and Rovers taking thirteen men to Dawlish, and the papers were full of tales of brine baths and massages and runs along the beach. There was also doubtless a little night life along the way for the likes of Alan Williams and Bobby Etheridge, and the City lads were buzzing with the news that on the Saturday, Weston's Winter Gardens were hosting the Six-Five Special, the BBC's revolutionary new rock and skiffle show. Top of the charts on February 15, Cup tie day, was one of the Six-Five's great protegees, Michael Holliday, with *The Story of my Life*; though on the terraces it was all rather more sombre, and little of the talk strayed much beyond Munich.

As always at this time, Rovers were faring the better in the Second Division, and heading for a top ten finish; but City had beaten them three-two at home in October (Atyeo two, Walker), and drew the return fixture at Eastville three-all in April, so there was no reason for John Atyeo or anyone else to see them as out-and-out favourites. Close games and plenty of goals, then, and so it proved this time, with City again hitting three. Unhappily for the hordes of reds in the 39,160 crowd, Rovers got four, despite the absence of Alfie Biggs through 'flu. City followers still swear the Rovers winner was offside, but maybe it is time to move on after all but fifty years...

At the end of the season there were inevitable farewells as Peter Doherty did the job any incoming manager has to do. Cyril Williams simply picked up his boots and was gone to manage Chippenham Town, while Alec Eisentrager made off for Merthyr Tydfil, convinced then, as today, that John Atyeo was the greatest of them all. 'I played with lots of good players, including Ivor Guy, Ernie Peacock, Tommy Burden, Jimmy Rogers, Jack White and Dennis Roberts,' he told John Thompson of the *Bristol Evening Post* in 2005. 'But John Atyeo was the best. He was a big man, strong and quick, and he scored fantastic goals, some of which were set up by me. He was good enough to play for England, and would have starred in the Premiership today, because he was the perfect target man.'

The level of football to which such great servants of the club as Cyril and Alec descended left even their most ardent admirers in no doubt that their time in the League really was up, but the manager was still prepared to give thirty-three-year-old Ernie Peacock a few more games at the beginning of 1958-59, while Tommy Burden, at thirty-four, played the whole of that season at wing-half. If Doherty liked the cut of your jib, whether it was for your fighting spirit or creative skills, he would not let age be a barrier; he was also prepared to overlook Tommy's part-time status in this instance, and maybe lived to regret that decision.

Walter Atyeo died on the evening that Bolton Wanderers beat a patched-together Manchester United in the 1958 Cup final. 'He meant so much to me and had helped me all through my career,' said John, and this is no place in the book to debate the pros and cons of that help. John felt lost and confused, and was grateful early in 1959 when an 'offer he could not refuse' came along for the shop and he and Ruth could move back to live with his mother. He spoke of being glad to be there to comfort her, and as we have hinted, he was acutely aware of his new role as the head of two generations of his family. He had always in one way been the king of the house at Glenthorne – Jack Boxley, in the build-up to John's wedding, had gone to see him there and been amazed at just how much life revolved around him – but now he felt his responsibilities weighing heavily on him. Playing cricket began to seem less important, and over the years, Phil Fussell became no longer such a close companion. Nevertheless, John still felt warmly enough about him to name his only son after him, years later.

The sale of the shop brought a brief flirtation with the idea of buying a farm near Swindon that bred mink – 'small animals whose skins are used to make winter wear for the idle rich', as Peter Godsiff put it in the *Evening Post*, leaving no-one in any doubt about where he stood on the fur trade issue, even before it *was* an issue – but the cost of it and the labour involved put John off the idea. 'It would have meant a great deal of hard work, and quite honestly, I think it would have interfered with my football,' he said. 'The heavy cost would have enabled us to start off only on a small scale, but I still think there is a big profit to be made from mink farming.' Instead, with the shop gone, quantity surveying behind him and an unusual diversion into farming exotic weasels put on the back burner at the very least, John took the quantum leap of signing new terms with Bristol City as a full-time professional. The move was widely welcomed, and understandably so, but to put his decision in context, it would probably never have happened if he could have bought more minks for his money.

In the light of his deep and heartfelt mourning for his father, we can only speculate on the kind of form he might have shown for England in the World Cup in Sweden in June, had he made the cut; his team-mates would doubtless have found him an introverted and distracted young man. A break from football was never more welcomed by him, though even the balm of the familiarity of playing cricket for Frome was marred by the fact that his father was not there in the pavilion willing him on. Later in the year, not long before Christmas, John went along to the Angel Hotel in Westbury to accept his father's thirty-five-years' service award from the British Railways St. John Ambulance Association at a prizegiving for its Westbury and Frome classes. There could scarcely be a more graphic illustration of his commitment to family and roots than this.

Back at Ashton Gate in the summer of 1958, City signed all but one of the squad of boys who had helped Bristol win the English Schools Trophy the previous season (by beating the decade's dominant though not particularly English team, Swansea). The word on the street was that their parents had been 'looked after' by Harry Dolman. The exact nature of this looking after is now lost in the mists of time, though it is safe to assume that the little terraces of Easton, Bedminster and Knowle did not suddenly sprout Rolls-Royces and Bentleys. It was fondly imagined that these lads could form the basis for a home-grown City team for years to come, and there was some alarm when Peter Doherty then brought in several of the youth side from Doncaster Rovers, slightly older and more battle-hardened players. Bert Tindill saving the club from the drop was one thing; a dressing room full of 'teddy boys with Yorkshire accents' was another.

On paper and from this distance, season 1958-59 looks a remarkably settled one for Bristol City. Peter Doherty used fewer than twenty players all season for the first time in more than fifty years, and eleven of them each made thirty-four appearances or more, making up a core team of Tony Cook, Gordon Hopkinson, Mike Thresher, half-backs Peter McCall, Alan Williams and Tommy Burden and forwards Wally Hinshelwood, Bert Tindill, John Atyeo, Bobby Etheridge and Johnny Watkins. Whatever was to happen the following season – and as we shall discover, almost anything that could happen, did – the new manager could not be accused of not giving the players he had inherited a chance. In the close season he had gone back to Doncaster to sign their twenty-five-year-old right-back Hopkinson, in effect to replace Ernie Peacock, making it two of his former players in the squad, while his only significant signing during the course of the season was the Belfast-born left-half Tommy Casey, who had impressed him in Northern Ireland's colours in Sweden. Casey, at twenty-nine, had been most high-profile as a Newcastle player, but had signed for Portsmouth immediately after the World Cup and had spent a miserable few months with them in their wretched 1958-59 relegation season, and grabbed the chance to link up again with his national boss. He saw out his League career at Ashton Gate, staying three seasons after Doherty had departed, and among the players, at least, he was the most popular of the manager's later signings – 'full of blarney and a great character', as John Atyeo recalled him; the fans were by no means as keen.

Season 1958-59 began well but ended in disarray and unhappiness. City started like an express train, beating Rotherham six-one at home on the opening Saturday (Hinshelwood two, Tindill two, Atyeo and Etheridge), and following it up with a seven-four hammering of Barnsley at Oakwell, eight of the goals coming in a dizzying second half (Atyeo three, Tindill two, Etheridge and a Johnny Watkins screamer). Lol Chappell scored all four for Barnsley, while Arthur Kaye, briefly seen by Blackpool as the next Stanley Matthews, was another of the home side's stars. There was a surprise for John Atyeo when one of his non-footballing friends, on honeymoon in Yorkshire, saw that City were at Oakwell and took the bus over to watch them. He was so delighted by what he saw that he could not control himself and ran on to the pitch to congratulate the man he was proud to call his mate. 'What are you doing up here?' asked Big John, astonished to see such a friendly face at a midweek game two hundred miles up country. 'Come and have a pint. I'll see you in the players' bar afterwards'; an unusual conversation between a footballer and a spectator in the middle of a Football League match.

The City team stayed in Yorkshire for their game at Sheffield United three days later, when they came down to earth with a bump and a four-nil hammering. Somehow those first three results came to symbolise the whole season, with lots of goals scored and just as many conceded. The final table shows City in tenth place, with forty-one points from their forty-two games, having won seventeen, lost eighteen and drawn seven. Seventy goals were conceded and seventy-four scored, of which Atyeo got twenty-six, Tindill nineteen and Etheridge thirteen. In the F.A. Cup, fate brought Bristol City and Doncaster together in the third round, and Peter Doherty was happy to come away from Belle Vue with a two-nil win (Tindill, Watkins). This paved the way for the replayed match against Blackpool, and the unscheduled stay at the Norbreck Hydro in the fog.

Despite their up-and-down form, City were still in the top six going into the new year, but the season trailed off into mediocrity, and a depressingly low gate of just over 10,000 showed up for the last home game against Lincoln, a routine one-nil win in which John Atyeo scored his final goal of a season in which he had been below par in the latter stages. Still, the faithful mused, as they streamed out into the springtime evening, there might be a few surprises up the old club's sleeve next season; if they had known the exact nature of those surprises, some of the more nervously disposed of them might have taken a leap off the parapet into the Cumberland Basin there and then.

CHAPTER 12

A CAMP DIVIDED

When the retained list was announced at the end of 1958-59 there was
a big shock: Johnny Watkins, Bristol-born, at the club since 1951 and
a first-team regular for the past two-and-a-half seasons, had been
released at the age of twenty-six. The peripheral players always fretted
about their last pay packets of the season, wondering whether they
would also contain a dreaded letter of dismissal, but Watkins had not
seen one coming. 'On the day he received his letter, Johnny sat next to
me in the dressing room with tears in his eyes,' John Atyeo recalled.
'He was a good friend of mine, and I remember telling him that
perhaps it could turn out for the best. Within four months he was
tearing us apart playing for Cardiff City, who snapped him up for a
bargain £4,000; Cardiff went into the First Division, and Johnny did
well for them – so it did turn out all right for him in the end.'

As for Watkins, he has always understood that John Atyeo sped up
to the Brecknell, Dolman and Rogers factory as soon as he had seen
his team-mate's plight, asked the chairman what was going on and told
him he was making a mistake. It was to no avail, but before long Harry
Dolman was forced to accept that the release of the winger was far
from the best piece of business he ever did. Johnny Watkins felt a great
deal better when ambitious Cardiff City came in for him – ironically,
after their hopes of signing John McCann had been dashed – and even
more so when he was told he could continue living in Coombe Dingle,
one of north Bristol's most pleasant suburbs. He immediately enjoyed
a wonderful promotion season with Cardiff, and although he was not
quite First Division material in the long term, it was a happy and
rewarding move for him. He certainly did not have to wait long to draw
first blood; City's fifth game of the season was at Ninian Park, where
they were thrashed four-two, while they lost at home three-nil to the
Welshmen (and honorary Welshmen) in January. For the first game,
Johnny shared a railway compartment both ways with some of his old

137

team-mates, including John Atyeo, Jimmy Rogers, Mike Thresher and Tony Cook. Cardiff went four up in twenty-five minutes, with Watkins, captain for the day, getting one of them. On the way home the compartment door slid open and Peter Doherty stuck his head in, about to speak. The sight of Johnny Watkins there left him dumbfounded for one of the few times in his life.

Another big move: Bert Tindill and £14,500 went Barnsley's way, and in exchange came left-winger John McCann and inside-left Malcolm Graham. Atyeo hated the upheaval. 'We were aghast,' he told friends. 'We'd never before met (the two newcomers) as players, and at the same time we were very upset about Johnny Watkins.' In his newspaper memoirs of 1970, however, his tone was somewhat softer. 'The coming of McCann and Graham looked a bold, progressive buy on Peter's part, but regrettably, the old City buying jinx cropped up again,' he reflected. 'The club seemed to make a habit of buying high and selling low, although I can never find the reason. Graham was a very good player, but his mysterious injury meant he didn't make his debut until October 31 at Stoke City. By that time the club were in the doldrums and at the bottom of the table. Mind you, his debut was worth waiting for. He scored twice in a three-one win, the first time we got three all season.'

Nobody, Atyeo included, could ever get to the bottom of the fiasco of Graham's injury, but it was certainly one of the factors in Peter Doherty's rapid departure later in a season in which the club was already doomed to relegation back to Third Division status. The mystery made the headlines in the local sports pages – 'Time City told the truth about Graham' – and the *Evening Post*'s Peter Godsiff, always a keen conspiracy theorist, grumbled: 'Why all the secrecy? Getting vital H-bomb plans from the Government would have been easier than getting some facts about Graham from Ashton Gate... This week, manager Doherty has been harder to contact than the Prime Minister...' The fact was that Graham, in his prime at twenty-four, was suffering from an ailment that did not prevent him from being the fastest sprinter in training or kicking a ball powerfully, yet meant he could still not be risked in a game or even a training match; this was obviously a huge embarrassment to Doherty, after spending so much of the club's money on him. The word went around that Harry Dolman had taken the young man to see a Harley Street specialist, and the verdict was that there was nothing about his suspect knees that prevented him from playing football; whatever his problem, it was not in his physical condition.

In fact Graham and his young wife, away from South Yorkshire and their families and friends for the first time in their lives, were desperately worried about the health of their little boy, who had apparently serious leg problems. There were very real reasons why going out and kicking a ball around was low on his list of priorities, but of course Bristol City could not have been expected to see it that way, and it was at their request that a five-man League commission met officials from the two clubs to thrash out just what would and would not happen if he proved unfit in the long term. City came away by far the more satisfied club, with all their demands for safeguards upheld. It was agreed that they would pay Barnsley Graham's transfer fee only if he was trouble-free within the next three months, and that was how it worked out. A couple of days later he played for the Reserves away at Leyton Orient, and then he was straight in the team for the away game at Stoke City.

As for the City players, they looked at Graham and saw not a man in torment, which he undoubtedly was, but someone who had done pretty well – better than most of them had – out of football and the transfer market lottery. They took in his elegantly cut suits and Daimler saloon, and as his weeks on the sidelines lengthened, they let odd little myths grow up around him. They decided that as well as his being an inside-left, everything about him was inclined to that side of his body. He wrote with his left hand. When he got on the team coach he sat on the left, and they would be watching out for him to do just that; silly stuff, really. On the other hand, they also knew that he had some pedigree, and had once been taken up to Newcastle with the clear intention of joining United. He wanted to go, the Barnsley chairman Joe Richards wanted to cash in on him – but when he and his opposite number Stan Seymour met with their solicitors, a deal simply could not be struck. In the end, Newcastle would not meet the fee Barnsley were asking for Malcolm Graham.

Several legends still abound about Graham's eventual debut at Stoke. As the coach turned into the Victoria Ground car park, he spotted an advertisement with an innocent little pun, urging fuel-buying fans to 'Stoke up with Coke'. 'Stoke up? Grrr, I'll give 'em Stoke up,' he growled, with a vehemence that seemed totally out of character to his new team mates. Then, in the dressing room, he spent so long padding himself with cotton wool and swathing his feet in bandages that some of the lads were muttering darkly about the Curse of the Mummy; but he did the business out on the pitch in that game, played in the next three and scored two more goals before his knee problems put him out again until early February. He ended the season with a grand total of eight League goals from just fourteen games, which made him third top scorer, compared with sixteen each for John Atyeo, in his first full season as a full-time pro, and Jimmy Rogers. The fact that John was overall leading marksman by dint of a goal in the three-two F.A. Cup third-round home defeat by Charlton Athletic was no comfort to him at all at the end of a wretched season in which he at least notched his two hundredth League goal, at home to Plymouth Argyle on December 28.

Even that milestone was a painfully long time coming, since he scored his 197th on November 7, went six long games hitting the woodwork, defenders' backsides, the back of the stands and indeed anything but the net, and then put it right with three in three days against Plymouth, away (two) and home (one), over Christmas. The two hundred goals had been delivered in 366 matches, and scoring does not come much more clinical and consistent than that. As for Malcolm Graham, at the end of the season, by which time he had long been accepted by the younger players in the dressing room as a decent guy, he was off to Leyton Orient and legendary status as one of the brave boys in blue of 1961-62 who won the club a single but unforget-table year in the First Division. The fee was £5,250 and the board was happy to get that, given the blight his various woes had cast on his stay at Ashton Gate. When Leyton won promotion there were many at Ashton Gate who smiled wryly, because the role he played so well at Brisbane Road was exactly what he had been brought to do at Ashton Gate – playing as a deep-lying prompter between the midfield and a dangerous forward line of Atyeo, McCann and Rogers.

John McCann was another unhappy signing who made scant impact and was on his way back to Yorkshire and Huddersfield Town after little more than a year. A Scottish B international with plenty of skill and trickery, he was unlucky to break his leg in the four-one win at Plymouth on Boxing Day, a result all the more remarkable in that the home-grown and imported players were by this stage at loggerheads with each other and all of them, to a man and with John Atyeo very much to the fore, were livid that they had had to travel south on

Christmas afternoon. As we have noted, at least John took it out on the world with two goals. Early the following season, McCann's move to Huddersfield brought Jack Connor down to City, a transfer that was soon to have a happy outcome. McCann moved clubs three more times in the next four years, rarely settling anywhere for more than a year; but despite this, and despite the fact that his signing is a crucial element in the split camp folklore, the then emerging Bobby Williams looks back on him today as 'a smashing lad'.

A much more controversial pre-season incomer was Tommy Cavanagh, Doherty's right-half at Doncaster, a £2,500 signing who was quickly made captain, played twenty-four games through the season and found himself instantly redundant after the manager's summary departure. This tough Irish Liverpudlian found few friends in the Ashton Gate dressing room and was the least liked of the Doherty signings. On a personal level, most of the players got on well with the now departed Tindill, Casey, McCann and Hopkinson, as well as the emerging Roger Collinson and Archie Taylor, the most talented of the welter of teenagers brought down from Belle View; as we have noted, they even liked Malcolm Graham well enough, when they knew where he was coming from, which suggests that whatever went awry in what is now notorious as Bristol City's split camp season was founded on something more complex than out-and-out personality problems.

Was it partially down to parochialism and small-mindedness? Certainly. Was there some religious bigotry there? At first the suggestion seems preposterous in a non-sectarian city such as Bristol – what, did they all sit around in the bath debating the theological pros and cons of the transubstantiation of bread and wine? – but yes, religious bigotry was indeed there. Several of the City board were Freemasons, and the Masons and the Roman Catholic Church to which Peter Doherty and a number of his players belonged were mutually incompatible at that time; these days, both organisations make more conciliatory noises, but essentially, the tenets of each are still such that it is well-nigh impossible for a man to be a faithful member of both. Looking back, it seems plain that Doherty was mistaken in bringing in so many players from his former club – a club with no great pretensions in the football world; it was an insult to the players he inherited in Bristol to imply that so many of the boys he had left behind could do a better job than they could.

Over and above this, at a dressing room level, a sufficient number of the newcomers were Catholics or of Irish descent to prompt mutterings about left-footers and Micks and priests walking the corridors, and the Freemasons in the boardroom felt no compulsion to try to quell such rumblings. Jantzen Derrick – Bristolian through and through, an ex-England Schools international, a groundstaff boy and not seventeen until January 1960 – was living his dream as a player at Ashton Gate, but he hated watching what his seniors were up to: 'I'd see the first-team players choosing to split into two groups as they ran round the ground. I couldn't understand it, but it made me feel uncomfortable.' Older locally-born players would tell their friends in the press: 'It's like trench warfare in there.'

So much of the unrest centred on Tommy Cavanagh, and his instant appointment as captain. The locals simmered with rage. He presumably knew Peter Doherty had this role in mind for him before he agreed to move south, and had the option to decline it, but then again, it would be flattering to any journeyman footballer to be asked by one of the most famous and skilful players in the game to join him hundreds of miles away and serve him as his right-hand man. If nothing else, the manager must have seen leadership qualities in Cavanagh, and had a belief in his ability to win over the dressing room. In Bristol today, Cavanagh is still seen very much as the villain of the piece, as a captain most of the players simply could not believe in. Unsympathetic team-mates swore that he visibly foamed at the mouth when he got into a lather. 'Take it from me, my son, Tommy Cavanagh was a very bad influence on Bristol City Football Club,' John Atyeo told one of the authors of this book not long before he died.

On the other hand, let us see it from the new man's point of view. He joined the club in July 1959, and this is what appeared in the first home programme of the season, against Rotherham on August 29: 'I saw Tommy Cavanagh this week. He has this to say: "Despite the Irish look of my name, I'm an Englishman born at Liverpool, and I'm an Anglican, and since coming to Bristol I've gone to St Francis Church." It was all very forthright, but Tommy's like that – direct, decent, matter-of-fact, dedicated.' The writers of this book have between them been reading football programmes for more than ninety years (sad but true), and nowhere else has either of them remotely seen a pen-picture of a new player in which he has instantly had to explain away his name or discuss religion. It is an insight into the extraordinary pressure

Cavanagh must have been under from the start, and it would be hard-hearted not to have some sympathy with this unsophisticated young man, having problems at work and trying to find his feet in the south of England for the first time with his homesick wife and three little children.

The family had a club house near the ground, and the then only recently rebuilt church of St Francis of Assisi in North Street, Ashton Gate, would indeed have been a logical place of worship for them, if that had been one of their instant priorities. On the other hand, not even this satisfied some doubters; the brick-built church looked as if it could have been Catholic, sounded as if it could have been Catholic and was indeed built, along with several others in the inner-Bristol suburbs, to cater for worshippers on the Catholic wing of the Church of England. Poor Tommy would have been better off if he had declared himself a Methodist.

Alan Williams, at City almost since childhood and only just turned twenty-one at the beginning of the season, was one of the home-growers worst affected by the wind of change sweeping the ground, so disoriented that in the end a move to another club was the only solution for him, even after Doherty and most of his signings had moved on. An experiment that put him at centre-forward alongside John Atyeo did nothing to make him feel any more at ease. The first time it was tried was at home to Middlesbrough at the end of September, after a few days' training and team bonding near Paignton. The visitors' man wearing number nine was Brian Clough. Will scored, Cloughie missed a few, and it ended two-nil for City. Reality returned the following week with a three-nil walloping at Derby County, and that was the end of that little fantasy.

'I sometimes think there's a lot of exaggeration talked about the split camp season,' Alan Williams says today.

'Yes, Alan, but you were a good side, and you ended up bottom of the table. Something must have gone drastically wrong somewhere.'

'Yes, there's no getting away from that.'

Another point of friction in that fractious season was money, at which point enter John Atyeo, Tommy Burden and Mike Thresher. More than a decade on, details of the drama were still sharp in John's memory: 'Doherty believed in a sliding scale, so players would lose money if they lost form and were out of the side. It was a matter of principle on both sides. When the side was promoted (in 1955) Mr

Dolman promised that the players in that side would always be on top money as long as they remained with the club. The three of us were the only surviving members of the team when Peter introduced his sliding scale. We held out, eventually Mr Dolman returned from holiday and it was settled amicably. We wanted top money, which was £20 in the winter and £17 in the summer. Peter wanted us to take a £3 drop during the season if we were out of the team. Mr Dolman reached a compromise. We signed for the sliding scale but were promised the £3 would be made up if we were dropped. In my case it did not apply, for Peter was the only manager never to drop me. I particularly admired Tom Burden's stand over this issue. He was due for a benefit the following season, but was always a man of principle. He was prepared to sacrifice his chance of a benefit for something he believed was right.'

What John turns a blind eye to in this account, of course, is the undermining of Peter Doherty's authority through Harry Dolman's wheeler-dealing. Whatever happened that season, Atyeo, Burden and Thresher must shoulder a considerable share of the blame for the unrest, and thus for the relegation. There is a remarkable team photograph from that season with the three of them at the centre of the front row, Burden in the middle as if still captain. The real captain, Cavanagh, is second from the right on the back row, in which Rogers, Etheridge and Cook occupy the three other central places. Hopkinson, Casey, Hinshelwood and McCann are the four outermost players. The message could hardly be clearer.

The dispute – during which the three 'rebels' did not report for training – was certainly an inauspicious start to a season which the national press, as excited by the signing of Graham and McCann as the Ashton Gate faithful, had believed could be City's year. Even Bristol Rovers' captain Norman Sykes admitted that the players City had signed, combined with Big John on form, Alan Williams, Tommy Burden, Mike Thresher, Tony Cook and the like, really did look to be in with a reasonable chance of stepping up to the top flight – and the bookmakers agreed with him. They made Liverpool, Cardiff City, Aston Villa and Bristol City the four favourites at the top of Division Two.

Peter Doherty shared their optimism early in the new season, and he believed John Atyeo would play a major part in a campaign that would be looked back on as his finest ever. His assessment of his star player in the *Bristol Evening Post* on August 22, 1959, made plain all his admiration for him – but at the same time betrayed his ambivalence towards his attitude. That said, he was confident that John's new status as a full-timer would sweep away all the doubts. 'By my reckoning, Atyeo should have been one of the finest inside-forwards of the post-war years,' Doherty wrote, to the irritation of hordes of City fans who were convinced that he had been just that for the best part of a decade. 'He has far more ability than most who have claimed the headlines. He is modest, keen, charming – a quiet, loyal member of the City. But I sometimes wonder whether all the virtues which make Big John such a pleasant chap do not detract from him as a footballer, for John Atyeo is *too* modest. He seems to have little idea how good he is.

'In training sessions, John has worked like a navvy. He has finished with notions of being a part-time player, and is now completely on a full-time basis. He has hammered away at the training routines all day and every day. He is as keen as a new razor blade. All he wants now is encouragement to be as good as he can be. I am told that Ashton Gate fans saw him at his best in the promotion year, and that form will come back again. It is up to everyone with the good of the club at heart to see that Atyeo gets a helping hand on his way back to the top bracket. In all sincerity, I believe that Atyeo can again stake his claim for a place in the England side. The international team will probably be rebuilt, and John is young, strong, talented and experienced. His best seasons could still be in front of him.'

So much for early season dreams. In fact, as we have reflected, this was a very disappointing time for John – but in retrospect, should the club have expected more from him? Should he have grasped his colleagues by the scruffs of their necks, banged their heads together and ordered them to battle as one for the sake of Bristol City Football Club? To look to him for that, says the writer David Foot, is simply to misunderstand him: 'He was a team man, not a leader of men; he could inspire his colleagues by scoring uplifting goals, but he was not the one to be urging them on a bad Tuesday night at Bradford City.' City ended 1959-60 three points adrift at the bottom of the table, with a record of won eleven, drawn five, lost twenty-six, goals for sixty, against ninety-seven, points twenty-seven. The points equivalent today would be thirty-eight from forty-two games, and when it is considered that fifty from forty-six are by no means a guarantee of safety these days, it can be seen just how far off the pace the team was. There were brief moments of joy, including a one-nil home win over Liverpool in the fourth game of the season, a two-one beating of Bristol Rovers at Ashton Gate (Atyeo two – some say two of the greatest goals of his career) and the double over Plymouth at Christmas; but nine times they let in four goals or more, including six at Huddersfield, Middlesbrough and Swansea and five at home to Aston Villa (without reply) and at Sheffield United and Brighton. It was after the latter, a five-one whipping at the Goldstone Ground in early March, that the recently widowed Harry Dolman had seen enough of Peter Doherty. Harry was staying with his sister in Sussex that weekend, and had ample time to ponder on what was going wrong. Open dissention between the players had broken out in the F.A. Cup third round game against Charlton, which was lost three-two after a two-nil half-time lead had been squandered (Atyeo, Cavanagh), and this time it had been even worse.

Herbert Gilliam, the *Western Daily Press's* long-serving man at Ashton Gate, was alarmed to see the lack of discipline at Brighton. 'I witnessed one of the worst displays of football from City,' he wrote. 'They were roundly bickering among themselves. Once or twice I looked across to the directors' box... When it went to five-one I phoned in my last report, said a hasty farewell to my colleagues in the press box, chased along the streets to Hove to get the Brighton Belle to London and catch the connection to Bristol. I knew that Harry just had to do something.' As in the Charlton game, Cavanagh was the butt of the Bristol players' ire, with almost all the team excluding him from the play. 'I've been running around for forty-five minutes, and I haven't touched the ball,' he raged at half time. 'Then stand still,' Les Bardsley replied coldly, bringing the feud more into the open than ever before. Stand still is exactly what Tommy Cavanagh did; after the final whistle, he never kicked a ball for Bristol City again.

Dolman's conclusion was simply one many supporters had reluctantly reached some time before, not least because rumours were rife about full-on fighting among players in training: Doherty must go. He had even pulled out as manager of Northern Ireland in an attempt to bring matters back under control at Ashton Gate, but he had lost the confidence of the dressing room – both sides of it – and ultimately he had lost the support of Harry Dolman, who had once fought so hard to secure his services and had delighted in his company both at the ground and out and about in the West Country. The morning Doherty went, John Atyeo drove into the car park with his car horn blaring. As he arrived, the Doc was walking out with his typewriter. 'Well, we got you in the end,' said Atyeo, and he would tell the tale for the rest of his days, seemingly oblivious to the fact that it did not cast the most kind light on his legendary loyalty to the Bristol City cause. The day after Doherty was sacked, Dolman took John Atyeo, Jimmy Rogers, Mike Thresher and Alan Williams out to lunch, and assured them that there would be changes for the better. Les Bardsley, who had succeeded Wilf Copping and Eddie Nash as trainer, was put in charge of the team, but with just ten games left it was all too late. Neither was Bardsley helped by the back-up services of a committee comprised of Dolman, vice-chairman Bill Kew, director F.C. Vyvyan-Jones, a high-profile Church of England clergyman in the city and Tommy Burden, who was instantly reinstated as captain in place of Cavanagh. It must be said that results got no worse under their auspices, and four of City's eleven wins came in those last ten games. On the other hand, there were some strange and disturbing things going on as the season reached its climax, and they haunted John Atyeo for the rest of his days.

Leaving those aside, momentarily, City had a handful of games left in which to turn things around. The following Saturday they were at home to Lincoln City, and there was no place in the team for the three contentious northern players or for Wally Hinshelwood, who along with Cavanagh never played for the club again. Derek Virgin, long-serving Somerset-born reserve and Ashton Park schoolmaster, turned out at inside-right in one of his rare first team outings, Bobby Etheridge came back at right-half and Jantzen Derrick made the fourth appearance of his long career out on the left wing. Lincoln were sunk one-nil by a Jimmy Rogers goal, and the crowd went wild. The following week, a two-nil defeat at Portsmouth served as an early warning that no miracles could be expected; and though a poor Sunderland were beaten at Ashton Gate, with John Atyeo playing one of his best games of the season and getting the winner, defeat at Villa Park in front of 38,556 continued the pattern of one step forward, one step back. Champions-elect Aston Villa were one-nil down at half time, thanks to the one and only goal of right-back Roger Collinson's career; it was not a bad place for him to perform the feat, but two hotly disputed penalties in the second half sent City home pointless.

Late on, as the season unravelled, Cardiff City's home game against Plymouth Argyle on Easter Tuesday took on massive significance for

the Robins. Cardiff were promotion-bound, Plymouth in the doldrums
with City, and John Atyeo, Bobby Etheridge, Tony Cook and director
Vyvyan-Jones took the short trip to Ninian Park to cheer themselves
up with the sight of their fellow strugglers losing two more points. The
previous day they had won with a convincing looking scoreline over
Ipswich at Ashton Gate, so the right result tonight would be the icing
on the cake. Johnny Watkins was injured, and they sat with him in the
stands, buoyed by his reassurances that his promotion-bound team-
mates were right up for it, and the points would go their way. Of
course, football being the funny old game we all know it is, the boys
in blue missed two penalties, the boys in green pinched the winner, and
they went on to finish the season comfortably clear of both City and
Hull, the other relegated team. The match that sealed the Robins' fate
for all except the most optimistic mathematicians in the world –
among whose number Big John was most certainly not – was at
Brisbane Road in the third game from the end of the season, when
mid-table Leyton Orient cruised home three-one. Caretaker manager
Les Bardsley looked back on that afternoon and concluded: 'I have
never come back from an away game with such a low-spirited bunch
of players. We came back on the Tube, right the way across to
Paddington, and sat on the platform waiting for the carriages to be
shunted in. I have never sat with a more dispirited, depressed, utterly
defeated eleven lads. Harry Dolman went off to a hotel somewhere and
came back with half a dozen bottles of champagne. "Look, we'll go
down in style," he said. "We'll be back, don't worry, we'll be back." '

So they were, five long years later, by which time only Jantzen
Derrick and John Atyeo of City's Leyton eleven were still in the team.
The final game was at home to Stoke City, where the season's lowest
Ashton Gate crowd, 9,103, saw their favourites beaten two-one. All
was long lost by then, of course, and while it was a time for large
numbers of the club's followers to express their apathy by staying
away, many of those present vented their anger in a way that rocked
both the players and the board. Clearly, there could never again be
another 1959-60.

Before then, however, the Easter programme brought three matches
in four days about which rumour and speculation began to circulate
almost from the start. The theory was that attempts were made to bribe
key opposition players to throw the games – away at eleventh-placed
Ipswich Town on Good Friday, April 15 (won three-one, Atyeo two,

Rogers); at home to sixth-placed Huddersfield Town on Easter Saturday, April 16 (lost three-two, own goal, Atyeo); and at home to Ipswich on Easter Monday (won five-one, Atyeo two, Rogers two, Bobby Williams). There had also been talk of the away game at Swansea Town on April 26 – Swansea allegedly 'owing City one' for a supine performance at Ashton Gate that had given the Welshmen two points and last-gasp salvation on the final day of 1957-58 – but since City were already down by then, and a youthful and inexperienced home team won six-one, it can be safely assumed that whatever might have been planned for that one did not go ahead.

John Atyeo was among those at the club who picked up on the proposals for at least some of these games, and the memory of them disturbed him until the end of his life. In the summer of 1990 a West Country-based football writer (who does not figure elsewhere in this biography) was granted an interview with John at his home in Warminster on the proviso that it would not take more than a few minutes. Typically, the big man warmed to the task, the two found they had much in common despite a generation gap, and their conversation continued until late into the night. In the darkness, out at the garden gate, Atyeo surprised his guest by suddenly beginning to unburden himself in a somewhat confused – and certainly confusing – way about the end of 1959-60, and how much he had hated what he had seen and heard at that time. Should he make public what he knew? He was urged not to, and he never did; but straight-as-a-die as he was, he never ceased to be haunted by this glimpse of a side of football that disturbed and appalled him.

CHAPTER 13

THAT SINKING FEELING

Relegation brought the end of five years of Second Division football at Ashton Gate and the beginning of five more back in the Third, though for City it was a first taste of life in the national third tier, with the scope to drop one more step down the League ladder if all went awry. In truth, that fate never looked remotely likely for the team over those five years, and it was not until 1982, in their third relegation in three seasons, that they tasted Fourth Division football for the first time. Of course, balanced against the fact that that ignominy never befell the club during the time Harry Dolman was at the helm and John Atyeo was battling up front is the sad reflection that neither did they taste life in the top division, as Alan Dicks and his red, red Robins did between 1976 and 1980, before it all went so disastrously wrong.

Instead, in the summer of 1960, Dolman must have felt that, for all his dreams, he was back to square one. 'Relegation was a terrible set-back for all of us, but I think Mr Dolman felt it more than anyone,' Atyeo mused years later. 'After having a taste of the Second Division and being on the brink of the First Division, we were back where we started, with a disgruntled band of supporters and a disillusioned team. Something had to be done, because spirits were at a low ebb. It was the worst moment I had with the club in fifteen years, back to the bottom of the graph.'

The priority was a new manager, and despite the fact that stories of the dressing room friction had spread far beyond the West Country, no fewer than sixty experienced football men fancied their chances at Bristol City. At first Fred Ford, the Bristol Rovers coach, was not one of them, but he found himself at Lilleshall on a coaches' and trainers' course with City's Bill Harvey and Les Bardsley, and they told him the job was as good as his for the price of a phone call to Harry Dolman. After he had talked the matter over with his close friend Bill Shankly, Fred got in touch with Harry and said: 'If you'll let me do things my way, I'll join you.' On July 14, 1960, after keeping quiet about the deal to Bert Tann all summer, he signed a three-year contract worth £2,750 a year – wonderful money in the game when it is considered that in the following January football all but came to a halt when players from Danny Blanchflower, Bobby Charlton and Jimmy Greaves downwards threatened to strike for the right to earn more than a maximum of £1,040 per annum.

It was certainly not that the club was flush with money. In fact it was facing life in the lower leagues with a debt of £55,000, a sum which Harry Dolman wiped out, through a donation of shares in Brecknell, Dolman and Rogers. When he handed the money over, Les Bardsley told him: 'If you'd listened to what we told you, you could have kept your £55,000.' On the other hand, Harry told the press: 'If I'd given it to the Tory party, I'd probably now have a bloody knighthood.' He also took the opportunity to do a spot of boardroom reshuffling and score-settling by making part of the deal the resignation of his fellow directors George Jones and the Revd F. C. Vyvyan-Jones, who so recently had been a part of the interim management committee. Dolman had a hernia operation in the summer of 1960, and Lionel Smart, who farmed as a neighbour of Acker Bilk near Pensford, was in hospital at the same time. Harry opened a copy of Charles Buchan's *Football Monthly*, wrote in it 'How would you like to join my new-style board at Ashton Gate?' and passed it along the corridor to him, and he took little time in saying yes. Another new director appointed at this time was one of Harry's close business associates, Graham Whittock. Whittock, of course, was already close to John Atyeo, and Smart soon would be.

The summer brought inevitable exits from the dressing room, with perhaps the two most contentious Doherty men, Tommy Cavanagh and Malcolm Graham, going to Carlisle and Leyton respectively. Wally Hinshelwood, finding life as a thirty-year-old flying winger an increasing struggle, moved back home to London and a brief stay at Millwall, though more Hinshelwoods left Bristol than had arrived four years earlier. Wally's son Paul, a great Crystal Palace stalwart of the future, was born in the city. Even after these departures, however, the players were still at sixes and sevens when they returned for the new season, and on his first morning of training in Ashton Park, Fred Ford found himself throwing his weight around to stop a scuffle between two of the senior pros. He lined the entire squad up against a wall and read the riot act

– and though the blunt message 'You *will* be a happy crew' is not one that is easily enforced, it can be if the man management is right, as it most certainly was in Ford's case.

Alan Williams, still at odds with himself and the club in the wake of the disastrous relegation season, was one of the few men at Ashton Gate who could not get on with the new boss, and was at loggerheads with him from that first day of training. Good enough to have been chosen for England Under-23s in a game that was unhappily postponed, this proud Bristolian, whom many thought would never leave his native city, struggled through the whole of a season during which he scarcely played – and when he did, occasionally found himself floundering up front. When he signed for Oldham in the early summer of 1961, just turned twenty-three, many of his friends wondered what lay in store for him. In fact he quickly became a Latics regular and played 172 League games for them, before going on to rack up a further 250 or so with Watford, Newport County and Swansea, adding up to a career total of 550-plus matches. He captained each one of those last three clubs, and had indeed been named by Peter Doherty to skipper Bristol City in place of Cavanagh in the Doc's last throes at the club. The manager was fired before this could be implemented, and of course Tommy Burden was the new regime's man for the job.

At first, City supporters did not know what to make of the signing of Rovers' coach as their team's boss, but to the players he was just another football man to be judged on his own merits, and they soon decided that he had plenty of those. 'We made a fresh start under Fred – everyone always called him Fred – and I liked him from the word go,' John Atyeo recalled. 'When he came, I remember talking to Geoff Bradford about him, and he told me: "You can't go wrong now. He's the best man you can possibly have for the job." Every player who ever served under him, with the odd exception, has the same opinion. He was as straight as a die and as hard working as can be. He set about the task with a will, although he didn't have much to work on to start with. The gates slipped, there wasn't much money and the whole club had to be rebuilt.'

The admiration was mutual, but the relationship got off to a fragile start, through the fault of neither man. In the first match of the new 1960-61 season, a two-nil defeat at Valley Parade, Bradford, John Atyeo picked up an ankle knock that put him out for nine of the next eleven League games, the first lengthy lay-off of his largely injury-free career. He felt particularly down about it: 'It was a difficult time for Fred to come to the club, and he probably pinned a lot of his hopes on me, because I was going to carry the brunt of the forward work. Then came this, in my very first match of our season back in the Third Division...' It was Fred Ford who at last made Atyeo captain at Ashton Gate, when Tommy Burden retired at the end of the 1960-61 season, a decision made all the easier by his full-time status.

'He was skipper by example more than by forceful personality,' Ford later reflected. 'He was the most skilful player in the side, and a modest man. His modesty showed in his play; he never attempted the flashy or the impossible, and neither did he do anything that was unnecessary, or seek glamour, on or off the field. The example set by a senior player is a tremendous asset to any manager. John Atyeo always seemed to attract the company of the youngest newcomer to the side. He never drank or smoked or went in for the bright lights – a natural athlete. For much of the time I was his manager, his main asset to the side was his touch – his instinctiveness in front of goal, his ability to lay the ball off for a colleague. It was first class – international class. I never once saw John greedy to score a goal. If another player was in a better position, no matter how slight, John would pass the ball to him. This became a feature of Bristol City's style over John Atyeo's last seasons. We did not have a selfish player on the books.'

The long trip to Bradford on the opening day of the 1960-61 season gave John Atyeo plenty of time to reflect on football's fates. On the same afternoon that injury was disrupting his Third Division season until early October, his close friend Johnny Watkins was making a scoring debut in the First Division for Cardiff. By the time John was properly back in action the team had sunk into the bottom half of the table, and there they stayed, rarely fluctuating from the fourteenth position in which they finished, and depressingly unimpressive on their travels. Apart from making John captain at the end of the season, Fred Ford returned him to his favoured inside-right spot by spending the proceeds of the Graham sale on Alex Tait, a ginger-haired centre-forward and occasional winger who by now had convinced Newcastle that he was not the next Jackie Milburn. Still, he scored thirty-eight goals in the 117 League games he played for City, including fifteen in this debut season.

For John Atyeo, however, Tait was more than a polished ally in the forward line. He was also a schoolteacher, a part-time player, and John got on very well with him, sympathetic, as he was, to men who looked beyond football as a career. A full-timer since 1958, he knew by now that he operated best when he had things going on outside the game. 'There's a lot more to life than this,' he would tell those who cared to listen, and in Alex Tait he had an intelligent colleague who did not need to be convinced, even though – familiar story – it was precisely that attitude that led to his parting of the ways with Newcastle. Alex played a major part in persuading John that teaching could also be the way ahead for him – a conviction on which he acted in the autumn of 1963, when he shocked Fred Ford by reverting to part-time status and taking a place at teacher training college.

Despite his injury-afflicted season, John ended it as top scorer once more, with nineteen goals in thirty-seven appearances plus a further seven in the F.A. Cup and three in the Football League Cup in its faltering inaugural season. He was the first to admit that this overall haul of twenty-nine for the season made flattering reading, as the F.A. Cup goals came against non-Leaguers Chichester City in the first round and Kings Lynn in the second. The eleven-nil rout of Chichester at Ashton Gate saw him score five for the one time in his senior career, but the defending was so naive that he could not take too much pleasure from the feat. 'I was ashamed to take some of the goals that day,' he recalled. 'I scored five goals in a match for the only time, but I'm not so certain it was much to brag about.' The South Coast amateurs were there strictly for the day out and their share of the proceeds of a 12,000 gate. When the teams walked out on to the pitch the Chichester boys wanted their photograph taken with the City players, so certain were they that they were never going to do this kind of thing again; eight-nil down at half-time, at least they had been realistic about their chances. Everyone came away convinced that the eleven goals could have been more if John and the forwards had not shuffled the ball around in a vain attempt to give Jantzen Derrick his first F.A. Cup goal; that was the only way in which they did fail that afternoon.

John scored his first three in eleven minutes towards the end of the first half, and although he was disparaging about his feat that day, the *Bristol Evening Post* reported that his second, a volleyed lob from Connor's pass into the top corner of the net, 'would have beaten most goalkeepers'. On the other hand, there was quite a sting in the tail of the *Post*'s praise for the big man's performance that day: 'Atyeo's mobility, his chasing back and his excursions to both flanks to collect the ball impressed the onlookers and produced the hope that he would show a similar yearning for work in future – especially away from home.' The last sentiment, in a season in which City won away only twice, is a reminder that John never shook off mutterings about his level of commitment on 'wet Tuesday nights' at Bradford, Bury, Grimsby, Scunthorpe or wherever. Does it really always rain non-stop in those places when Bristol City are in town?

Kings Lynn in the next round were a different proposition. In the first game, in East Anglia, goals by Atyeo and Rogers had put City two-nil up at half time and in the driving seat, but with an East Park crowd of nearly seven thousand roaring them on, the Linnets pulled one back. All of a sudden City's little stroll became a frantic battle, made a great deal worse by the fact that Tommy Casey was limping with a dead-leg and wanted to come off. Fred Ford would have none of it. 'Run it off, lad, run it off,' he ordered. Casey was switched out on to the wing, but he was no more than a passenger out there, and still bickering vehemently with the bench. With minutes to go, Kings Lynn conjured up an equaliser. They and their fans were high as kites, and in the tunnel afterwards one of the home lads started telling Big John how lucky his side had been to hold on for the draw. 'Just you simmer down, my son, and save your breath for Tuesday night,' Atyeo advised him. 'You're going to need it.' Unhappily, back in the dressing room, his calming influence made no impact on Fred Ford, who showed the players for the first time that when it came to swearing, cup-throwing, door-kicking football managers, the then still juvenile Alex Ferguson, Barry Fry and Peter Reid had a great deal to learn.

The tactic obviously worked, since the replay at Ashton Gate turned out to be the formality John had predicted it would be, with City running out three-nil winners through Atyeo and Rogers (two), whose days as a prolific goalscorer were over. In the next round, a goal by the emerging Bobby 'Shadow' Williams despatched Plymouth Argyle at Home Park, but Leicester City at Filbert Street were several bridges too far in round four. The first match was abandoned at nil-all at half time in some of the worst rain and waterlogging John and his colleagues had ever encountered, but the First Division team were far too good for them in the replay, scoring five and having the decency to give City an own goal in reply. Leicester went on to reach Wembley, where they took their place in history by allowing the 'Glory, Glory'

Spurs to clinch the first League and Cup 'double' of the twentieth century.

City had a shorter run in the new League Cup, drawing their first ever game one-all at Aldershot but winning the replay three-nil (Atyeo two, Adrian Williams); the goal at the Rec was scored by Jack Boxley in his very brief return to City, for whom he had first signed a few months before his friend John Atyeo. Depressingly, after that night, Big John was never on a winning League Cup side again. Nottingham Forest, from the First Division but still a club run by a committee, rather than a limited company, were the Robins' next opponents in mid-November. Unique among the top teams, they were still without floodlights, which put them at something of a disadvantage in this specifically midweek competition, and the authorities would have none of it when they tried to have the tie switched to Notts County's ground. The upshot was that only 3,690 of their fans deemed watching Forest beat Bristol City in what seemed a meaningless competition a worthwhile way to spend a grey Tuesday afternoon, and John Atyeo's consolation goal in a two-one defeat was scored in front of one of the smallest crowds of his senior career.

Back at base camp, at least these games were a distraction from a League season that saw City win seventeen, draw ten and lose nineteen, with a goal tally of seventy for and sixty-eight against. Their points total of forty-four was a country mile behind champions Bury's sixty-eight. The main transfer business of the season, in October 1960, saw John McCann go to Huddersfield in return for the big Cumbrian centre-half Jack Connor, who had been recommended to Ford by Bill Shankly. In fact McCann had not played since the spring, and Fred put him in the team for four games just to show Huddersfield what they were getting. They took him on the strength of it, but the move never worked out for him; sad to say, he was never the same player after that broken leg at Plymouth.

Fine defender though Alan Williams had been, it was Jack Connor who became City's defensive rock for years to come; he was one of those men who played the game with a smile on his face, but not many centre-forwards ever got to see the joke. 'The first season under Fred was no more than average,' John Atyeo recalled, 'but there was a lot of work needed to be done, and without much money, Fred settled for stop-gaps and cheap signings. He pulled off a master stroke when Johnny McCann went to Huddersfield Town in a straight swap for Jack

Connor. It was probably the club's most significant business deal of the decade, unless you consider the signing of Mike Gibson for £5,000 from Shrewsbury Town [April 1963]. Jack's performances through the years were faultless. He was a great fellow to have in a club, easy-going, friendly, and nice to get on with, and a darned good player into the bargain. His distribution was perhaps not all that was desired, but he could stop a centre-forward. Those long legs could reach anywhere, and he was exceptionally good in the air. I'm glad I met Jack in football.' Connor and Gibson also struck up a great rapport, both on field and off. 'Les Bardsley used to say I had to play if Jack Connor was in defence, because I was the only one who could read his own goal attempts,' Gibbo recalled. In the last match of 1960-61 John scored a hat-trick at home to Brentford in a three-one win, and said he was proud to have done so well in Tommy Burden's final match. The following week, City beat Rovers three-one at Eastville in the Gloucestershire Senior Cup in Atyeo's first game as captain, and he got two of the goals. As he went into the summer of 1961, quietly proud of being the skipper of his beloved Robins, he felt a hundred times more at ease than he had done twelve months earlier: 'We were gradually picking up the threads, and the club was becoming organised once more.'

An offer for John, the last serious one, came in that close season. It was said to be for around £15,000 and came, ironically, from Portsmouth, for whom he had played fleetingly when they were League champions. No longer; in the top grade until 1959, they had just been relegated to the third for the first time since winning the Third South championship in 1924, and they saw Big John's goals from inside-right, combined with the high-scoring heroics of Ron Saunders at centre-forward, as a sure means of bouncing back right away. He and City would have none of it, though Pompey, to their credit, went on to win the 1961-62 Third Division title without him. With the lifting of the maximum wage early in 1961, bringing Atyeo a few more pounds a week but no more than that, he was more settled in his role at the club; always paid the maximum wage permitted by the Football League, he was also one of the few at the club to be paid travelling expenses. 'You'd have thought he was coming from China,' some of the lads would grumble.

One legitimate way a leading club could make life easier for its players in the maximum wage years was through supplying creature

comforts beyond the reach of lesser teams – generous housing
allowances, training gear and laundry, 'civvy' clothing in the way of
blazers and suits, travelling expenses; at Burnley, under butcher Bob
Lord, it did not do for you or your family to be vegetarian. John Atyeo
was no stranger to perks, but in the summer of 1961, his sense of well-
being went a good deal beyond a feeling of financial stability. Alex
Tait had begun to point him towards a future in teaching, a thought that
pleased and intrigued him, even though, at this stage, he probably did
not know that he would be embarking upon training for it before his
playing days were through. He had not long turned twenty-nine, but
was quite certain that the wage revolution had come too late to earn
him riches in the game, either at City or elsewhere. In one respect he
was right, in that Arsenal, Chelsea and Liverpool were no longer
beating a path to Harry Dolman's door and talking telephone numbers.
On the other hand, Johnny Haynes, admittedly a couple of years
younger than John, was happily pocketing his £100 a week at Fulham
– while, fast-forwarding to 2003, it is interesting to reflect that David
Beckham signed his £150,000-a-week deal with Real Madrid at very
much the age Atyeo was when the maximum wage was abolished in
'61. Becks certainly did not believe he was too old for a profitable
move.

Season 1961-62 was a better one for City, who finished sixth and
briefly reached second place in a February and March in which they
never went lower than third. They started slowly, but the first two
games served notice that this would be a year of ups and downs. Away
at Notts County on the opening day, they were sunk by a last-minute
penalty; three days later, at home to Northampton, a yards-offside
John Atyeo was played on by a careless backpass, he said 'thank you
very much' and City had got their first two points of the season. They
were down to nineteenth place after they had lost at relegation-bound
Bradford Park Avenue in late September, but ironically, it was a six-
one whipping of the same opposition in February that briefly pushed
them up into the second promotion place. Swindon, coming together
into the exciting home-grown 1960s team that is still remembered with
affection today, were beaten five-three at Ashton Gate (Shadow
Williams two, an Atyeo cracker, David Noake and Tait). City did even
better at the County Ground in mid-March, when an Atyeo hat-trick
helped them to a four-nil win, which was followed instantly by a four-
one at home to Torquay United.

Great stuff – but sad to say, these two cheering results were sandwiched between top dogs Portsmouth at home and away, and a four-nil beating at Ashton Gate and five-nil at Fratton were proof positive that City were destined for another year on the third rung down. Of course, there was a huge crowd for both games, with Ashton Gate buzzing with anticipation, and there were plenty around to groan 'typical City' when it all fell apart.

It turned out to be another prolific season for John – for Bristol City, thankfully, not Portsmouth – with twenty-seven in the League and three in the F.A. Cup. He was particularly impressive in December, with one of the most vibrant goalscoring bursts of his career: nine goals in five games through the month, including braces at home to Bournemouth and at Crystal Palace and four at home to Notts County just before Christmas; one of the big chart hits that early winter was Jimmy Dean's *Big Bad John*, about a mean and silent stranger who sacrificed his life to save his fellow miners; parallels with John Atyeo seemed fairly scant, but it was played endlessly over the tannoy at around that time, and City's own Big John would smile in the dressing room when he heard the crowd singing along to it at half time. Alex Tait at number nine chipped in with a useful thirteen in the League and another five in the Cup that season, but the real revelation, at inside-left, was Shadow Williams – he ghosted around like one – who got twenty-one in League games and another one in the Cup. Aged twenty-three when the season started, he was in his second year as a first-team regular and complemented Atyeo so perfectly as a schemer with an extraordinary flair for goals that the fans looked forward to enjoying his artistry for years to come.

Not surprisingly, large numbers of them were shocked when he went to Rotherham for a meagre £9,500 early in 1965, just months before promotion back to Division Two – and so was John Atyeo, who was relishing hunting in a pack with the cunning Shadow and the forceful Brian Clark. Back to 1961-62 and young Clark was given eight starts, including the last three games of the season, and posted up his intentions when he scored a brace in a three-two win over Coventry at home in late April and then all three in a Gloucestershire Senior Cup beating of Bristol Rovers a few days later. Rovers were on their way down to join City in the Third Division, the Robins had found a new hero to batter defences alongside Big John, and suddenly life was beginning to look rosier. At the other end of the age spectrum, it was the end of the road for Jimmy Rogers, after nearly three hundred games and more than a hundred goals for the Reds. He had had his prolific moments over the years, but this season he contributed just four to City's impressive total of ninety-four goals, a tally bettered by only two other teams in the division.

'We really did only just miss out on promotion that season,' Jantzen Derrick recalls today. 'I joined City in 1958, fifteen years old, and up until that time I had watched the team from the terraces. I was pitched into a troubled dressing room under Peter Doherty, and as a young boy of sixteen this was a particularly daunting experience. Fred Ford got to grips with the problem, instilled a steely discipline and gradually sorted things out. It so nearly paid off in 1962.'

Other high-scoring games in City's favour included four-three at newly-promoted Peterborough and against Halifax Town both at home and away, and five-nil at home to Reading. The goal John Atyeo scored in that game was his last as a player in his twenties, since it was his thirtieth birthday the following day. Three days after that, he was out on the Ashton Gate pitch again for that six-one drubbing of Bradford Park Avenue, and he wasted no time in grabbing his first goal as a 'senior citizen'. Set against these big wins was the small matter of a seven-three reverse at Barnsley – and not on a wet Tuesday night, either – which went some way to making the Oakwell crowd forget that strange seven-four mauling three autumns earlier.

As in the previous season, the Robins twice met non-League opposition in the F.A. Cup, and again they made heavy weather of one round while strolling through the other. Their first opponents were Hereford United, among the aristocracy of the Southern League and a team capable of springing a surprise on more distinguished teams than Bristol City. Alex Tait grabbed the very late second-half goal that gave them a draw at Ashton Gate, and nobody much fancied the return at Edgar Street. Bobby Etheridge, as was his wont when games were in that part of the world, hopped on to the team coach at Gloucester, and refreshed by such a short ride through the countryside, he helped his team to a five-two win with one of his increasingly rare goals from midfield. Two more from Atyeo, another from Tait when he shot home from an impossible angle and a Shadow Williams special sent most of the 11,222 crowd home miserable, and rather surprised to boot. Hereford might have been non-League, but this had been a battling

Familiar face: John on a selection of
trade cards from the 1950s and '60s,
plus, above, a modern retrospective
tribute to him

John relaxing at the seaside with both Ruth and the team. She seems to have captured the holiday mood, but there is something about John that suggests that that smart blue blazer is not far away

City on their travels, with John fourth from the left. Trains were a popular option for long-distance journeys, though missed connections could still make for tiresomely long days

The best Atyeo goal of them all? One factor in favour of John's strike at Villa Park in the F.A. Cup in February 1957 is this famous picture of it, which even in grainy press cuttings captures all its drama. Playing the part of the helpless custodian is Nigel Sims

Before the storm, season 1958-59.
Back row: A. Williams, Atyeo, Cook, Thresher, McCall.
Front row: Hinshelwood, Hopkinson, Tindill, Burden, Etheridge and Watkins

But are they listening? Peter Doherty, right, addresses a somewhat distracted looking set of Bristol City players

Going down, but looking cheerful before defeat by champions Aston Villa at Villa Park in April 1960: Back row: Williams, Collinson, Etheridge, Cook, Casey, Thresher. Front row: Rogers, Burden, Atyeo, Graham and McCann. Another split camp season photograph shows the pay rebels Atyeo, Burden and Thesher in the centre of the front row, with captain Tommy Cavanagh and the rest of the imports pushed out on to the periphery

Summer 1960, and Harry Dolman, third from left, with the new Bristol City manager Fred Ford. To the left of them in the picture are directors Bill Garland and Norman Jones, and to the right, secretary Syd Hawkins and director Arthur Amos

A new team begins to take shape, 1961-62.
Back row: Casey, Briggs, Connor, Cook, Etheridge, Thresher.
Front row: Rogers, Tait, Atyeo, R. Williams, Derrick

By 1964, Big John's brown boots were part of the folklore. Here he polishes them up on a Friday evening with the help of his little daughters Carol and Julie

A bedtime story for the girls, November 1964. It was not until 1970 that the Atyeos, including his mother Effie, moved from Dilton Marsh to a house built and owned by Ruth's family in Warminster

For by no means the first time, John was the supporters' club's player of the season in 1963-64, and the look of respect and admiration on the face of the presenter of the award says much about the esteem in which he was held. The picture also immortalises the legendary fawn mac

Left
Duel in the sun: John battles it out
with Norman Sykes of Bristol
Rovers in the opening game of the
1963-64 season at Ashton Gate

Below
Just what I always wanted... John
had so many mounted footballs
for hat-tricks and goalscoring
milestones in his career that the
floor of his loft was groaning. This
one was presented to him by the
supporters' club chairman Dick
Richards before the game against
Barnsley in March, 1964, when he
proceeded to net two more

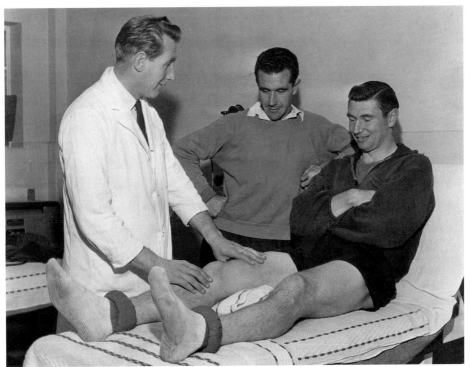

September, 1964: Physio Les Bardsley is the man with the magic fingers, old pal Mike Thresher the giver of moral support

Promotion bound – though they did not know it at Walsall in December, 1964.
Back row: Bush, Ford, Gibson, Briggs, Low.
Front row: Savino, Clark, Atyeo, Sharpe, Peters, Connor

The euphoric scenes after the home defeat of Oldham Athletic on the last day of the season, April 24, 1965, clinched Bristol City promotion from the Third Division by 0.11 of a goal. John's late goal decided the issue after Brian Clark had put City ahead, and the last seven minutes of the match passed in a daze as far as most spectators and players – including, fortunately, Oldham's – were concerned. John's tears were taken to be a sign of his joy and relief at the club's final emergence from the dark days of 1959-60. No amateur psychology was needed a few minutes later, however, when he and the team emerged to acknowledge the roar of the crowd

Above
Maximum embarrassment factor: John walks out to the applause of Ipswich Town and Bristol City players for his final League game, on May 10, 1966.

Right
He feels more at ease by the time he is greeting old team-mates from his first season at Ashton Gate, 1951-52, who were also part of the reception committee. Here he is congratulated by Dennis Roberts, watched by Fred Stone and Jack Bailey

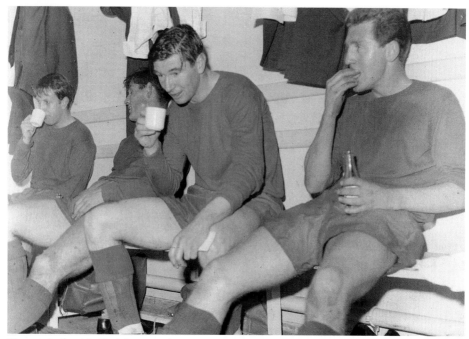

Shattered after his final League game – though his young colleagues do not look a great deal livelier. A pensive John is flanked by Jantzen Derrick, Terry Bush and Brian Clark

The last League line-up, May 1966.
Back row: Connor, Ford, Parr, Gibson, Briggs, Low.
Front row: Derrick, Sharpe,Clark, Atyeo, Bush and Bartley.
The presence of a substitute (in this case, Gerry Sharpe) was a reminder to John of how much the game was changing

An inscribed gold pen and pencil set was the supporters' club's gift to John on his retirement, presented by chairman Dick Richards, next to Ruth Atyeo on the left. Harry Dolman is on the right with Beryl Fudge, the supporters' club's assistant secretary

John with his first son and last child Philip in the snow in the garden in Warminster in the early 1970s

Still a commanding presence, John Atyeo as many will remember him in his later years

From one legend to another: The testimonial brochure tribute to John from the *Daily Express's* Roy Ullyett, arguably the leading sports cartoonist of the 1950s and '60s

Ways we remember John: top, and most prominently, the Atyeo Stand at Ashton Gate, seen shortly after it opened in 1994 with the chairman of the day, Scott Davidson. The Atyeo sculpture at Baltic Wharf, not far from the ground, is the work of the leading Bristol-born sculptor Stephen Cox; and a red-leafed maple planted at Kingdown School, Warminster by two grateful pupils has still to reach its full majesty and maturity

SOCCER HEROES
By Philip Neill

JOHN ATYEO
Bristol City

This print is number 30 in a limited edition of just 30

A Soccer Hero, indeed. This colourful A4 limited edition print by Philip Neill is a reminder that when it comes to looking back on what many see as the golden age of football, John Atyeo is right up there with the best.

The print costs £12.99 signed by the artist, who can be contacted at 33 Bolton Road, Chorley, Lancashire PR7 3AU midweek away win for City, and you did not often hear that said around that time.

In the next round, Dartford fared a little better than Chichester had done some twelve months earlier. They were sunk eight-two, with Big John – maybe still covered in embarrassment over some of his Mickey Mouse goals against the South Coast amateurs – helping himself to only one. Alex Tait was not as fastidious, and got a hat-trick, Jimmy Rogers scored his last in the competition, and Jantzen Derrick grabbed his first – first two, in fact – at his sixth time of trying. He netted again in the third round, against Second Division Walsall, but the Saddlers went through four-one at home after a nil-all draw at Ashton Gate. The League Cup, as it was to prove to be until the last years of the decade, was a complete non-event, a three-nil thumping in front of two men and a dog on a Wednesday evening in York; nobody now can even remember what the weather was like, but as far as the result was concerned, it might as well have been a wet Tuesday night at Bradford. Oh, how John Atyeo blessed the visionaries at Lytham St Annes who had dreamed up the League Cup.

So to 1962-63: in the summer, Fred Ford was taking a keen interest in the Preston North End centre-forward Alfie Biggs, who was desperate to get back to Bristol, and the two had always had a good working relationship during the first of Alfie's two long spells at Eastville. He had been transferred away from Rovers just a year earlier as a replacement at number nine for Tom Finney, and that proposition would not have been as absurd as it might seem to those who do not remember Alfie, if only he had been able to settle in the North. Jim Milne, the Preston manager, always swore he was the best player he ever bought, and his twenty-two goals in forty-nine Second Division games for Preston were proof that however rootless he felt off the pitch up there, he was perfectly at home on it.

A Knowle West boy, he should have gone to City straight from school, anyway, but the story was that when he turned up at Ashton Gate to sign on, he was kept waiting, grew tired of it, and hopped straight on a bus for the other side of town to join Rovers instead. While he was pining for the West Country throughout 1961-62, the Biggs-less Rovers were plunging into the Third Division. Player and club clearly needed one another, and that is what happened in October 1962, when he went back to Eastville for the best part of another six seasons and scored even more goals than he had the first time around.

Perhaps City were always destined to miss out on him, but there was a time when the prospect of landing Biggs looked a possibility, and John Atyeo would have relished it. He knew about Alfie's reputation for boozing and gambling and chasing the girls, but like the Preston manager Milne and most other thinkers in the game, he admired him mightily for the sheer quality of his play: his strength, courage, pace, vision, selflessness, sure touch and fierce shot with both feet. John was also aware that, for all his Jack-the-lad image, Alfie was like him in one respect, a devoted son who lived with his mother and gave her great love and support. There was also the comforting thought that since Biggs was a famously snappy dresser, known to one and all as 'the Baron', there would never have been the remotest chance of he and John mixing up their clothes on their adjacent pegs.

So much for dreams; in the event, John Atyeo found an exciting new strike partner in Brian Clark, but he himself had the most wretched season of his career, with niggling knee and ankle injuries keeping him out of sixteen of the forty-six League games, and leaving him third top scorer for the season. His sixteen strikes in thirty matches were right up to standard, of course: an average of more than a goal every two games was and remains the mark of an outstanding forward, and all the more so when you consider that Atyeo saw his role in the second half of this disrupted season as that of creator. Nevertheless, there was Brian Clark at the top of the tree come April 1963 with twenty-three from forty-two, while the skilful, scheming Shadow – spurred on in the weeks before Christmas by massed ranks of fans roaring out the Susan Maughan hit about wanting to be *Bobby's Girl* – did brilliantly well with nineteen out of thirty-eight. John was back at centre-forward this season, playing between the two of them, and was typically generous when he told the *Bristol Evening Post*'s Peter Godsiff about the experience. 'I enjoy it tremendously,' he said. 'When I started in football, the older players took an interest in me, and helped me all they could. I try to do the same now. These two lads learn very fast, and quickly pick up things. They both have very good footballing brains and you can see your work used to the best advantage. The style of these two players suits me – the short, quick-passing game. Brian and Shadow play this type of football as well as any pair I have seen.'

John was staying more deep, with these two livewires up front and Jantzen Derrick acting as another creative force of nature when he was on song; Jantzen – his mum saw the name on swimwear while shopping in town when she was expecting him during the war, and liked it despite its Germanic ring – was by now the player at Ashton Gate most in tune with Atyeo in terms of a footballing brain and pure skill, when his inconsistencies were not creeping in. Despite playing behind the two strikers, however, Big John still made it clear to Peter Godsiff that he would never be happy with anything but a number eight or nine on his back; there was enough talk about 'deep-lying' inside-forwards in football by this time for him to accept the role as still very much part of forward play, but any suggestion that he should go into midfield as a wing-half was anathema to him.

He agreed that, this season at least, he had adapted his play to a creative role, rather than that of an out-and-out goalscorer: 'This sort of thing comes to practically everyone throughout football. When you get older, you gain experience. Maybe you lose some dash and verve, but you try to make up for that by looking for the ball in midfield and setting up things for others. It all comes back to the players around you. You start to base your game on them. If we had two deep-lying ball players, I would probably have to try and get through on my own a bit more, but that's not the case with Brian and Shadow alongside me.' Asked whether he had ever fancied playing at wing-half, he replied: 'I've never considered any other position [than in the for-wards] seriously. I've never played wing-half, even in practice matches. I have always fancied myself as more of a creative than a destructive player, an attacker rather than a defender.' With the benefit of hindsight, we can see that John's attitude was rooted in the percep-tion then current that midfielders, however creative, still had fifty-fifty attacking and defending duties. A skilful out-and-out playmaker, how-ever 'deep-lying', could only have a number on his back that marked him as a forward.

Jantzen Derrick and Alex Tait also reached double figures as City plundered a hundred goals that season; unhappily, they managed to concede ninety-two, and any promotion potential 1962-63 might have had had petered out by the end of October. John Atyeo declared his intent with eleven goals in the first eleven games, including braces at home to Millwall and at Shrewsbury and Reading; but only four of those games were won, and though three five-two wins – at Bradford Park Avenue and Carlisle and at home to Barnsley – set some City fans dreaming, there were far too many bad results in between for any kind of confidence to build up. It was a happy day on September 15, when

Fred Ford took the team to Bristol Rovers for a League match for the first time since he had left Eastville, and The Handshake, much anticipated by the local press, took place between him and Bert Tann with no accompanying fisticuffs. Better still, City won two-one through goals by Clark and Etheridge (penalty), and at the end of the afternoon they were third in the table.

That did not last for long. Too many draws were hindering progress, including successive home games with Coventry and the emerging Swindon Town. Away defeats at Peterborough and Coventry followed, but though a home demolition of Barnsley gladdened hearts a little, there would not have been much joy around Ashton Gate that season if the fans had known what was to come. John Atyeo's goal in the five against the Yorkshiremen was his fifteenth of the season – the fifteenth in seventeen games – but from then on, injuries would restrict him to just thirteen more matches. In the next game, the first-round F.A. Cup tie with Wellington Town, he twisted his ankle so severely that he was out for the next half-dozen games.

It was at Ashton Gate on November 10, the first game of his absence that season, that nemesis came in the form of Queen's Park Rangers. At the end of the season they finished only one place higher than City's fourteenth, but they were often a bogey team and they certainly were this afternoon. They scored first, but City equalised before half time through Terry Bush, in for Atyeo and still then only a very spasmodic first-teamer, and were battling well enough before goal-keeper Tony Cook broke his arm for a second time in an accident that all but ended his long career. Bobby Etheridge went in goal, but two late goals took the game beyond brave City's reach. Twelve matches between Boxing Day and early April brought Atyeo not a single goal, and though of course he was playing a deliberately deeper role, it was a great relief to him, when he came back for the last game of the season against Reading after missing the previous nine, that he scored in a four-two home win.

There were times, repeated times, during that barren spell, when his future as a footballer was being seriously questioned. City's board had been alarmed when just 6,656 spectators had turned up to see them beat Shrewsbury on the notorious shopping Saturday just before Christmas, and despite John's return for the visit of Brighton on Boxing Day, there was still precious little bonhomie in a crowd that barely crept above 9,000; the visitors made sure there was none at all come twenty to five, when they headed east with both points.

There is no doubt at all that John Atyeo was still struggling desperately with his injuries during those dozen mid-season games, and should never have played in any of them. What prolonged his agony was the fact that the action dragged on into the second half of May, because of the Big Freeze that allowed City just two League games in the whole of January and February and no away fixture between December 15 and March 2. Ten games in March and April, when all the teams in the League were playing catch-up with their fixture lists, typified City's crazy form that season. They won six of them, lost three and drew one, with a goal aggregate of for, thirty-one, against, twenty-two – and oddly, their goalscoring was all the more prolific towards the end of that run, when John Atyeo was on the sidelines once more. It is hard to imagine the Robins scoring six, four and five in successive games without Big John, but that is what happened.

The four came in a home win over a Bristol Rovers still rocking from the bribes scandal that brought the life suspension of two of their brightest stars, goalkeeper Esmond Million from Middlesbrough and inside-forward Keith Williams, who had been unfortunate enough to have been in contact with the betting syndicate's ringleader Jimmy Gould during his time at Plymouth. The Sheffield Wednesday trio of Tony Kay, Peter Swan and David 'Bronco' Layne were the most high-profile casualties, gaoled and suspended for so long that their careers were virtually ended there and then, but in Bristol, all the shock waves were around Million and Williams. It was a salutary reminder to others beyond the confines of Eastville that playing around with the rules of the game could lead to dire consequences.

In the F.A. Cup, City were lucky in drawing non-League opposition in the first and second rounds for the third time in three seasons, and this time both of them were at home. Wellington Town put up a spirited show and were one-all at half time before going down four-two (Atyeo two, Derrick, Etheridge penalty). What ruined the game completely was Big John's ankle injury, and when Tony Cook suffered that even more serious injury in the very next game, morale was at its lowest at any time in Fred Ford's reign. Everyone knew there would be at least as fierce a battle in the second round of the Cup, when the crack amateurs Wimbledon were the guests. There was indeed, but without the injured Atyeo, City scraped through two-one. That gave them a third round tie at home to Aston Villa, against whom they led one-nil at half time (Clark) before being held to a replay. This they lost three-two in front of 23,718 at Villa Park, little more than a thousand more than had seen the first game at Ashton Gate – and all but forty thousand fewer than had been on that great old ground to see John Atyeo's wonder goal there in 1957. John played in both games against Villa, but it was in the depths of his injury struggle and there were no fireworks from him this time; he missed one, when the ball bounced off his shinpad, that had the prophets of doom questioning his future in the game like never before. In fact we know what happened to those predictions, and the most interesting fact about that third-round tie today is the length of time between the first game, on January 16, and the replay, on March 7; seven weeks to get a Cup tie finished tells us all we need to know about that desperate winter of '63. John also appeared in City's sole League Cup game, lost at home to Rotherham.

While there were those who were prepared to give John due creative honours during his goal-less spell, the man himself was as aware as he ever had been that, for him, being an inside-forward still meant rattling the back of the net as hard and as often as possible. It was to the relief of all that he at last got that one in his one-off comeback game on the last day of the season in mid-May. City fans had long since seen enough of football for the summer and only a handful over 7,000 bothered to watch the Reading game, but those who did cheered Atyeo's goal to the echo. His career had never seen anything like those dozen goal-less games, and at least he had something to take into the close season – the chance of a full return to fitness, and his name on the scoresheet, where he knew it belonged, for the first time in the League since late October.

He discussed the goal famine at some depth with the *Evening Post*'s Peter Godsiff, and while he was happy to take some credit for the bright form of Brian Clark and Bobby Williams, he knew the fans expected far more from him than a fatherly supporting role. 'I do worry about not scoring goals, especially when nobody else does. I just can't seem to get the ball in the net lately,' he mused on March 30. 'I've had bad patches like this before, you know, and have always got over them. I suppose I've been written off by some people each year for the past four or five seasons. It's true I haven't put in so many powerful shots over the past few weeks. Perhaps I'm not timing the ball so well – that's the main reason [for powerful striking] in any sport. If you hit the ball just right, it flies off fast and true.' He assured fans that he would be back among the goals again soon: 'I certainly hope so. This is something I believe is bound to come again, in time. Sometimes it takes longer, but the main thing is to keep going. If you continue fighting against it, things are bound to turn out right. It's a bit depressing when I look back on a match we lost or drew and think to myself: "If I'd taken this or that chance, we would have won." My ankle is not as good as it was at the beginning of the season, but it's getting better all the time. I had two setbacks – the original injury against Wellington and then when I slipped on ice on the tarmac at the ground. It's not 100 per cent, yet, but I'm hoping it will be before long.'

Godsiff was writing after a four-one win at Watford in which Clark had got a hat-trick and Williams the other, and he insisted that this game alone had proved Atyeo's worth. 'Anyone who saw his tireless exhibition of masterly midfield play on Tuesday night would have immediately put away his vitriolic pen,' he opined. 'I do not think Atyeo is finished, neither do his team-mates, manager Fred Ford or the player himself. I believe he will still be a first team player at Ashton Gate in another four years' time. He has missed more and easier chances than any other forward, but at no time has he ever deserved to be dropped, as many fans believe. He is as important now, as the mid-field link with Brian Clark and Bobby Williams, as he was when he averaged twenty-eight goal a season himself...' That said, Peter Godsiff agreed that John was having a bad spell in front of goal: 'It must be many years since he has gone so long without scoring... It seems most likely that Atyeo's reign as leading scorer has gone, but he still has a future at Ashton Gate. His job as the architect behind a close-passing, intricate footballing side is now as vital as anything he has done for the club in bygone days. Atyeo has declined as a footballer. He has lost his zip and speed, but he has gained in maturity and experience. Even today, at his age (thirty-one), his value in the transfer market would exceed five figures. Let us not forget that Atyeo, in his prime, was an England class player. It would be fatuous to pretend that he is still in that category, but he is still a force in the Third Division. Make no mistake, if Atyeo were available for transfer, a queue of clubs would be on the City's doorstep.'

Nevertheless, it must have been a jolt for John to see such *Evening Post* headlines as 'Atyeo *not* finished' and 'Written off as a has-been?

Nonsense!' It was the first time in his career that he had needed a sympathetic press to convince his public of his worth. Journalism produced at a breathless pace, as was Peter Godsiff's, does well to stand up to scrutiny, decades later, as strongly as these words do. He was right about so many aspects of John Atyeo's play, he was nearly right about his still being with City four years on – but where he was wrong, and supremely happy to be proved wrong, was in writing off his goalscoring genius. In the three seasons left to him, two in the Third Division and one in the Second, John would smash in another threescore goals or more, head the club's scoring charts in two of those three campaigns and miss out on doing so in the other by a whisker. Yes, it is all very well making chances for other people; but it is goals Bristol City fans worship John Atyeo for, and in the years between 1963 and 1966 they came by the dozen – goals he never forgot, and his admirers never will.

CHAPTER 14

FALLING INTO PLACE

The good times began to roll again in 1963-64. Fred Ford had been at the club long enough for it to be running his way, and it was a fit, athletic and skilful young team that was emerging under his tutelage. They finished fifth that season, only five points behind champions Coventry City and runners-up Crystal Palace, and though that was their highest position all season, talk about mounting a serious promotion push next time never rang more true than it did in April 1964. A true joy was the return to fitness and form of John Atyeo, who played in every first team game in League, F.A. Cup and (inevitably fleetingly) League Cup, and ended the season as top scorer with twenty-one plus another six in the cup competitions.

It would seem, on the surface, that you could not be much more of a full-time footballer than that – yet this was the season when he reverted to being a part-timer, announcing to a genuinely shocked Fred Ford in the summer that he planned to study teaching, and would be enrolling at the training college in Redland, Bristol that autumn. Those who feel they know something of what made Atyeo tick are convinced that this renewed sense of purpose off the pitch contributed to his resurgence of form on it, after the miseries of the previous season. As the years ticked by, his part-time status certainly did nothing to lessen his influence on life at Ashton Gate. One day out training in Ashton Park, Bobby Williams was aware of the big man growing increasingly fed up with running routines: 'Let's have the ball, Fred, let's have the ball.' Fred Ford said nothing, but a couple of minutes later his whistle blew: 'Right, lads, a bit of ball work...'

Flanked again by Brian Clark and Shadow Williams, but now hunting as a pair with Brian and happy to see Shadow snapping up all the knock-downs and rebounds that came his way, John helped them amass nineteen and twenty goals respectively, felt rejuvenated by their presence and took a quiet pride in showing them that whatever they could do, the 'old feller' was not quite ready for the bathchair, either. Brian was the son of Don Clark, a big-scoring City centre-forward immediately after the Second World War and the club's very supportive assistant manager in John's younger days, and the big man had followed the boy's progress since he had arrived at Ashton Gate from technical school. In fact he knew him years before that, when Brian used to stand around the players' entrance after home games. 'Your dad will be out in a minute,' he would tell him, as Don was putting the finishing touches to his afternoon's work in the office. It made the big man all the more happy to be playing a part in the young man's blossoming career. 'I helped him learn the trade of a professional footballer, saw him mature and had the pleasure of playing beside him and travelling with him for three years,' Atyeo said later. 'He was a good listener, and always ready and willing to learn; he was also modest, and one of the most dedicated players I have known.' With happy memories of Clark Senior, he concluded that: 'I know where Brian gets his natural and friendly character from.' In fact Brian loved to be with John – to soak up football lore, as much as technical advice: 'It was great sitting with him on the coach, listening to his stories about his England years, and memories of the likes of Johnny Haynes and Jimmy Greaves.' Those two players were among those of his generation whose play he admired the most, one for his passing skills and the other for his goal sense, though he remained indifferent to Haynes as a person to the end.

Atyeo's relationship with Bobby Williams was equally fatherly. 'When I first arrived at Ashton Gate in 1958, John asked me what my ambitions were,' Shadow recalls today. 'I said they were to play in the first team, to play alongside him and to play for England. When I moved to Rotherham early in 1965 I turned to him and said "Well, John, at least I achieved two of the three".' To some supporters, Bristolian Williams's departure at the age of twenty-five for £9,200, just months before the dream of promotion was achieved, was an outrageous piece of business. By then, however, he had been ousted from the team by Gerry Sharpe, dismissed as too delicate a player, according to some, for the rough-and-tumble of the Third Division. When Shadow first heard of the possible move, he was reluctant to go north and refused to do so four times before asking John Atyeo for advice. John, knowing that the transfer would not be without its financial reward for his young colleague, said well, he might as well look into

it. Bobby Williams looked and said yes, but – not for the first time –
he was a West Countryman who did not flourish in South Yorkshire.
Neither, in truth, did Bristol Rovers' style suit him when he returned
south not long afterwards, and it was at Reading where he ended his
career and stayed on as a coach.

John loved to hear the crowd on his side again, singing his praises.
There was a rhythm and cadence to the name Atyeo that lent itself to
mass chanting. He had not heard that eternal, doom-laden Ashton Gate
brickbat 'Come on, yer pie-can' directed at him very often over the
years, but it had happened just occasionally in recent times, and he did
not like it; better by far to be serenaded with such early-1960s classics
as these, recalled by Peter Lomas of Filton:

(To *Daisy, Daisy*)
City, City, bound for Division Two,
We go crazy over supporting you,
We may not have Stefano,
But we got Johnny Atyeo,
So ring your bell and rattle like hell,
On the terraces made for you.

(To *Onward Christian Soldiers*)
Onward Bristol City to Division Two,
With Big Johnny Atyeo scoring one or two,
Jantzen sends 'em over,
Johnny heads 'em in,
And they all run back to the centre spot,
Doing the Ashton fling.
Onward Bristol City to Division Two,
With Big Johnny Atyeo scoring one or two.

(To *Robin Hood*)
Atyeo, Atyeo, riding through the glen,
Atyeo, Atyeo, with his band of men,
He's got the ball,
He's scored a goal,
Atyeo, Atyeo, Atyeo.

Oh, well, perhaps you had to be there at the time...

None of the young players could resist smiling, behind John's back,
at least, about his legendary brown boots. Low-slung continental

football boots had begun to creep into the English game in the mid-1950s, and the German Adidas brand, with its three white stripes, used the 1958 World Cup as a platform to spread its image far and wide; Puma, with the kind of streamline stripe more often seen on the side of motor coaches, or painted on optimistic young men's Austin A30s to make them go faster, were not far behind. For John, however, the only possible boots were big, brown, with a toecap like concrete and great protective flaps well above the ankle, and he would polish them diligently before every game. He certainly struck Terry Bush, who was coming into the team at this point, as a battle-hardened pro from the old school: 'Those brown boots were so much a part of him. They were part of the shape of him. It just wouldn't have been him without them.' Terry also remembers shuddering at the sight of Big John scrubbing grass and earth out of grazes on his knees with a nail brush when the grounds were hard. Opposing defenders, sophisticates from the football academies of Carlisle and Rotherham and the like, in their Adidas and Pumas, would snigger over John's ancient footwear, but it only served to make him try that little bit harder to have them laughing on the other side of their faces. 'That's what bloody brown boots can do to you,' he would growl as another shot whistled into the net. After his friendly rival Alan Ross in the Carlisle goal had been having a go at them all one afternoon, John simply grinned and gave him a little wink as the ball whizzed into the rigging.

Back to the autumn of 1963, and looking around the dressing room, John recognised only Mike Thresher from the promotion squad of 1954-55; after the first handful of games it was the end of the long trail for Tony Cook in goal, aged thirty-four come the October and ring-rusty after his long lay-off through injury. There was talk that he might go across the city to Eastville in the wake of the Esmond Million fiasco, but Rovers were prepared to give their reserve 'keeper Bernard Hall his chance, and he served them well and bravely for several seasons. Cook hung up his boots a one-club man, with 320 games behind him, and his going left Atyeo the longest-serving man on the books.

Fred Ford, always buzzing around the country in his Morris Minor in search of talent, moved to replace or at least find cover for Cook in April 1963, when he signed Mike Gibson from Shrewsbury Town for £5,000. John Atyeo, while sad to see his old mate Cookie go, was happy with the move, since Gibson had been outstanding when he had played against him in the past. 'You've got a good 'un there, Fred,' he told Ford, though at first quite a few people at Ashton Gate had their doubts about that. Fred Ford took one look at his new goalkeeper and pronounced him about two stone overweight, and it was not until the third game from the end of that long season, at home to Crystal Palace, that he made his debut in a one-all draw. On the following Saturday at Port Vale, still not in tune with his fellow defenders, he let in two soft goals, and endured with the rest of the lads a Fred Ford half-time tirade in all its table-kicking intensity. 'I'll buy the lot of you a suit of armour.' the boss fumed. 'You're the biggest bunch of cowards I've ever come across.' John Atyeo was still injured, but watched from the stands and winced. 'When I saw Gib in that game I wondered if Fred had made a bad decision after all,' he said years later. 'I've never been so wrong.' Cook was back for the last game of the season, but made just three appearances at the beginning of 1963-64 before a four-one away defeat at Port Vale saw him make way for Mike Gibson for the last time.

Of course we know now that 'Gibbo' was between the sticks for City right through until the early 1970s, when Ray Cashley took his place at the beginning of a fresh wave of glory-hunting at Ashton Gate, but back in 1963-64 the new goalkeeper was simply another piece in the promotion jigsaw of the following season. John Atyeo liked the way the team was shaping up, though like many older men in any group of colleagues, he could not help looking back fondly on some of the names from the past. 'Tony Cook was the greatest character to play for the club in my time,' he mused in 1970. 'I thought Cookie went too early. Another player who went too soon, in my opinion, was Jimmy Rogers. What a pair those two were. Twink Cook had the natural ability to make you laugh. Those two thought life was a big joke – especially Cookie, who considered a pint, a fag and a game of football all part of living. Fred wouldn't allow smoking on the coach or before a match – not that there were many smokers in the side. We played at Coventry City one day and Twink went into the toilet to have his usual smoke before the game. He shouted out through the door: "Give me a programme. Is Fred about?" "No," grunted Fred; but Cookie recognised his voice, and we were all in stitches. Cookie was the sort of bloke who would have a cup of early morning tea in his bedroom and then doze off while he was drinking it, spilling it all over the bed.' Cook's version of the tale was that the programme was passed into the cubicle to him by the unmistakable hand of Ford, who had lost two fingers during the war.

There were other bright new faces apart from Gibson. The summer of 1963 brought outside-left Peter Hooper, who had terrorised City for years in the blue and white of Bristol Rovers. He had moved to Cardiff only the previous summer, but despite having had a tremendous season with them – his twenty-two goals from out wide were more than a quarter of the team's total – he had major problems with his manager George Swindin and asked three times for a transfer. Fred knew him from Eastville, he knew Fred, and he served City tremendously for that one season, contributing thirteen goals and, as we have noted, impressing John Atyeo with the power of his shooting. With Hooper and the three inside-forwards firing on all cylinders, and Jantzen Derrick continuing as a tremendous creator at his brightest and best, City had a forward line that looked as lethal as any that season. Unfortunately for Peter Hooper, the years were catching up on him, and his influence on the following year's promotion push was minimal.

Since the demise of Tommy Casey, the position of left-half had been a problem for City, and it was in the October of 1963 that lofty Gordon Low at last made the position his own. He had moved down to Huddersfield as a kid from Aberdeen a few months after his school mate Denis Law in 1957, but Denis was already plying his trade in Turin, unhappily but lucratively, by the time Gordon moved to Ashton Gate early in 1961. He had taken time to settle in Bristol, and any early hopes of playing alongside his old team-mate Jack Connor on a regular basis were soon dashed; but now was his chance, and he grasped it with both hands. After a good win, he would be in the supporters' club talking them through it, with what came to be known as a famously selective memory that specialised in singling out all the heroics of G. Low. For all this, the fans in general never took to him greatly; they thought he was slow and unspectacular, not very skilful and no great rouser of the troops.

Here, though, was one of those 'players' players', and when Atyeo retired he was a popular dressing-room choice as City's new captain. Even before then, it would be at Gordon's house at Bedminster Down that some of the lads would gather after training, playing with his little children while his wife Brenda cooked them bacon with eggs newly bought from the boot of Big John's latest Hillman Minx. Since graduating to Minxes he had taken to replacing them frequently, but never would he run to one with a heater in it. 'It would have cost him a couple of pounds extra, but he wouldn't have it,' Jantzen Derrick recalls. 'Instead, he would roll up from Wiltshire in the middle of winter wrapped up in his overcoat, scarf, gloves...'

Most players would go into the supporters' club to enjoy the back-slaps only if they had won, while John Atyeo would make straight for his car after a game, whatever the result, knowing that he would spend the next half-hour signing autographs and talking to well-wishers, any-way. A blind man would stand close to the players' entrance, and when he heard the hubbub that accompanied the big man's appearance he would call out: 'Is that John? Is that John?' Atyeo would always walk over to him, shake his hand and talk to him about the game, before he turned his attention to the autograph hunters. 'Can you sign "Best wishes"?' was the eternal request of the kids with their *Football Monthly* pictures and scrapbooks, and he invariably would, asking 'What's your name?' when he had time to add a personal touch. 'To Alan, Best wishes, John Atyeo', every letter legible and a signature as clear and simple as a bank clerk's: hundreds of men all over the country, many of them reaching retirement age, can still rummage around among their souvenirs and come up with something of the sort. 'Got this when Bristol City played here,' they will tell anyone interested enough to listen. 'He got bags of goals, played for England a few times. Huge guy. Great big fawn mac, he was wearing...'

In at right-half early in the 1963-64 season, succeeding Bobby Etheridge, was Gordon Parr – swarthy, super-fit and a kid who was leaving John Atyeo and the rest of the old hands behind on training runs long before he made the first team. When he did, there were times when all he seemed to do was keep on chasing – all over the pitch, and to no good purpose; but he calmed down to become a very valuable member of the team, a tackler and destroyer *par excellence*, and though in the following year's promotion push he found himself sharing the number four shirt with Chuck Drury, he and Connor eventually formed a formidable centre-back partnership.

Season 1963-64 got under way with a three-nil hammering of neighbours Rovers at Ashton Gate, with Atyeo making it the third successive season he scored City's opening goal. By December Rovers had begun to put their lives and their season together and won the return four-nil at Eastville, after going three up in the first ten minutes;

both games attracted around 20,000, but that was deceptive. A big problem for City this season – the biggest it had been for years – was the apathy of the Bristol public. For all their battling it out in the top half of the table, the crowds stayed around 7,000 or 8,000 – the odd decent gate pushed the season's average up to just under 10,000 – and Harry Dolman and the board knew like never before that five-figure attendances were a thing of the past unless something really spectacular was going on on the pitch. City started to put it together in late October and early November, and by Christmas they had moved into the top six. There was a farce at home on Boxing Day, when fog descended at half time, the referee and the linesmen stood on the centre spot, looked up and down the pitch and walked off to go home. As City were three up at the time, and everyone wearing red in the ground swore they could see the length of the pitch with one eye closed, nobody slunk away feeling particularly Christmassy that afternoon; at least City won the away fixture two-nil at Loftus Road two days later, and when the rearranged home game was played in March, justice was done when the points duly went their way.

There was a highlight for John Atyeo at home to Walsall in February, when he not only scored a hat-trick in a five-one win, but with it his three hundredth goal for the club in all major competitions. He had neither the room nor the inclination to keep all the commemorative footballs presented to him over the years, but he kept that one. The following week, visitors Wrexham were beaten four-nil (Clark two, Atyeo, Hooper), but although other bright results followed, there was never the consistency for a serious promotion bid; a four-all draw at Hull, after being three-one down, was a fighting effort, but at the end of the day it was only a point. The biggest attendance apart from Bristol Rovers' visit was the 13,914 attracted by Mansfield Town on Good Friday. Mansfield had been as afflicted as Rovers had been by the game-rigging scandal, but their recently departed manager Raich Carter had put together a good side, sparked by Ken Wagstaff's goals, and they were having a decent season. Then again, City had won their last five home games, most of them handsomely, and their fans saw no reason why it should not be six come 4.40 p.m. Some hope; Mansfield tore the Reds apart and raced into a three-nil lead at half time. City pulled it back to three-two, but Mansfield's Welsh goalkeeper Colin Treharne held firm. In the club's five years in the Third Division in the early 1960s, few results at Ashton Gate are more painful than

Portsmouth's four-nil win in 1962 and Mansfield pulling the rug from under the Robins' feet that Good Friday. The next day they were at home to Colchester United, and beat them three-one, goals by courtesy of Atyeo, Clark and Williams, but this time, only 7,779 bothered to turn up, and when Mansfield won the return four-nil on Easter Monday, that, very much, was that.

Just one last excitement in this season of frustrated hopes: City's final away game was at Millwall, who stood a chance of escaping relegation if they won that Monday evening. City had nothing to play for, as they had proved a couple of days earlier in a wan one-all draw at Wrexham, and the Lions were fired up with the prospect of securing the two points that would have seen them survive. Also on the relegation fringes were Luton Town, where the former Ashton Gate coach Bill Harvey was nearing the end of his second season as manager. Somewhat unconventionally, into the dressing room shortly before kick-off came Bill, who impressed on the City players just how useful it would be to him if they did their stuff that night. They had liked Harvey, a kind and caring man, and it seems that what went on between them and their old coach was better than any pep-talk Fred Ford could have given them. 'Come on, lads, we'll do our best for Bill's sake,' said John Atyeo, and that is what they did, in front of 12,000 hostile witnesses who were willing them to fail. A second-half blaster of a penalty by Peter Hooper, leaving Alex Stepney helpless, sent the crowd into waves of fury, and both sets of players were glad of the refuge of the dressing rooms on the final whistle. 'We'll stay in here for half an hour,' John told his team-mates. 'Just sit tight.' In the showers they could hear bricks, stones and bottles rattling around Cold Blow Lane, but to their relief, the hostility was all directed towards the home team. The coach was parked a good distance away, and it was not until ten o'clock, with the disgruntled hordes dispersing, that it was felt safe to bring it around to the players' entrance. Then it was fish and chips on the Old Kent Road, out with the cards and back at Ashton Gate by half past one in the morning, mission accomplished.

In the F.A. Cup, City progressed to the fourth round before being whipped six-one at Sunderland the day after the night of big Atyeo eating already discussed. In the first round at Corby Town, on the worst pitch John said he had ever played on, they battled to a three-one win, and in round two, away, he scored twice to despatch Exeter City. There was a two-all away draw in the next round, at Doncaster (Atyeo,

Clark), but City got through in the replay two-nil, with another goal from Big John and a Peter Hooper penalty. By the time of the second game, the draw had already been made for the next round, and a big crowd went home from Ashton Gate with dreams of a spot of giant-killing at Roker Park. So much for dreams.

The attendances at City's four F.A. Cup ties that season are a reminder of just how strong a grip the competition still had on the public imagination. There were 4,000-plus at Corby, 15,000 at Exeter, 18,000 and 20,000 for Doncaster, 46,000 at Sunderland. Nobody saw this as a contest for second-class citizens in those days. On the other hand, everyone saw the League Cup as a no-hopers' competition, but nobody more so than Bristol City, who accordingly performed like no-hopers in it year after year. This time it was Gillingham's task to perform the formality of putting them out of their misery, four-two at Priestfield, with Atyeo scoring his fourth, fifth and last goals in the competition.

Third Division champions in 1963-64 were Coventry, followed by Crystal Palace, and those two success stories had a special resonance with Harry Dolman, who was great chums with both chairmen, Derrick Robins and Arthur Wait. Each would propel a club still most closely associated with the Third Division South into the First Division before the end of the decade, and Coventry, in particular, were famous for their glitz and razzmatazz, their fans' trains complete with disco and photo opportunities, all orchestrated by their love-him-or-hate-him young manager Jimmy Hill; most people not bedecked in sky blue plumped for the easier hating option. When Bristol Rovers went to Highfield Road in 1963-64 and turned the form book upside-down with a one-nil win, there was Jimmy Hill on the pitch, at the end of the game, bathed in the BBC spotlight. 'Come on, how about me?' Bert Tann bleated plaintively. 'I'm the manager of the winning side.' He should have known that when there was J.H. to be talked to, he did not stand a chance.

Harry Dolman and his new wife Marina would holiday with the Robinses, and when their two teams met there was always a jokey rivalry between them. The two men talked about anything and everything to do with football, and would chuckle about all the new tricks Jimmy Hill was coming up with to keep the club (and Jimmy Hill) in the headlines. Robins would also tell Dolman about the rest of the backroom team there, including this sharp London boy Alan Dicks, who had not had the most distinguished playing career but was fast emerging as the bearded wonder's right-hand man.

Out on the field, life was a good deal more earnest, but John Atyeo and Coventry's craggy, crew-cut captain and centre-half George Curtis had learned to admire and respect one another. Curtis ranked Atyeo among the best he had opposed – a list that took in John Charles and other formidable strikers of the time, such as David Herd and Fred Pickering – and praised his strength both in the air and on the ground and a surprising burst of speed for a big man: 'You could think you'd curbed him for ninety per cent of the game, and then he would pop up with a goal from the slightest half-chance.' One day at Coventry, John played a joke on a still rookie Brian Clark. 'I was at inside-right and he was at centre-forward, and as we came out of the tunnel he said to me "Look, we'll do a tactical switch this afternoon. You play centre-forward, and I'll play inside-right." I knew he must have good reason for this, so of course I said O.K. Then, when we were lining up, I looked down the pitch and saw this great six-foot-eight Goliath with his knicks up round his thighs glaring back at me. Beside me, John was shaking with laughter. Of course, we switched back to as we were.' Atyeo never forgot his duels with Iron Man Curtis: 'I still have a few scars, and many vivid memories,' he recalled. 'He never committed a nasty foul – though he always tried to let you know he was around.' Happily, come season 1964-65, it was at last Bristol City who were letting people know they were around.

CHAPTER 15

THE MEN MOST LIKELY

The squad was picking itself as the big kick-off neared in August 1964: Mike Gibson, Tony Ford, Alec Briggs, Gordon Parr, Jack Connor, Gordon Low, Terry Bush, Jantzen Derrick, Ray Savino, Brian Clark, John Atyeo, Bobby Williams, Gerry Sharpe, Lou Peters and the newly arrived Chuck Drury were beginning to look like the men most likely to succeed. Mike Thresher's time was all but over, giving his career a strange symmetry: into the team towards the end of the championship season of 1954-55, out of it at the start of the promotion year of 1964-65, leaving John Atyeo the only one to have battled it out over the whole of both those campaigns. Peter Hooper, too, played nothing like the role he was expected to, dogged by injury and not as young as he used to be. Ray Savino, a right-wing flier, had been at the club for two years, after signing from his native Norwich, and this would be the one season in which he played with any kind of regularity. Up-and-down in form – 'You should be selling ice cream on Weston pier' Fred Ford would growl at him in his lesser moments, ignoring the fact that his previous work had been in the rather less Italian-stereotypical surroundings of a sheet metal factory – he broke his leg at Carlisle four games before the end of the season, and never again got a decent run in the team.

Ray shared his club house in Shirehampton with his wife Carol, their little daughter and various prize rabbits, which travelled far and wide to win cups for him regularly. Some of the lads used to say that if the team was on platform one of Temple Meads station waiting for a train, as likely as not some of Ray's rabbits would be on platform two, bound for far more important contests of their own; it was just as well that they were on different trains, since their pedigree would hardly allow them to share their compartment with mere Third Division footballers.

Chuck Drury, who signed on the eve of the new season, arrived after more than 150 first-team games with First Division West Bromwich

Albion. Harry Dolman sent one of his directors, Lionel Smart, to do the business at the Hawthorns, and though his background was in cattle dealing, he proved to be no slouch at haggling over footballers, either, when he managed to halve Albion's initial asking price to £8,000. Contributing at least partly to this was the fact that Drury was injured when he arrived; it meant that after a single try-out very early on, Drury did not kick a ball in the League until February, by which time the more superstitious were feeling that the ghost of Malcolm Graham was stalking the corridors once more; not so, and although his career at City was not long, the midfield authority he gave them in the last third of that season did much to steady the ship in the final push towards promotion. He gave tremendous support and encouragement to his colleagues on the pitch, leaving them with more time to ponder on such weighty question as to why, since they presumed he had inevitably picked up 'a bob or two' in his move from West Brom, he still found the need to line his shoes with cornflakes packets.

This season marked the end of the prolific Clark, Atyeo, Williams inside-forward partnership – but two out of three was not bad, and Brian and John proceeded to plunder forty-seven League goals between them, sharing them almost equally down the middle but with the younger man getting the extra one. Clark also scored in the F.A. Cup, compounding his position as top scorer, while Terry Bush weighed in with sixteen. Clark was bang on target from day one, bagging a brace against newly promoted Scunthorpe United at the Old Showground. Unhappily, the home team got five, and though optimists with absurdly long memories reasoned that City had let in five on the first day of 1905-06 and still got promoted, not many of the Ashton Gate faithful were getting too carried away with the logic of this; they were much more bucked up on the following Tuesday and Saturday, when successive five-one results for the right team, against Barnsley and Walsall at home, put them in a far happier frame of mind, and after seven games they were at the top of the table. They put four past Southend without reply home and away and beat Workington five-nil in Bristol. At this stage, after those seven matches, they had scored twenty-seven. Clark was responsible for eleven of them; Atyeo failed to net in five of the seven games, but made amends by grabbing hat-tricks in the other two, at home to Walsall and Southend. Since six of Clark's eleven had also come from hat-tricks, the fans were wondering how many more they would see that season. The answer was none, but

Big John went one better by scoring four late, late on in the season, when a five-one win at Shrewsbury on Easter Monday allowed them to revive their impossible dream of promotion. By a quarter to five the following Saturday, the glorious truth had dawned.

In between these two key phases of the season, all was not plain sailing. For long enough a position between fourth and eighth was as much as they could muster, and when Mike Gibson went down with 'flu in late October at Boundary Park, Oldham, a ground nicknamed Ice Station Zebra with good reason, they were hammered seven-three and dropped out of the top ten for the first and only time. In the first part of the season it was never Fortress Ashton – Gillingham, Carlisle and Hull all made off with both points before the end of January – but seven victories and two draws in their last nine home games were a sound enough platform for success. Bristol Rovers were doing equally well for most of the season, and the fact that one of City's wins was over them, a tight two-one in front of 23,053, was cause for extra satisfaction. When the Reds had gone third just before Christmas, it was Rovers who had been lording it over them at the top. Better still, the two points from Rovers came at the end of a run of six defeats and two draws that had even Harry Dolman wondering in public whether the chance of promotion had again slipped away, and which had seen John Atyeo dropped – for the first time as an established first-teamer – for the two-nil beating by Gillingham the previous week.

There was even a rumour that Dolman was about to fire Fred Ford. A board meeting was called for the Thursday before the Rovers game, but this time no action was taken, perhaps because it was felt that luck had not been on his side. A two-one home defeat by Hull City during this poor run was particularly galling. In front of their biggest crowd of the season to date, 14,131, City played the best they had done for weeks, and took the lead just after half time through a Lou Peters goal. Hull counter-attacked, and when the referee awarded them a free kick on the edge of the penalty area, Gibson was still deploying his troops when Ken Wagstaff, that eternal thorn in their side, stepped up and chipped the ball out of his reach into the rigging. As Jack Charlton memorably moaned when Gary Sprake threw the ball into his own net: 'You can't give a goal for *that*, Ref.'; but that ref. could, and so could this one, and when Hull then broke away and scored the winner, there had not been as much uproar at Ashton Gate for years.

On the whole, however, it was City who got the lucky breaks, and John Atyeo always remembered a goal scored by Terry Bush at Grimsby, after everything had previously gone wrong that night: 'The coach lost its way, we were late getting to our hotel and the rooms were freezing cold. The ground was virtually empty, it was an icy night and for twenty-five minutes we were given a real hammering. Then Terry chased a loose ball down the right, hooked it into the middle from the dead ball line and it hit the inside of the far post and spun a foot over the goal line. It was the most incredible goal I've ever seen, and it was greeted by utter silence.' Presumably you could have heard the hush down on the fish market.

The F.A. Cup brought some relief from the promotion drive, with wins over Brighton at home and Bournemouth away before Sheffield United of the First Division were drawn at home in the third round. One down at half time, City equalised through a Tony Ford penalty, but were overwhelmed three-nil at Bramall Lane two nights later. The most notable feature of the match was going on behind the scenes. With Gerry Sharpe injured, Shadow Williams was given a rare chance at number ten, and among those impressed by him in the big South Yorkshire crowd that evening were directors of Rotherham United. In the boardroom afterwards, they sounded out two City directors about his availability, and they quickly brought Fred Ford in on the conversation. 'Talk to Harry Dolman,' he said, and at the first opportunity they did; the end result was that the Cup tie in Sheffield brought them in the best part of £10,000 more than they thought it would – though, as we have reflected, it lost them a player many thought they should have kept. In the League Cup, those nice men at Lytham St. Annes thoughtfully handed City a trip to Carlisle on a Tuesday night in late September: four-one to the Blues, and another interminable ride home.

So to the final promotion push, in which four games in nine days saw City rise from the fifth in the table that had been their final lot twelve months earlier to the second place that sent South Bristol crazy. On Good Friday, at the Carlisle United ground of recent unhappy memory, they scrapped for a point against the champions-elect after Savino had broken his leg and the home team had cancelled out a strike by Bush. Many who were there still swear that this was goal-keeper Gibson's finest hour, but then again, a host of other games vie for that accolade. City were lucky in that the Easter Monday game at Shrewsbury was an evening kick-off, and when they stopped for tea and toast near Leominster, their murmurs of approval turned to an excited babble as they listened to the afternoon's results on the radio and heard scoreline after scoreline going in their favour. 'If we beat this lot tonight, do them over at Ashton Gate tomorrow and then get two points at home to Oldham on Saturday...' Everything was far from cut and dried, and in the end it could all come down to goal average, but for the first time in months, the chance was there again. Big John was pretty well in the realms of higher mathematics, trying to perm all the different scoring scenarios, but two things were certain: City needed three wins, and they needed lots of goals.

A big City following at the Gay Meadow gave the Reds more vocal support than the home team, and it was a good deal noisier before the night was over. Poised at one-all at half time, this was one of those midweek games on a foreign field at which John Atyeo could not have been more pumped up. A goal early in the second half, after 'keeper Alan Boswell had got hopelessly stranded from a throw-in, sent the big man's adrenalin sky-high, and it was vintage Atyeo as he lashed in three more for the team's first five-goal tally since that early-season flurry. All the way back John was again tinkering around with the goal computations, but with a happier face than he had been doing a few hours earlier. Come the big game the following night – this was a time when much of the Bristol workforce still liked to see Easter Tuesday as a day off work – more than 16,000 made merry at Ashton Gate to watch City do the double over Shrewsbury with the greatest of ease. Or nearly the greatest; their three-nil lead (Atyeo, Bush, Clark) was built up before half time, and they would dearly have liked to have seen a few more go in in the second half. Nevertheless, with a game to go, the result had pushed them up into a promotion position for the first time since mid-September, and now it was simply a case of waiting to see what Saturday would bring.

Simply a case? The four days leading up to the weekend were unbearable, and by mid-day on the Saturday the streets and pubs around the ground were thronging with people who simply could not stand the wait any longer. In the dressing room, the hubbub in the car park told the players that something very special was going on out there. In the midst of it all, in his own oasis of calm, was the defender Tony Ford, of such a placid temperament that by this time he was the club's first-choice penalty-taker. John Atyeo, at the end of a week of harrowing tension, glanced across at the composed figure on the other side of the dressing room, compared how he felt with how this man looked, and just had to laugh. 'Look at him,' he said, nodding towards Ford. 'Bet you hope we get a penalty in the first minute, don't you, Tony?' 'Oh, yes, it'd be good to be one-nil up nice and early.'

There were 28,248 on the ground, and not many of them were shouting for Oldham Athletic, in whose ranks that afternoon were old boys Alan Williams and Peter McCall. On the other hand, the noise for City was deafening, and if that did not make the players edgy enough in the early stages, news that Mansfield had gone two up at Barnsley in the first twenty minutes set their nerves jangling even more; the rule of thumb was that, to go up, Mansfield had to score three goals to every one by City. This did not seem so bad a proposition for Robins fans before the kick-off, but when the other lot had got two up before your lads had even settled down properly, it was suddenly not looking nearly so rosy. Gibson boosted his colleagues' confidence by coming out for a difficult cross and handling it immaculately, and Brian Clark, after missing an open goal, made amends in the best possible way by netting on the stroke of half time. Sharpe floated a high centre from the right into the penalty area, Peters got in a shot with no great force, and Clark was there to knock it into the net. It was only towards the end of a riotously rowdy half time that some of the fans down that end looked at one another and muttered: 'I thought Clarky looked a bit off-side, didn't you?' No matter; the ref. did not see it that way.

The object of the second half was to get another goal, and of course keep Oldham out. The latter task was not proving so difficult, since the visitors' attacking ambitions were few, but it was still not easy breaking them down at the other end. A couple of chances came John's way; first, he was not at his sharpest when Bush headed across the face of the goal, and when he did get his shot in it was straight into Ron Swan's arms. Then a slip by Williams almost let him through, but his sharp hooked shot was well saved by the goalkeeper. Urban myth has it that Alan Williams, an old friend and admirer, was not the most formidable of opponents that afternoon, but Will will not have it that he tried anything but his hardest. In fact he was not technically marking Atyeo, but centre-forward Terry Bush, and in *The People* the following morning, the sports writer Graham Russell concluded: 'Time and again [City] were foiled by Alan Williams... He had a magnificent game against his old colleagues, taming Bush and often subduing Atyeo as well.' What Williams does say today is that John was venting his frustration at him more and more as the game went on: 'Aw, we're never going to do it now, Will, we're never going to do it.' In the end, Atyeo and the crowd were looking for a footballing miracle – and seven minutes from the end, that is exactly what they got when he dredged up his last reserves of energy to swivel and smash a glorious drive into the top corner of the net from eighteen yards.

It went down quite well, really; since pens far more fluent than ours would be hard-pressed to describe the pandemonium that ensued, let us simply leave it at that. Everyone was in a daze for the last few dying minutes, tears were flowing down John Atyeo's cheeks, and the scenes of jubilation that met the final whistle were not seen again on the ground for another eleven years, on the warm April night when City at last reached the heights that always eluded John and his colleagues. Nevertheless, there seemed nothing second-best about their achievement that evening, compounded by Mansfield winning by just three-two; it meant that the Robins were up by 0.11 of a goal.

There is something almost iconic about two images of Atyeo that emerged from that afternoon. In one, his face is crumpled in tears of joy as he is mobbed by the crowd, the expression and his tousled hair making him look like some big kid; in the other, he stands in the directors' box with his hands held high, glorying in the adulation of the crowd after thousands had chanted 'We want John. We want John...' 'These pictures, like no other, tell us just what success for Bristol City meant to John Atyeo,' says the sports writer David Foot. 'It wasn't a great game, but it was a team performance, and John saw it romantically as a triumph for all eleven of them. He never lost his feeling for the team ethos of football.' Looking back on the game, Atyeo recalled: 'I was on holiday from Redland Training College at the time, and it was just as well. I just moped around for the week, hardly eating a thing. I got so carried away with it all that I wasn't in a fit state to play. It meant a lot to me, because I had had serious thoughts about finishing at that time. Saturday came, and 28,000 fans crowded into Ashton Gate just to see us win. Nothing else mattered, only the result. Oldham were a poor side and it was just another match for them – but the goals wouldn't come. Then, just before half time, Brian Clark scored a goal that had a dubious look about it, but it counted. We wanted another goal just to make sure. I hadn't done much in the game, but near the end I had a dip and the ball ended up

in the top right hand corner for our second goal. I couldn't remember
the last few minutes. I was crying through sheer joy.'

Back in the boardroom, the champagne was flowing. It was the
beginning of a party that Mike Gibson looks back on as 'the only night
in my life I drank myself sober'. For him, as for the rest of the City
players, the game had been almost unbelievably tense. When he came
out that afternoon, he had stuck firmly to his usual ritual: a wave to the
crowd, four steps in from his right hand post and a leap up to touch the
crossbar. The fans always counted those four paces and greeted the
leap with a mighty cheer, but the way they responded then was a
reminder to him just how much promotion would mean to the whole
Bristol City constituency – not just those hordes gathered there then,
but tens of thousands more spread throughout the city, the region, the
country, in pockets throughout the world. What followed, according to
Gibson, was eighty-three minutes of hell, before John Atyeo's strike
made all their dreams come true. 'We were a group of characters who
enjoyed life off the field as well as on it,' Gibson recalls today. 'We
used to socialise together, and that was very important in building
team spirit. Although we wanted promotion for the club and the
supporters, we wanted it even more for each other. It was like a big
family, and a far cry from today's game with its huge amounts of
money.'

Before it all got completely out of hand, Harry Dolman and John
had a few serious words together. 'I hadn't planned to carry on playing, but this changed the whole picture,' Atyeo recalled in 1970. 'I
wanted to finish in the Second Division. I'd finished my two years at
Redland and had qualified as a teacher. I was glad about that, because
those were two tremendously hard years for me, doing virtually two
jobs. With maths and physical education to offer, I had little difficulty
in getting a job. I was accepted at Kingdown School in Warminster,
and the headmaster, Peter Kay, assured me that I could go on playing
as long as I wanted. I decided to continue for one more season.'
Atyeo then went on to a rather more sobering meeting with Fred Ford,
shortly after Dolman had slapped the manager on the back and offered
him a job for life: 'Fred called me down to his office. He was looking
through all the names of the Second Division clubs. "Where are we
going to get any points?" he asked.' Big John, never one for undue
optimism, even on such a night of nights as this, found it hard to give
him an answer.

CHAPTER 16

END OF THE ROAD

There were no big-name signings for Bristol City's return to the Second Division, and some of their supporters were anxious about that. Certainly, at the end of the previous season, Fred Ford had talked of needing one or two extra players, with a winger at the top of the list, and Harry Dolman gave the fans the assurance that 'Mr Ford will strengthen the playing staff where he thinks necessary.' In the long term, his decision to keep the purse strings tight cost him his job, but in that first season back up it simply seemed shrewd. The team was never out of the top ten from late October onwards, and there was a time, when they went fourth in mid-February, that the impossible dream seemed within the realms of reality to some. It never quite got as good as that, but in finishing fifth, the Robins comfortably exceeded most people's expectations. As in the previous season's promotion campaign, they used just seventeen players, and eight of the eleven who kicked off the season with a two-one home win over Rotherham (Atyeo, Hooper) were there on the last game of the season to despatch Ipswich four-one (Atyeo two, Bush, Parr).

Gibson, Ford, Briggs, Connor, Low, Peters, Atyeo and Clark were the backbone of the side, with important contributions from Derrick, Bush, Sharpe and Parr. In losing only eight games, City's record was bettered only by champions Manchester City, but they were also the draw specialists, ending up all-square seventeen times. If they could have turned four of those tied matches into wins – or, as we shall see, had better luck against Southampton over Easter – it would have been them and not the Saints who went up in second place. The Robins' defensive record – forty-eight conceded – was the third best in the division, but their goal tally of sixty-three was only three better than when they had gone down in 1960, and while the Atyeo-Clark partnership ticked over nicely in this higher grade of football, there was nobody much else to help them out. John, in his final season, reminded defenders that he could still cut it with nineteen goals in thirty-five games, while Clark, in his first year in this grade of football, ended with fifteen out of forty-two.

An early sign that the Reds would make the grade came at Maine Road in the third game of the season, when they drew two-all with Manchester City (Atyeo, Drury) and should have won. City had taken their first step to glory by signing Mike Summerbee from Swindon in the close season, while Colin Bell would follow from Bury in March. Francis Lee arrived some time later, but more than half the side that would win the First Division championship in 1968 was already in place, and Atyeo and co. gave them a good run for their money that afternoon. 'The happy, contented side Fred had built up in the previous four years was a pleasure to play in,' John reflected. 'He got the maximum amount of ability and effort out of every single one of us during the promotion year and our first season in Division Two, yet he did it all on a shoestring budget. We had some wonderful wins that 1965-66 season, and we used to go away expecting to bring back at least a point.' In fact there were some very fine away wins in 1965-66, with four goals scored against Charlton, Portsmouth and Leyton Orient on their home patches and two points also taken from visits to Bury, Bolton, Rotherham, Plymouth and Birmingham; they all helped City run up a season's total of twenty-two away points, and that was good going by anybody's standard.

In comparison, City's home form was dreary, with two defeats and a depressing nine draws, and an average gate of 15,000 or 16,000 at the beginning of the season had dropped to 10,000 or 11,000 by the end. What is more, Ashton Gate's was coming to be seen as a hyper-critical crowd, with their ire and often audible abuse aimed at the team, individuals and manager alike. John Atyeo pinpointed the Easter games against the Southampton of the likes of Tony Knapp, Terry Paine, Martin Chivers, Jimmy Melia and John Sydenham as the death knell for promotion hopes. 'Those two games finished us off, but we came so close,' he recalled. 'On Good Friday we lost one-nil at home, when Jack Connor put through his own goal. I reckon we had about ninety per cent of the play without scoring, and a four-nil win for us wouldn't have been unfair. After winning at Plymouth the following day, when Danny Bartley gave Tony Book one of his biggest chasings of all time, we went to the Dell for the return with Southampton on the Monday. Again we played well and were leading two-one until injury time, when Terry Paine broke away to equalise in about the ninety-fourth minute.'

Southampton's win at Ashton Gate was one of those two home defeats inflicted that season, the other being against Wolves on December 28. An odd coincidence: City had sold their first set of floodlights to Burton Albion, and this home game three days after Christmas saw the belated switch-on of the new ones, which had cost £27,000. When Wolves had launched the original lights it had been as lofty heroes from another planet doing their lowly hosts a good turn. This time they were merely Second Division rivals who ended the season a place behind the Reds in the table, but they had the better of things that evening.

City had come so close that by the end of the season there was genuine disappointment at the club that promotion had been missed. On the other hand, to do what they had done had been a great achievement, maybe an over-achievement, whatever some of the fans thought. 'Fred Ford deserved the manager of the year award for what he did with that team,' John said. 'The argument has often been raised over whether or not he should have bought that season. It would have been difficult to know who to leave out if another player had come, because this was essentially a bunch of fellows playing together as a team – and the happiest team I can remember, as well. Buying could have had a reverse effect at that time. Anyway, the two Southampton games were after the transfer deadline, so it didn't apply, then. It was still a wonderful achievement to finish fifth.'

By that time John had made the firm decision to end his career, though he later confessed that if promotion had been won, he would not have been able to resist staying on and seeing what he could do with one last season in the top grade. It would have given his career a bizarre twist – First Division football in his first season and his last, when in each case age would have prevented him from playing anywhere near his best – but in the event, it was not an option. It was on the train back from Cardiff after a two-one defeat in mid-March – with sixteen-year-old John Toshack clipping in a beauty for the winner – that he had quietly told Fred Ford that he planned to hang up his boots; he wrote a letter to Harry Dolman at much the same time. The fact that Cardiff's hero that night had been half his age with some months to spare would not have passed him by. Neither manager nor chairman offered any objection, or tried to dissuade him – until after a few matches had been played in the following season. It was a month later when the news was broken in the press. 'I don't think I can go on any longer,' he told Peter Godsiff of the *Bristol Evening Post*. 'I've had my mind made up for some time, now, but decided to postpone the announcement until the club's chances of promotion had virtually gone. I felt Fred Ford would have enough to cope with, without my retirement being sprung on him. All good things come to an end. It's a sad decision to have to make, but I didn't think it wise to plough on for another year, and perhaps go downhill. I've always said I would retire while I was at the top. Now City are back in the Second Division and have consolidated their position this season, I thought it an opportune moment to retire. I felt I should now make room for the younger ones. Someone else is entitled to my place in the side.'

He was echoing what a lot of people thought – that there would still be a good deal of talent at Ashton Gate after he had gone. City had played at Birmingham City without him late in the season and come away with a resounding three-one win which left many concluding that maybe they would not miss the old fellow much at all. On the other hand, the cry was going up, as it did twelve months earlier, that the Robins really would have to buy this time. Two forwards of class were needed, 'and that means players costing £30,000 upwards', Peter Godsiff concluded. Odd to think that that had been the kind of notional fee attached to John Atyeo ten years earlier, when £30,000 footballers were the very cream of the crop.

John Atyeo's last and 645th appearance in the Football League for Bristol City was at home to Ipswich Town in the final match of the season, a rearranged evening game on May 10, 1966. He needed two goals to reach his 350 for the club in senior competitions, and in emotional scenes recalling the promotion decider against Oldham twelve months earlier, he got them. The ceremonies began before the teams came out, when John's testimonial appeal was launched by John Arlott, the cricket commentator with the Hampshire burr to whom the Atyeo brand of steadfastness and loyalty appealed greatly. It was a poignant address, listened to with deference by the moderate crowd of nearly 14,000. The Ipswich chairman, the brewer John Cobbold, was friendly with Harry Dolman, so it was inevitable that the visitors would play their full part in the pomp and ceremony that then followed. After the match they presented John with a silver tankard – 'a wonderful gesture, and one of my many treasured memories', as he later reflected, with his usual generosity of spirit. At twenty past seven the two teams minus Atyeo filed out side-by-side, a custom at that time reserved for showpiece games, and along with them were nine of the City team he had appeared with in his debut season fifteen years before. Only when they were lined up on either side of the centre spot did John walk out between them, hugely embarrassed and clutching a football like Linus with his comfort blanket. Once out there, though, he was soon in his element, greeting Cyril Williams, Jack Boxley, Alec Eisentrager, Ernie Peacock, Pat Beasley, Fred Stone, Twink Cook, Dennis Roberts, and Jack Bailey from the class of '51, and making sure they would still be around for drinks after the final whistle. Then there was just time for a team photograph, and the action began.

He nodded the ball into the net after only three minutes but was ruled offside, and it was Ipswich who went ahead not long after that through Ray Crawford, another man who did not need a street map to find the back of the net. City were not behind for more than five minutes when Terry Bush snatched an equaliser, and when they took the lead through Gordon Parr with just over twenty minutes to go, it looked as if they might at least end the season on a winning note. There was just one snag: for all their high ranking, they had not scored more than twice at home all season, and at two-one up with fifteen minutes to go, there was no good reason to imagine that John would turn an emotional night into a legendary one by bagging the brace he so desperately craved. Then again, he always did have a sense of the dramatic for someone with his feet planted so firmly on the ground, and if two goals were what the crowd were willing him to get, then two goals it would be.

The first came from a corner on the right, a Danny Bartley inswinger that brushed off his forehead into the net at the far post. Or did it? Yes, it did, and those who had the temerity to suggest that the ball had gone in straight from the corner were shouted down loudly. More to the point, referee Ken Burns was clear in his mind: the last two goals of the match were scored by John Atyeo. There was certainly no doubt about his second, the 350th of his career, with six minutes of the game, the season and his career to go. By this time, according to Peter Godsiff, 'rather than an ageing veteran, he became a youthful teenager bubbling over with enthusiasm', and he was rewarded when a Gordon Parr shot was blocked, the ball spun out to him and he was able to pounce on it before his marker to bang it home. He was only about eight yards out, but his arms were in the air in triumph before it hit the back of the net.

Before the match, John had said: 'Records have never bothered me, and I shall not be disappointed if I fail (to score two goals) tonight.' In the vernacular of the twenty-first century, yeah, right. The game was all over minutes after that, and it was yesterday once more. The final whistle blew, he was mobbed by as many of the thousands on the pitch who could get their hands on him, and they all knew that his eventual disappearance down the tunnel, arms still upstretched, would not be the last they saw of him. 'We want John,' they chanted once again. 'At-ee-o, At-ee-o.' They sang *Auld Lang Syne* and *For he's a Jolly Good Fellow*, a pleasant (or maybe depressing) reminder of just how much football fans have changed in forty years. Then there he was up in the directors' box, with Harry Dolman and vice-chairman Lionel Smart standing proudly beside him. 'We'll never see his like again,' Harry pronounced. 'There may be more spectacular players, but few will equal him as a man.' Down on the pitch and in the stand, however, the crowd made it quite clear that 350 goals were quite spectacular enough for them, thank you very much, Mr Dolman, and they shouted themselves hoarse in praise of their hero one last time; well, until his testimonial match in October, anyway.

The treasured tankard from Ipswich was not John's only memento of his retirement. The directors presented him with a 'hundred-guinea gold watch' before the Gloucestershire Senior Cup final a few nights later, a one-nil defeat by Bristol Rovers in which he played no part, and he and Ruth were at the supporters' club's dinner and dance at the newly opened Top Rank Suite, where he received an inscribed gold pen and pencil set 'for outstanding services for the club'. The National Federation of Supporters' Clubs sent him a message declaring that 'his sportsmanship and club loyalty are an inspiration and credit to soccer'. As the season ended, Atyeo also found himself involved in the kind of ambassadorial work he might have imagined would be his lot at Ashton Gate for years to come. Bedminster boy Geoff Merrick, the fifteen-year-old England schools captain who was about to join City, was welcomed to the ground by a Big John looking more like a teacher than any the lad had left behind at Southville School, with his checked sports jacket and woolly pully. By now, of course, with a year's teaching under his belt, he was getting a firm grip of what made teenagers tick, and was able to make them feel instantly at home.

Chris Garland, just seventeen and from the new tower block flats overlooking the ground, signed at much the same time, and was another player whose career Atyeo followed and nurtured where possible. These boys had still been in primary school when John blasted home the goal that took England to the 1958 World Cup finals, and with the 1966 finals to be enjoyed in England that summer, eight years ago must have seemed like ancient history. This time, John was just as much a distant spectator as the rest of us as Bobby Moore's boys blazed their trail to everlasting glory. 'My TV set took a real hammering over those three weeks,' he joked.

Come the new season, 1966-67, and he was still very much around the club, with a prominent column at the front of the programme and an open-ended brief to be about the dressing room as much as he liked. Fred Ford welcomed him aboard the team coach for away games, and as with his encouragement of the youngsters, his involvement with the club he loved was shaping up very much as had been expected. Once again, and even more surprisingly, in the absence of the big man, Ford did not avail himself of Harry Dolman's chequebook, but talked instead of a 'triangular spearhead', with Brian Clark and Terry Bush supporting Gerry Sharpe, and the likes of Jantzen Derrick and Danny Bartley also firmly in the frame. He even spoke of the kids Chris Garland, Dickie Down and Johnny Giles being given opportunities in the first team, which was seen as desperately optimistic, and rightly so.

Chris's time would come, as we know, but not until towards the end of the following season, while Dickie and (this particular) Johnny Giles were never quite up to scratch and soon on their way to the terminally floundering Bradford Park Avenue. Fred admitted that the transfer market was not his forté: 'I know much more about buying and assessing players than I did three or four years ago, but it's not an easy task these days. I was at Wolves on Monday watching a Central League [reserve] match against Bury. So were representatives of about twenty other clubs, including Ron Greenwood of West Ham. That's the state of football now.'

All this was disturbing enough for those calling for team strengthening even before a ball was kicked – but when the action began it went from bad to worse, with straight defeats and just two goals in the season's opening four games. At the third game, a home loss to old foes Cardiff, the programme notes were ruminating: 'Already several people have declared that we will miss John Atyeo. Any club is bound to miss a player who scored 350 goals in his career. These comments were anticipated when John decided to retire. John was offered a contract for this season but he felt that his fitness would not stand up to another full season. He has given way to younger players. This is an inevitable progression in football and in any sport. We respected John's wishes, as we respect his opinions now. He has made himself available to give whatever assistance may be required, and he travelled to Huddersfield last Saturday with the team.'

In fact the clamour for his return was genuine and heartfelt in some quarters, and there were those who believed that his loyalty was such that if relegation really did threaten, then he would polish up those old brown boots and start banging in the goals again, as he banged them of yore. The speculation went right on up to his testimonial game in October, for which he had to retain a certain level of fitness, and only after that was it accepted by one and all that it was truly time to let go; John himself had known it from early spring.

Fund-raising for his testimonial was now well under way. At home games there was a 'Beat the Clock' competition, based on the timing of the first goal, with a £25 prize. You could send a cheque or postal order to a subscription fund c/o Brecknell, Dolman and Rogers, Pennywell Road, Bristol 5. Testimonial ties were 12s 6d (62.5p) each, and a brochure was being got together by John Davies, the *Daily Express* man in West Country football, who also found time to organise 'Beat the Clock'. In his programme notes, John thanked the supporters' club for its help, and noted enigmatically that 'I have some very willing Senior Scouts and several other friends who work very hard on my behalf'. He declared himself 'most satisfied' with the forthcoming brochure, but 'it certainly makes my career more glamorous than I'm sure it really was'.

The opposition for the testimonial game on October 10, 1966 were Leeds United, whose decade of dominance of British football under Don Revie was only just beginning; their collection of silverware from those years – two League Championships, one F.A. Cup, one League Cup, two European Fairs Cups – massively undersells their power and influence at that time, largely because of their uncanny knack of finishing second when the chips were down. The fixture had come about as a result of a remarkably glowing newspaper tribute to Atyeo written by Revie in a Yorkshire football paper the previous March. John had read it as the team was on the train heading home from a defeat at Middlesbrough and was overwhelmed by its generosity; he had played with Revie only occasionally on the England fringes and knew him well enough to chat on the odd occasions they met, but he was no bosom buddy. Besides, the future national manager was simply not usually the kind of man to make those kind of pronouncements.

In the event, and strangely, for a former player who was frequently at odds with his bosses and always moving on, Revie presented the Atyeo philosophy as if it had been dictated to him from Dilton Marsh. Comparing John with Joe Baker, who had just completed his latest big-money move, he wrote: 'These are two of the finest centre-forwards Britain has produced since the war, yet they come from poles apart as far as professional soccer is concerned. Atyeo has had an astonishing career with a club which, with no disrespect to their manager, Fred Ford, is not among the most glamorous and influential throughout the League. Over the years, Atyeo has stamped himself as one of the most loyal players ever to grace the game in this country, and at the same time, in my view, he has lost the chance of making himself a rich man. For those who do not know Atyeo personally – and I am proud to count myself as one who does – his insistence at staying with Bristol City when he could have had his pick of any club in the country is difficult to understand. The reason is simple. To Atyeo, happiness has been worth more than monetary gain or personal glory. He has been happy playing for Bristol City. It is as clear-cut as that. I wonder how many players with class potential would take such a view today, when the rewards for someone at the top are much greater than when Atyeo was first making his name as a goal taker supreme.' Revie hailed the dedication and loyalty of John and Portsmouth's Jimmy Dickinson as 'the perfect illustration to any young player just making his way in the game', and drew the conclusion that 'he would have been a regular member of the international side in the 1950s if he had been with a more fashionable club. To my mind, it was a mistake for England to discard him after only six games. He has a rare talent, a knack for being in the right place at the right time. Jimmy Greaves has this same sixth sense.'

Revie paved the way for a letter from the testimonial committee when he concluded: 'When Atyeo retires from playing – and I sincerely hope that it will not be for some time, yet – I am sure that City will give him a great testimonial game, perhaps one of the greatest ever in England. It would be a fair reward for the years of service he has put into the club, and a substitute for the more dynamic rewards he would have gained had he taken that step up the ladder.' In response to the article, by which he said he felt 'most flattered' John paraded before the local press his usual reasons for not moving, with all their familiar ambivalences: 'In a First Division team I might have become a better player, but there again, I might have found the competition so fierce that I might not have won a first team place at all. The only way I might have earned more money would have been by getting more caps, and thus more international fees.' The last assertion is a classic piece of Atyeo evasion. Was he really suggesting that in the five years since the lifting of the maximum wage, he had earned as much at City as he would have done as an established favourite at one of the moneybags clubs? If that really was the case, he must have been picking up more, one way and another, than even his most imaginative colleagues might have dared guess at.

The testimonial brochure *John Atyeo King of Goals*, priced 2s 6d (12.5p) was an attractive and well presented publication with a welter of tributes, some of which have already been touched upon in this book. The Football League president Len Shipman, Bert Tann of Bristol Rovers, George Curtis of Coventry, Gordon Low, Matt Busby, Joe Mercer and uncle Alfredo di Stefano and all lined up to pay homage to the man of the moment, not that Alfredo sounded as if he was a regular around Bristol 3: 'I never played against John Atyeo,' the Real Madrid legend confessed, 'but any player who could score 350 goals in English football deserves praise.'

Don Revie did not let John Atyeo down. He brought his full first team plus a number of substitutes who would become household names in years to come: Sprake, Reaney, Charlton, Hunter, Gray, Madeley, Johanneson, Harvey, Lorimer, Storrie, the other Johnny Giles: they all turned out for Big John in a game they won four-two. The City goals came from Gerry Sharpe and Jantzen Derrick but not, alas, the man of the night, whose compensation lay in a wonderful crowd of 17,000 who paid £3,930 for the privilege of being there, with tickets at 12s (60p) in the stand and 5s (25p) in the enclosure. A ball-park figure of £5,000 has been put on John's total benefit cheque – maybe not the breathtaking bonanza speculated upon by Revie, but a decent sum, nonetheless. It was augmented on New Year's Day, 1968, when John was one of seventeen long-serving players, recently retired, to be paid £1,000-plus each by the Football League Provident Fund; in all, 385 ex-professionals shared a pot of £104,733, and his companions among the four-figure beneficiaries included Johnny Gordon, a club-mate at Portsmouth at the start of his career.

Back to the benefit game, and Big John was getting used to all the fuss that was made of him on these serial 'nights to remember' by this time, and showed no sign whatever of not enjoying it. At the ground that evening was the World Cup, the Jules Rimet trophy that will always be the only World Cup to England fans of a certain age, and John found himself parading it around the edge of the pitch with Jack Charlton and Norman Hunter, the latter of whom was one of the unsung England squad members who were not out there against West Germany on that famous Wembley afternoon. There were no winners' medals, either, for that shadow XI, but Norman knew what was expected of him and dutifully trotted around the ground with the other two. He and Terry Cooper would come to know it a good deal better in the years ahead.

As for John, the sight of the trophy in his hand was a touching reminder of Dalymount '57 and all that, a goal that had grown in significance among England fans over the years as the status of the World Cup had taken off in their minds; the Irish, of course, had never been in the slightest doubt about its importance. The *Bristol Evening Post's* Peter Godsiff's assessment of Atyeo's performance in the game that followed was that he did not look fit – but this was 'something which could, if necessary, be rectified'; on the other hand, he did show many of his old touches, 'the kind of craft which could still be an asset to the team'. Even this hard-headed reporter, with a record of being consistently realistic about Atyeo's declining powers, could not quite accept that this night really was the end of the road. There was the familiar rush for the tunnel at the final whistle, the chanting of the thousands, the figure clad in red appearing in the directors' box with his arms held aloft. Surely there could not be yet one more last hurrah after this one? No, there could not, but it was still a wonderful evening, rounded off by a banquet at the Grand Hotel in Bristol.

First to speak at that was Harry Dolman, who said: 'I've had wonderful times watching him play. He's given thousands of people enjoyment with his football. John Atyeo will go down in history as one of those wonderful footballers in Bristol, like Geoff Bradford and Fatty Wedlock. He is a credit to himself, to Bristol City and to the game as a whole.' Next up was Denis Follows, the Football Association secretary, who compared him with other one-club players of the calibre of Billy Wright, Tom Finney, Jimmy Dickinson and the Sheffield United full-back Joe Shaw: 'Other people have scored more than 350 goals, others have made more than 645 appearances, others have played fifteen years with one club, others have never been sent off or reported by referees, others have gained more caps for England; but the only player to achieve all these distinctions is John Atyeo.'

Harry Reynolds, the Leeds United chairman, added: 'Everyone is telling us what a great honour it is [for them] for Leeds to play in this testimonial match. But *we* consider it an honour and a privilege to have been asked to come along this evening and do something to help make the night a success.' Finally, it was the turn of John Atyeo, who had been sitting 'sheepishly' through all the praise, to stand up for a few minutes to speak 'fluently and unemotionally', after first thanking all who had helped in both his football and his testimonial appeal. 'I've had more luck than I deserved in my career,' he claimed. 'I've had luck all the way through, culminating with Leeds coming down here tonight.' The Leeds chairman presented him with a silver salver to add to his growing collection of mementoes, while the Bristol press came up with a clock to complement the club's gold watch.

After that, it was back to reality; but as has been noted, John was still very much a part of the Ashton Gate set-up, and his programme notes allowed the wider public to glimpse hitherto unsuspected aspects of their hero. For a start, he really did have a hard-nosed approach to money. On September 13, Swansea Town made history by being the first League team to cross the new (now old) Severn Bridge, opened just two days earlier, for a League Cup game. John's attitude was as pragmatic as could be, and those who always thought they detected something Corinthian in his play were forced to revise their view of his concept of the football industry. 'Professional players welcome the League Cup because it is always more enjoyable to play a midweek match than train for five days,' he wrote. 'It breaks the week up nicely to have an evening game, but perhaps the most important reason for players being fully in favour of this competition is the financial angle. Appearance money and bonus is offered by the club, which is equivalent to the man in the street being offered overtime. The bonus increases with every round, until a hefty sum is at stake in the final.' The result was one-all at Ashton Gate, and City lost two-one at the Vetch Field after extra time. John reflected that he had never played extra time in his life, despite having been involved in many replays: 'Perhaps it was just as well, because in the latter part of my career I was struggling to last ninety minutes, let alone play another thirty.'

A couple of months later there was a hands-across-the-water exercise with Hanover, the German city with which Bristol had been twinned since shortly after the war, when Hanover 96 came to play City in the Friendship Cup, donated by the *Evening Post*. Harry Dolman wrote a piece in the programme about building bridges and civic exchanges, 'with my wife acting as interpreter' as he arranged the visit and a trip by City to Hanover the following August. Marina, who presented the cup, had lived and worked for a German company in Hanover for two years, and was now a member of the twinning committee. Schoolchildren spent the afternoon decorating the boardroom in Hanover's green, white and black and City's red. As for John, his preoccupations, as the fans were coming to expect, were more feet-on-the-ground: 'Our players will welcome this type of game, because it gives them a chance to play a match without having the worry of vital League points at stake. The fact that bonus and appearance money is offered is an extra incentive...' As an afterthought, he added that they would also want to win 'from the prestige angle', though that clearly did not add up to very much for them, as they lost a rough game against boring opponents three-two in front of a miserably low gate. The club lost money on the match, barely taking half the £1,500 they had guaranteed their visitors. The Bristol-Hanover twinning continues to flourish in many ways, but not a lot is heard of the Friendship Cup these days.

CHAPTER 17

PLEASE, SIR

John Atyeo took up his teaching post at Kingdown School in Warminster in September 1965, aged thirty-three and just weeks into his last League season, and by the following March he was saying: 'I'm very happy teaching. This is the job I shall stick at.' Nevertheless, if he thought his previous two years as a full-time student and part-time footballer had been hard, he was soon to discover that being a novice teacher and a player in the Second Division was even tougher, making all the more unrealistic the expectations of some that he might stay around in the game for yet another season after this one. John went as a teacher in the mathematics department with additional duties in physical education, but from the start, and increasingly as the years rolled by, his priority was maths. In a way, he was in an awkward situation regarding P. E., unwilling to be put into a position in which he might be seen as stealing the thunder of staff members for whom it was their major discipline. He enjoyed coaching a variety of sports, he did his fair share of refereeing, and while he liked to keep his other life firmly in the background, he could see why some of the more football-mad boys might want to look at and touch his England caps and shirts, and would occasionally oblige. If it motivated them to greater sporting endeavours of their own, so much the better.

Kingdown, when he arrived, was a secondary modern, under an experienced head in Peter Kay. Stemming from a senior school in the middle of Warminster, it had not long been established at its edge-of-town campus, and beyond all the plate glass and fresh brick-work it clung on to traditional structures more tenaciously than many schools at that time. For instance, it set great store by the house system, to the extent that the teaching role of head of house had real meaning and involved real duties. The four houses were named after local topographical features – Wylye, Arn, Deverill and Cley – and the new Mr Atyeo was assigned to Arn, whose colour, surely far from

201

coincidentally, was red. Before very long he was head of that house, and proud of it. Under him, Arn flourished on the playing fields. 'John was very clever and cunning at getting the best sports boys and girls – in a nice enough way, of course,' his former colleague Roy Spurr recalls. 'Arn won everything for years and years.' The deputy head of the day, Penny Ealey, insists that this sporting success was down to more than sheer serendipity: 'John really did spend time with his teams, preparing them.' There was general amusement when he missed out on Rob Newman, who followed his elder brother Paul into another house. Nevertheless, the happy coincidence of Newman's arrival at the school in 1975 had a lasting influence for the good on John Atyeo's last years.

As a secondary modern, Kingdown had a very good academic reputation. It would put some teenagers in for their O levels in their fourth year, a practice rare enough even at grammar schools, and those who succeeded would then be able to concentrate on fewer subjects in the fifth form. John Atyeo's maths department was to the fore in this, along with English and biology, and it would give the staff much satisfaction to send a number of 'eleven-plus failures' on to sixth forms in Frome, Salisbury or Trowbridge. It also kept the teachers on their mettle, and that was fine by John Atyeo. He had been there for around five years when the school went comprehensive, and as the 1970s wore on, other changes were in the air, as they were in education all over the country. The decision to do away with the house system was met with dismay by a large number of staff members, and John took it as badly as anyone. 'I think that nearly broke his heart,' says Anne Spurr, who with her husband Roy put in some forty years' service in the science department at the school. 'Houses brought in that little bit of competition among the children, so there was friendly rivalry; among staff, too, because we were all allocated houses. It also transformed the enormous number in the big school to four manageable ones.' With a strong Army presence in the town, the school roll could fluctuate wildly – from around 700 up to 1,600 in John's time, and then back down to below 1,000.

His persona at Kingdown was rather different from his profile at Ashton Gate. As the years progressed he grew into a trusted if slightly eccentric elder statesman, but he was never the kingpin he had been at the football club. On the other hand, there were some echoes of the past. He kept his family life private, in spite of all his children going to Kingdown, and his wife Ruth, with a brood of five keeping her fully occupied, was rarely seen with him at school events and social gatherings. Colleagues knew he would do anything for the school, and was always there at functions and sports days, but he did not socialise much with them at other times. He also remained famous among his peers for being careful with money. 'If we had a meeting, it was always "Shall we go in your car?"' one former colleague recalls affectionately, 'and he would always be last through the door when it came to buying a round of drinks.'

The headmaster at Kingdown through most of John's twenty-four years there was Frank Heywood. It was his lot to turn the school into a comprehensive and introduce sometimes unpopular new systems that reflected the educational theories of the time, but John liked him well enough; he liked it even more if he could hit him for four or six on the cricket field. His days as a bowler were all but spent, but he was still very useful with the bat, and colleagues on the staff cricket and football teams and their foes alike would revel in the fact that, for perhaps the only time in their life, they could go home and tell their children they had shared the field with a sporting household name. 'It was fun to play cricket with him,' Roy Spurr remembers. 'We would be up against other schools, the police, the fire brigade, all a very casual sort of thing, and the other fellows would enjoy it as much as we did. Towards the end we used to have a couple of older boys in the team, because John was a fine coach in that sport, too, and it was a good way for them to bridge the gap between school and club cricket. It was part of my job to look after the grounds, and we had a wicket on which I lavished a lot of time and care. "You could play a county game on this track, Roy, no bother at all," John used to say to me.'

On the other hand, he learned tricks to keep pushy mums and dads, particularly dads, at bay. They used to come on parents' evenings and tell him: 'My lad's really good at soccer, and he wants to be a professional footballer. How can I make sure he's not overlooked?' The implication there was clear – 'Can you fix up a trial with City, John?' – but he would have none of it. 'Don't worry about your boy,' he would grin reassuringly. 'If he's anywhere near that sort of ability, the scouts will already have spotted him. They're out and about everywhere.'

Early in this book we reflected on the affection in which Mr Atyeo was held by the pupils at Kingdown, even those who knew nothing of his long-ago life in the headlines. It seems their high regard for him was well earned. 'He was one hundred per cent dedicated to the pupils of this school,' says Roy Spurr. 'You never saw him get angry with the children. I saw him cross, and ticking them off, but never really going for them.' Comments on a Kingdown former pupils' website seem to uphold this view, as these quotes make plain. From Jamie Henderson, who left in 1987: 'Mr. Ateyo [sic] taught both me and my mum. He was great. I learned so much from both him and Mr. [Phil] Bastin.' From Neil Dixon: 'John Atyeo was one of the most caring persons ever to grace the halls of Kingdown. He practically dragged some students into passing their maths O levels, and was persuaded once to show us his England caps.' From Kathryn Arbery from the class of 1989: 'Mr. Atyeo (is that how you spell it?): Crazy guy, did he really play for Bristol City with those funny shaped legs? My most vivid memory of him was pretending to have Tourette's syndrome during a maths class, and of course you always knew that the hangman word at the end of term was going to be "Bristol City" or "Football". Definitely the best teacher I ever had, and a great bloke too.'

Michael Green, who left in 1991, recalls: 'I was quite surprised one day when I was browsing through an encyclopaedia of football and stumbled across a photo of him. He was a cool character, never really spoke much about himself and always had the class's attention, although that may have been due to his fixation with whacking people on the wrists with his ruler.' From Emma Green, of the same year, there is the reflection: 'I was never taught by John, but I did know him, as he played football with my grandad for many years. He never failed to put a smile on my face, and always had a kind word for everyone. I will never forget him.'

Best of all are the recollections of Liverpool supporter John Moore, who left the school in the same year as John: 'I will never forget spring, 1988. I had spent weeks desperately trying to locate a ticket for the F.A. Cup final. Two days before the game, a messenger came to my tutor room to inform me that Mr. Atyeo wanted to see me over a disciplinary matter. Shaken, I cautiously and apprehensively made my way to see him. There I found not only Big John, but Mr. [Ian] Blackwood and Mrs. [Penny] Ealey – an intimidating trio, if ever there was one. I was convinced that I was in bad, bad doo-doo. John shook his head, muttered how disappointed he was in me and that I would have to be suspended from school. He claimed to be unable to even say the deed upon which I would fall, such was its dastardly nature. He produced an envelope from his breast pocket which, I was informed, contained written details of my misdemeanour. I opened said missive, feeling physically nauseous, and began to read: "F. A. Challenge Cup Final Tie, May 1988, Wembley Stadium, Admit 1". It was a Cup final ticket! The shock on my face was met with much mirth from the three senior mischief-makers, but it only got better when he produced yet another envelope, containing another ticket, as he felt I was too young to travel to Wembley on my own.' Then, after that, would you believe it, Liverpool went and lost to Wimbledon...

Lovely memories, but human nature being what it is, there were occasional irritating niggles. One day a pupil read about John's penalty miss against Brazil thirty or so years previously, and some of the boys took pleasure in reminding him of it. His son Philip, a better than average footballer at Kingdown School but obviously no John Atyeo, would be shaping up to take a penalty when one of the kids would sneer 'Are you going to miss it – like your dad?' 'The matter was brought up quite often,' Philip says today, with a lingering sense of exasperation and injustice. 'How many goals did he score – 350 or something?' Philip was with Warminster Town for a little while, but constant reminders that he was not as good a footballer as his father, as if he did not know it, led him to look to rugby for his Saturday afternoon's exercise.

Though John never lost his temper with the children, it could be different in the staffroom, says Roy Spurr: 'I've seen him get very, very angry, on several occasions, with staff members at meetings, when something was going on that he didn't like. He'd get incensed, and his face would balloon, and you'd see the veins in his neck. By this time he was a bulky chap and very florid, with a big red face and bulgy neck. We always said he was a candidate for a heart attack – and so it proved, sadly.' His last headmaster, John Lilly, was particularly adept at reducing him to fits of rage. While Atyeo was at Kingdown, pupils at the school included the offspring of the eccentric Marquess of Bath of Longleat, the stately home and visitor attraction just outside Warminster. Lord Bath's background was Eton, the Life Guards and Christ Church, Oxford, but as his children were born in the area, he was determined that they should be educated there – and not at the fee-paying Warminster School in town, either. Accordingly, after going to the local primary school, Lady Lenka Thynn, born in 1969, and her brother Ceawlin, later Lord Weymouth, born 1974, took their place on the school bus every morning from the age of eleven, and acquitted themselves at Kingdown well. Lenka, inheriting many of her parents' dramatic and artistic talents as well as a sharp academic brain, went on to Oxford entirely on merit and graduated with a degree in psychology in 1991. Ceawlin was of more average ability, but had no great problems.

One of John's loudest explosions came when the new head, feeling that the school's egalitarian approach might be detrimental to Ceawlin's learning, told a senior staff meeting: 'We've got to really watch this boy very carefully, and make sure he doesn't miss out on anything.' Atyeo was outraged. 'Aw, come off it,' he roared. 'This lad was born with a silver spoon in his mouth. It doesn't matter if he's the world's dimmest. He's going to be all right.' As Ceawlin was and indeed still is the heir to the 10,000-acre Longleat estate, and by no means the world's dimmest, anyway, most in the room apart from John Lilly felt that the big man had probably got a point.

If John Atyeo had worked on to State retirement age he would have left Kingdown at Christmas 1996 or Easter 1997. Instead, he was away by 1989, the result of a combination of factors. He was at odds with the headmaster for a variety of reasons, a significant one of which was that although he had served as acting deputy head, in the inter-regnum between Frank Heywood and John Lilly, it was made clear to him that he would not be promoted from the ranks to the permanent position. This is the stance schools take often enough, perhaps not unreasonably, but it upset and depressed him.

A good deal more bizarrely, he had been shaken by events in the maths department in the spring of 1987, when a colleague, fifty-year-old Heather Arnold, was found guilty of and gaoled for life for the brutal murder of the wife and baby daughter of another Kingdown staff member. John got on well with most of his senior colleagues, head of department Don Walters, Phil Bastin and the rest, but almost nobody in the school found Mrs Arnold easy company. Her only ally was a younger male teacher who travelled in from Westbury with her every day. Recently divorced, she grew to rely on his support increasingly, and she snapped when he told her, in passing, on the phone one day, that he planned to leave teaching to set up a dress-making business with his thirty-eight-year-old wife. Shortly afterwards, Mrs Arnold took an axe around to his house and all but decapitated the six-stone anorexic woman and the couple's eight-month-old daughter. This horrific crime made headlines all over the country and attracted sensational coverage in the West of England. People leading their everyday lives close to the heart of violent crimes as absurd and surreal as this often fall back on gallows humour to cope with the situation – 'You've got to laugh, or you'll cry'. The maths department and the staffroom at Kingdown generally did their best to keep their spirits up, but in the final analysis they knew that there was nothing remotely funny about what had been going on in their midst.

'We hear so much about counselling today, but then we were given not one bit of help as a school,' Penny Ealey recalls. 'We had to go in every day, dealing with the horror of it, and coping with ourselves and our students as best we could. The staff had to keep up a brave face; children were breaking down in lessons, and I spent half my time making cups of tea for them. One time, though, I just had to lock myself in the medical room and have a good cry. It was a terrible time.' It was made worse for John when the head objected to his talking briefly about the matter to the *Bristol Evening Post*. It did not take the paper long to realise that it was at John Atyeo's school that all this mayhem was going on, and an old contact on the news desk called him for a quote. John said very little, and what he did say was discreet, dignified and supportive of Kingdown, but John Lilly insisted that he should have been the one to have been talked to. He had a point, some might say a very good one, but whatever the rights and wrongs, it was yet something else to help wear John Atyeo down at a time of already high anxiety.

Already feeling below-par in health and disillusioned with the management of the school, he found the stress difficult to bear, and like several of his colleagues of much his age, he began to plan his escape. They were lucky: pupil numbers had fallen sufficiently to allow for reduced staffing levels, and it was the beginning of that time in education when generous redundancy packages were being put on the table. He took his, and never regretted it, but it is not quite true that this was the end of teaching for John. He later went back on supply to Matravers School, the comprehensive in neighbouring Westbury, and even, not long before he died, to fill a few gaps in Kingdown's timetable. That old Atyeo loyalty never deserted him; or the eye for a chance to add a little extra to the coffers.

Two Kingdown boys went on to wear Bristol City's colours in League football during John Atyeo's time at the school. The first – and the one who most caught the eye of school friends who did not know much about football but were dazzled by the sight of flamboyant attacking action – was Gary Smith, who made seven appearances for the Reds and another seven as substitute in 1980-81, their first season back in the Second Division after their fall from the top. Gary was still only a teenager, and in the financial chaos that was engulfing Ashton Gate at that time he was still barely twenty when he moved on to Bath City, never again to return to League action.

The other boy was the big midfield player Rob Newman, a couple of years younger, who signed apprentice forms for City in 1981 and had made all but four hundred League appearances for them, and another fifty-plus in Cup competitions, when he moved on to First Division Norwich City ten years later. There was so much of John Atyeo about Rob Newman as a schoolboy – a big, bright, friendly, strapping lad who excelled at all sports and developed into the natural 'games captain' type who led by popularity, dependability and example. He joined the school in 1975, and by the time he left in 1980 he had gained his colours in football, cricket, athletics, tennis, badminton, cross-country, basketball and hockey. His form teacher, Anne Spurr, also recalls him organising lunchtime table tennis tournaments, as if sporting action should touch every minute of his leisure time.

John Atyeo's part in Newman's progress is not quite as formalised as might be imagined. There is no talk of his giving the boy special coaching sessions, or discussing the technicalities of football. Until the house system broke down, he was happy to let his rival house master Ian Norwood rib him about 'the one who got away', while he was always keen to stress the role played in Rob's development by the head of P. E., Alec Davidson, who today is one of England's leading veteran tennis players. However, John was certainly useful to Anne Spurr as a shining example to this boy who knew from the start that all he really wanted to be was a professional footballer. 'Rob idolised John Atyeo,' she recalls. 'As his tutor I used to say look, you've got to get your O levels. You can see what's happened to Mr Atyeo; he's got another career, he's got a second string to his bow. If you stick to your school work and don't make the grade as a footballer, you could still have a good future as a P.E. instructor. John did the same. He used to nag Rob, as I did, and to the boy's credit he worked really hard. It's probably no coincidence that one of his best subjects was maths.'

John saw other parallels with his own early days. Rob had a wonderfully supportive family around him, father Roy kicking balls around
with him and driving him to games, mother Dorothy having the wash-
ing machine almost constantly on the go to keep up with his changes
of kit. Both would be on the touchline cheering him on, as would his
brother Paul, who was also a very good player, and their sister Tracey.
At the time of Newman's testimonial match, in August 1990, Atyeo
even surmised that he would go on to overtake his appearance record
for Bristol City, and 'I can think of no one more fitting to take over the
mantle. It would give me great satisfaction to pass on the record to
someone who has displayed such loyalty, reliability and modesty
throughout the past ten years.' This never happened, since Rob moved
on to Norwich for a £600,000 fee the following summer, some two
hundred games short of John's total. In one respect, however, it seemed
as if he at least equalled his master. In Newman's testimonial brochure,
Gary Penrice, who had been a youngster with him at Ashton Gate,
wrote: 'I hope he makes a lot of money – then perhaps he might stick
his hand in his pocket for the first time in his life'; and in the same
vein, David Moyes, later manager of Everton and once a defensive
partner at Ashton Gate, mused: 'If he stuck to attackers like he sticks
to money, Bobby Robson (the then England manager) would have one
fewer problem. What he does when I'm not around to buy the drinks,
I shudder to think.' Maybe it is just something in the West Wiltshire
air...

CHAPTER 18

THE FINAL YEARS

The statistics speak for themselves. In the four seasons after John Atyeo ceased playing for Bristol City, life in the Second Division was a constant struggle for them, and goals were hard to come by. In 1966-67 the team finished in fifteenth place only because, as the season wore on, the need for new forward power became so glaring that reinforcements simply had to be made. Fred Ford's 'golden triangle' of Sharpe, Clark and Derrick got thirteen goals between them all season, and Lou Peters, with nine in twenty-eight League games and two more in the F.A. Cup, was the season's unlikely top scorer. The first move towards rebuilding came in October, when Brian Clark, completely at sea without John Atyeo sniffing around the goal with him, was transferred to Huddersfield Town. 'My loss of form was very much down to John's leaving,' Brian says today. 'Not only the great service I got from him, but the way he would always occupy the attention of the dominant central defender. Even if he was having a quiet day, it would still be their best man who was looking after him. He had that aura, and I felt exposed when suddenly it wasn't there.'

Brian Clark's stay at Huddersfield was brief, and though not very pleasant, a crash-course for him in growing up and learning to stand on his own two feet, no longer looked after by his parents Don and Vera. It was a move back south to Cardiff that set his career firmly back on course, and with it a profitable striking partnership with an emerging John Toshack. Did Tosh and Atyeo have much in common? 'Well, they both had the same christian name, but that's where it stops,' he laughs. 'They were both top players, but Toshack was more an out-and-out finisher, in my time with him, at least, while there was so much more to Big John, with all his skills, his great skills, his creating chances for other people.'

Clark went to Huddersfield in return for the little Scottish veteran Johnny Quigley, who had successfully fought the kind of uphill battle

210

City were facing now at Leeds Road a couple of seasons earlier. His main career had been with Nottingham Forest, with whom he had gained an F.A. Cup winners' medal in 1959, and where his class and trickery prompted Bobby Moore to single him out as his most feared foe. Even at thirty-one he had a lot to offer, and a signing-on fee of £1,500, and a similar bonus if City stayed up emphasised just how highly Harry Dolman rated him. He was joined early in 1967 by his old Forest team mate Chris Crowe, another creative inside-forward with a good pedigree, while a couple of months later in came Hugh McIlmoyle, who had famously played for Leicester City against Spurs as an absolute rookie in the 1961 F.A. Cup final but since then had built up a goalscoring reputation with Carlisle United and Wolves. By the end of the season, then, with John Atyeo still very much around the club, the City attack bore no resemblance to the one he had left behind a year earlier.

Change was also soon to shatter the calm of Ashton Gate off the field. The beginning of season 1967-68 was as disastrous as it had been twelve months earlier, and after a four-two home defeat against Blackpool in mid-September had sent them to the bottom of the table, Harry Dolman and his directors had seen enough. City's record was played eight, won one, drawn two, lost five, goals for six, goals against nineteen. A case for bidding farewell to Fred Ford after seven years? The board certainly thought so, unanimously, and most of today's fans feel it was a reasonable decision – it was a record that closely resembled that of Brian Tinnion when he stepped down in September 2005. At the time, however, it was hugely controversial, and seen by large numbers as the betrayal of the man who had piloted the club back to Second Division respectability. Much was made at the time of the widely circulated report that Dolman had offered Ford a 'job for life' after the promotion game against Oldham in 1965, and maybe he did; maybe, in the heat of the glorious moment, any other football club chairman would have done the same; but then was then, and now was now, and since then Ford had constantly prevaricated in and misread the transfer market, 'sticking hold of Harry's money as if it were his own', as was often said. Now, after he had gone out and bought three excellent Second Division forwards in Quigley, Crowe and McIlmoyle, here were the Robins in last place in the table with nothing more to look forward to than another bitter relegation battle. 'We're not satisfied with things,' Dolman declared. 'We've been pressing Mr Ford to strengthen the team, but he hasn't done so. We've got to do something about it.' So what of Harry Dolman's so-called pledge to Fred? 'Well, that's football isn't it?' say those who were close to him, today; that just about sums it up, and few now would quibble over Ford's dismissal.

Back in the autumn of 1967, however, there was outrage. John Atyeo, still close to the club and contributing his high-profile column to its programme, said little in public, and much in private. His old team-mate Tony Cook, however, could not contain himself, and the former goalkeeper's reader's letter to the *Evening Post* chimed in closely with John's own views: 'I think to sack Fred Ford was one of the most diabolical things that has ever happened in football,' Cook wrote. 'I know I'm writing on behalf of all the players who have served under Fred at Ashton Gate... Ford was 100 per cent for Bristol City. None worked harder for the club, or put more into the job. This is a worse sacking than if Manchester United sacked Matt Busby. People say that Mr. Dolman is Mr. Bristol City. I always considered that Fred Ford was Mr. Bristol City... The decision has sickened me more than I can say. I have always said that Bristol City was the greatest club in the world – and it still was until Tuesday night. I'm afraid it has gone right down in my estimation, now. Where can the club hope to get another manager like Fred? I feel sorry for the man who has to take over.'

That man, after a short inter-regnum with the loyal Les Bardsley in charge, was Alan Dicks, Jimmy Hill's smart young lieutenant at Coventry City, who was still only thirty-three. Hill had left Highfield Road to take up his successful career in television, and it was clear that chairman Derrick Robins's replacement for him, Noel Cantwell, was too much his own man to want to inherit the club's senior backroom staff; a friendly word in Harry Dolman's ear, and the deal was done. The impact on John Atyeo was instant and painful; its most public manifestation came in his programme notes, which from October 28's match against Norwich City switched from the lead item to a slot on page thirteen. Pride of place on page three was given to *A.D. Writes*, soon to become *The A.D. Column*, and John's style changed from the idiosyncratic and personal to the straight sportswriting prose he used in the Plymouth *Sunday Independent* for a season or two before his death. 'Those columns, both in the programme and the newspaper, were very much his own,' says the writer David Foot. 'He wrote to me several times about the possibility of his being a journalist, and genuinely flirted with the idea of being one full-time. His writing was very much that of an average sportswriter.'

Only on March 16, 1968, with the visit of Portsmouth, was he allowed to reminisce a little – and a little inaccurately! 'I was fortunate enough to play a few games for the [Portsmouth] first team at the latter end of 1950-51,' he wrote. 'So that answers the many people who have asked whether I would have liked to have played in the First Division. I did, although it was only fleeting appearances, not stamped with great distinction.' The 'few games', of course, were two, one in the first half of the season and the second with several more matches still to play towards the end. After season 1967-68, John never contributed programme notes again.

Away from the public eye, matters were even worse. Alan Dicks took to his role of new broom with relish, and for him, it was a case of the bigger they come, the harder they fall. He made it clear that 'outsiders' were no longer welcomed on the team coach, and more hurtful still, he stopped John's little ritual of bobbing his head around the dressing room door at a quarter to three on a Saturday afternoon and saying 'Good luck, lads'. No more than that: he did not want to hijack the dressing room, give the team talk, big-time it; it was just that this small and harmless gesture had developed over the last couple of seasons, and now he had been ordered to stop it. Defenders of Alan Dicks say that any manager wishing to make a fresh start would have done the same, and doubtless so they would; but one of the authors of this book, with experience of having been blanked by A.D., can vouch for his cold disregard for his fellow man's feelings if the mood so took him. John Atyeo, on the receiving end of such treatment in the corner of Bristol he regarded as his second home, would have been a greatly saddened man.

This is where his drift away from Ashton Gate began. It was compounded by the exit of two directors, Lionel Smart and Graham Whittock, who were men of very different character but had in common a cordial friendship with the big man. Smart and Whittock, known to some as Tate and Lyle because of their close alliance on the board, left the club in a dispute with Harry Dolman over the cost of employing chief scout Tony Collins, whose roots were in Lancashire and Yorkshire football and who lived in Leeds. Those who favoured Collins, a man with extensive contacts in the game, argued that up north was exactly where he should be; City, surely, had connections

enough in the West Country and South. That was not the way Lionel
and Graham saw it, however, and off they went to Swindon Town,
where their Ashton Gate experience in ground development and con-
structing grandstands was of particular value.

As a result, there were times when John was far more likely to be
seen at the County Ground than in south Bristol; his son Philip remembers being taken there quite a lot in around 1980, when he was about
ten. Eastville was another ground where John would happily watch
football, and neither was he a stranger to Bath City's Twerton Park
when Bristol Rovers shared it from 1986 to the end of his life. Joseph
Murphy, a Rovers fan from St. George, was surprised to see him there
one night, 'well wrapped up', while he was making for his seat in the
stand: 'I said I bet he had a Bristol City top under there, but he just
smiled. We sat down and had a chat about life in general. I told him
that as a Rovers supporter I never had any trouble going to the City
ground. Why should I deny myself the chance to watch a great footballer like him? We agreed that it would be a great day if Bristol City
and Bristol Rovers fans just sat down together and enjoyed a local
derby, or had a bit of respect for each others' clubs. Some older Rovers
fans used to say City must have forgotten one of their greatest players.
They felt, like I did, that he should have had a position within the club.'

On the other hand, there was a time when John scarcely went to
matches at all. In a *Sunday Express* article in February 1974 he
declared that professional football disgusted him, with its yob
culture both on the field and off. Bristol City had just played Leeds
United, and he had been appalled by the feuding of the likes of Gerry
Gow and Billy Bremner on the pitch, and running battles between rival
supporters out in the street. This was a period when, in retrospect, the
game seemed truly to be losing its way, a time of mediocre play on
quagmires in front of seat-hurling fans. Today the 1970s are looked
back on with irony as an era of short shorts and dodgy haircuts, but
there was a great deal more amiss with the culture of the game than
that. Atyeo hated what he saw, and there was a time when he openly
declared that he preferred to be coaching schoolboys on a Saturday
than sitting in the stands at a football match; and coaching them in
rugby, at that.

As we have discussed, the emergence of Rob Newman as not only
a player but a genuine hero meant that John eventually returned to
City as a spectator, but his estrangement from the heart of the club

continued to the end. His relationship with Les Kew, the chairman in the last years of his life, was particularly problematical. The first time he was seen back on the pitch was against Bristol Rovers on New Year's Day, 1987, when he stepped out to a predictable hero's welcome from the holiday crowd; but on the Easter Monday before his death in the summer of 1993, he was reminded of just how cruel the situation had become when Wolves were the visitors. In the directors' box, and almost as close to the end of his life as John was to his, was his old England captain and room-mate Billy Wright; the two had met and embraced in the car park before the game, and Wright took it as read that the man his generation regarded as 'Mr Bristol City' would have a seat next to him among the other V.I.P.s that afternoon. Of course, he did not. Bearing in mind the iconic status Billy continued to enjoy at Molineux and indeed in the football world at large, he must have found it hard to understand why this club was treating with such distain its most prized asset of the post-war years, and very likely of all time. In his usual seat at the top of the steps, Atyeo for once vented his full fury at being on the other side of the fence.

He had far too much respect and affection for Marina Dolman and the memory of her husband to question her role as president of Bristol City, but why, he asked anyone within earshot, could the club not somehow use him in some way to the good of itself and the game? It was the dawning of the age of the F.A. Premiership, with its new-found user-friendliness towards the supporters (at a price), and well-loved players from the past were forever popping up in the executive boxes and refreshment lounges, mingling with fans who remembered them in their pomp and somehow feeling a part of the set-up, still. 'Hey, I was at Maine Road on Saturday, and guess who I had a drink with at half time – only Colin flippin' Bell.' For men of the baby boomer generation, memories of the drink would linger long after every last scrap of action on the pitch that afternoon had been forgotten. John Atyeo could have done all of that and a good deal more. It was true that he had had a very public falling-out with Harry Dolman after he had hung up his boots – but Dolman had been pushed upstairs to be president in 1974 and had died at the age of eighty in 1977. Besides, the two men had been reconciled long before then, and there were few more grief-stricken mourners at Harry's funeral than John Atyeo. It was a very different Bristol City indeed come the early 1990s, but one that consigned John to history while he lived; after he died, of course, and really was history, the club took significantly more kindly to him.

The rift with Dolman, inevitably, was about money, and Atyeo wrapped nothing up in his *Bristol Evening Post* life story in 1970, which blew the secret wide open. 'I'm out of football now,' he wrote. 'I have no ties with any professional club, although I still watch as many City home matches as I can. My team now is the school side, which I take on Saturday mornings. Yet I could now be a director of Bristol City, the club I still look on as the greatest in the West Country and the one that has the potential to rise to become one of the best-known clubs in the land. About three months ago I had a letter from the City chairman, Harry Dolman, asking me whether I was prepared to join the board. At last, I thought, when I quickly opened the letter, a dream come true. Since I finished playing three years ago, the talk about John Atyeo becoming a director had been bandied about quite often. Before I packed up playing, I said in newspaper and television interviews that perhaps my future in football would be as a director of the club.

'This was not just wishful thinking, because Mr. Dolman had told me earlier that he would like me to become a club director in due course – but when the invitation eventually came, a few weeks ago, it wasn't in quite the form I expected. I was one of the favoured few who received a letter from Mr. Dolman. I read most of the other names in the *Evening Post*, but for once I didn't get a mention. It was a cut-and-dried issue. If I had been prepared to put a "substantial amount of money" into the club, I would be considered for a seat on the board. I don't think the amount was mentioned, but I knew it was £3,000, as I had read about it in the newspapers.

'Why did I turn this chance down? There were several reasons. I have always felt that if I were to become a director, my asset would be my experience in football. I never really had any money to offer, certainly not in any quantity. But after fifteen years in the professional game, my contacts and friends could be a great help to the club. I thought this was of just as much value as a couple of thousand pounds. I never fancied staying in the game on the managerial side; it's too much of a rat race. It just didn't appeal to me, and I thought if I were to stay in the professional game, it would be at board level. I believed then, and I still do now, that I could put something back into a game I have enjoyed for so many years – and of course, with a club that was part of my life for so long. When it became really a question of money, I had to back out. Let's face it, a few people putting in £3,000 each isn't going to solve many financial problems. Still, Harry Dolman kept his word, and did invite me to join, as he said he would. It wasn't in the way I expected, but the offer did come at last.

'When I didn't hear anything for so long, I thought I had been forgotten. He told me that when the time was ready, I would be invited. It wasn't the right time when I finished playing, he said, because I knew so many of the players and had been with them in the same side. I was a little disappointed, I must confess, but I haven't given up hope. As things are at the moment, the requirement of new directors at Bristol City seems to be men with money. The club seems desperate for money, and it was made pretty clear by Mr. Dolman that large sums were required. Under these circumstances, I just wasn't the man. Maybe the time will come when my knowledge can be used by the club. Then I would be interested.'

John added that over the years, he had given great thought to football and its administration: 'I think the ideal situation in a club is to have a comparatively small board, say half a dozen directors at the most. Of these, three or four should really be wealthy men prepared to put money into a club. The other two should be people who know something about the inside of football, chaps who have been through the whole set-up of football, right from the bottom; an ex-manager, for example, would be an asset to most boards. I feel this would lead to a closer understanding between the directors, management and players.'

It rankled with John Atyeo that the £3,000 demanded by Harry would go a good way towards wiping out his 1966 benefit cheque. The need for money at the club was pressing, bearing in mind the £250,000 spent on the new stand that bore Dolman's name, which at the time struck many as impossibly grandiose, particularly in comparison with the vile and mean little shed it replaced. Of course, the chairman's foresightedness has been vindicated handsomely since then, even though the ground has never yet proved 'adequate for international games and F.A. Cup semi-finals' in the way he first predicted. In Harry Dolman's further defence, his reluctance to invite John on to the board on his retirement was based on sound judgment of the man and his loyalty to the team-mates he had so recently left behind. Time and again Atyeo had declared that ageing players had been allowed to go too soon – Cook giving way to Gibson in goal was one such instance, the retirement of Jimmy Rogers another – and Dolman knew that that was his instinct. What use would he be as a boss when it came to telling the likes of Jantzen and Lou – indeed, Gibbo himself, at the other end of his career – that it was time to move along?

Nevertheless, at that farewell banquet at the Grand Hotel after the testimonial game, Dolman had told the distinguished company: 'When John came to me a little while ago and told me of his intention to retire, he told me that he had just one more wish – to join the Bristol City board. Although I cannot answer that question tonight, I've got a feeling that Bristol City and John Atyeo will never part.' Of course they would never part; Messrs Denis Follows, David Wiseman, Sam Bolton and the rest of the top brass probably felt that the sentiment was so self-evident that it was hardly worth expressing... Nevertheless, as we have reflected, in his last years, and long after Harry Dolman had died, John continued to speak warmly to his children about his old chairman, perhaps mentally contrasting his intimate relationship with him, in both good times and bad, with the indifference of the current stewards of the club's affairs. 'I knew nothing about the dispute over the place on the board,' says Philip Atyeo, who was born in 1970, the year in which it happened. 'The way my father always talked about Harry Dolman, he almost made it sound like a father and son relationship.'

John occupied himself in various ways in his years of retirement from football, through the bulk of which, of course, he was far from retired from working life. As for his family life, it was almost only just beginning. When he retired from football he and Ruth had two little girls, Julie, who was five, and Carol, three, but Alison was born between his last League game and his testimonial match in 1966, Linda followed in 1968 and Philip in 1970. Philip is certain that his father definitely wanted a boy – as did his formidable gran, Effie – but it was more to carry on the family name, rather than for any dreams of future sporting glories. John had no grandchildren when he died, but now there are nine. Seven of them are boys, two have the Atyeo surname – but none has John as his main name. Philip recalls family holidays in rented houses in Lyme Regis and Torquay, where father was recognised almost as much as he was at home. John was no great traveller, and when his son was growing up he realised that he had never been to London, never been to Cornwall, and had never travelled farther north than Cirencester. He once expressed a wish to see a bit more of the country up north, but dad was dismissive: 'What do you want to do that for? I've been up there, and it's rubbish.' Wet Tuesday nights in Grimsby were clearly not easy to forget.

Big John kept in contact with a number of friends in the football world, mainly from City but also the likes of Geoff Bradford, always the best of foes. They would grumble about the wages being paid to the modern nonentities, but would always end with the mutually reassuring: 'I'm glad we were playing then, rather than now.' It is the single most repeated mantra of any ex-pro, whether he is forty or ninety, an abiding belief that only in his generation was there the right balance of sportsmanship, good fellowship and sheer fun that makes the game worth playing; Wayne Rooney will be saying it twenty years hence.

Beyond football, John stood up in the autumn of 1971 to organise a 602-name petition to help defeat plans for a proposed new road in Warminster, one that would have run intolerably close to his home. It was years later, in 1990, not long before the end of his life, that he was given permission to develop the orchard beside his family's old house at Dilton Marsh into a small close of six starter homes, and this transaction made a considerable impact on his finances; even old team-mates who knew how canny he could be with money whistled in surprise when details of his will were published.

On the sporting front, he turned to golf at the West Wilts club near Warminster, with its par seventy course up on the downs offering fine views as well as a demanding round with its tight little greens and fifty bunkers. He played with a small number of friends, among them Max Lines, a future captain and president, and Bertie Rogers, a teaching colleague at Kingdown who took the remedial class and used to lead it on country rambles around the periphery of the course, where, surprise, surprise, they stumbled across a great number of stray golf balls. John did not play competitively often enough to build up a credible par figure – he was in golf just for the fun of it, he would protest – but he was often put down as par eight, even though he was a good few strokes better than that.

Max Lines remembers the tremendous power of his driving, but mainly his skill on the fairway and green. 'His chipping and putting were brilliant,' he says. 'We both started at much the same time, in the mid-1960s, but he was soon playing with a great deal more confidence than I was. He could easily have been county standard. He used to miss putts on purpose, when I was playing him, just to take the mickey.' John was entirely self-taught; Bristol City, for all its camaraderie, had no great tradition of golf among its players, so most of what he knew he picked up only after joining West Wilts. He had a very peculiar drive. His son Philip says: 'His drive was more like a cricket stroke, with a very short swing, and he would somehow end up facing forwards. People used to laugh at him for that.' Max Lines does not admit to having laughed, but concedes that it was the kind of stroke that could have been played in a telephone box, so minimal was the backlift. Nevertheless, it helped land him the Captain's Prize after he had been at West Wilts for a couple of years, an occasion that gave the club its own little piece of Atyeo folklore. On accepting the trophy, John mused that football, after all, was easier than golf, because the hole was bigger. Everyone was tickled by this remark, which has been immortalised on a memorial bench at the third tee, presented to the club by Ruth shortly after her husband's death.

It seems apt that the memorial to him at the golf course is out there in the open air. He went to West Wilts to enjoy his sport in a recreational way, with socialising low on his agenda, so perhaps it is not surprising that there is nothing to commemorate him in the clubhouse. Refreshingly, Max Lines will not allow the usual Atyeo stereotype to extend to his conduct at the 'nineteenth hole'. 'I know what people say about John and money, but that was not my experience of him,' he says. 'He was no sponger. He always paid his corner.' The friends would get the county card to allow them to play on other courses, and revelled in playing two courses in a day: 'Ogbourne Downs and Marlborough, Tidworth and High Post, it was tremendous fun,' says Max Lines. For John it was not quite football for Trowbridge High in the morning, Westbury in the afternoon and Dilton in the evening, but sometimes it felt like the next best thing.

John was always quirky, and in his last years he grew just that little bit more so. His mother had moved with the family to the early postwar house in Warminster owned by the Harraways, and had continued to keep chickens there. John kept this up after she had died, but became exasperated by starlings that would swarm down and pinch the chicken's corn. One afternoon, watching television in the middle of the sitting room with one of the girls' boyfriends, he glanced through the open French windows, did not like what he saw, and proceeded to pepper the birds with a shotgun without moving from his chair. Each one ate more than its weight in corn a day, he grumbled. A resourceful starling might have argued 'Well, it's all right you saying that, matey, but just feel me – I don't weigh anything, anyway'. John would have none of it, but at least the boyfriend went home with a good tale for his mates, after he had recovered.

All of this, however, was against a background of deteriorating health. John was unlucky to be among the one in five or so people with psoriasis to develop psoriatic arthritis, which as with rheumatoid arthritis causes flare-ups of pain, stiffness and swelling in and around the joints. He was a regular visitor to the Royal National Hospital for Rheumatic Diseases in Bath, formerly and still popularly known as the Mineral Water Hospital or 'Min', which was founded in 1738 and remains a specialist hospital, even though it no longer offers aquatic treatment. The complaint was depressing in the extreme, but he tried to put a brave face on it; one time he came home jokily boasting to his golfing pals that he had never played snooker before in his life before his stay at the Min, and now here he was standing before them the hospital champ.

It was not so easy to jest about his heart problems. The first time he realised that something was amiss was in the late 1980s, when his son Philip was about eighteen. The two of them had been playing football on a field near their house with some young teenagers, and when John got home he began to complain of chest problems, which, as most people do in these circumstances, he chose to put down to indigestion. Of course they were caused by no such thing, and angina pills were prescribed. The family feels that a mild heart attack was equally likely, and wonders how much the drugs he had been taking for psoriasis might have brought it on.

It was on the early summer morning of Tuesday June 8, 1993, that John Atyeo died as the result of a massive heart attack at his home in The Avenue, Warminster, three days after he had been released from the Royal United Hospital in Bath. He had gone there following an earlier attack on May 26, and seemed to be faring well after being fitted with a pacemaker. 'Everyone thought he was on the mend – I was astounded,' said Les Kew, the Bristol City chairman, and that view was shared by many, not least his grieving family. His final appearance at Ashton Gate had been on May 14, at Chris Garland's benefit game against Manchester United, when as usual he took his place at the top of the steps, among the people he had come to see as the real supporters. Garland was in the stand being interviewed for television when John tried to slip quietly past him and the camera crew. Chris would have none of it. 'That's him, he's the real hero,' he shouted, bringing his questioner to an abrupt halt. 'That's the man who was my boyhood idol. That's the man you should be talking to.' The two embraced, and in the ground where John had shed so many tears in the cause of Bristol City over the prime years of his life – tears almost equally divided between pain and joy – the last ones to run down his cheeks were of pride in the warm recognition of a respected fellow-professional. The glow was still with him as he motored back to Warminster, that old, familiar trail, for the last time in his life.

The emergency services were quickly on the spot. The Wiltshire Air Ambulance landed on the playing field of the Avenue School, on the other side of the narrow lane from the Atyeo home. The paramedics worked earnestly and professionally, as good a team as any John had ever encountered, to try to revive him, but there was nothing they could do. He was sixty-one years and four months old. The cremation was the following Monday, within the week, after a service of thanksgiving at the Minster church in which he had been married. It was at the uncomfortably early time, for those travelling a distance, of 9.45 a.m., but despite this it was a very big gathering, with the field beside the church packed with cars. Those who think they know a thing or two about ex-pro footballers swear they stood out a mile – 'glazed eyes, black ties, dark suits, hands in pockets' – among other friends from the worlds of teaching, cricket, rugby and golf and the horticultural, business and local political circles of the Harraway family. Jack Boxley, Jantzen Derrick, Alan Williams, Mike Thresher, Jimmy Rogers and Tommy Burden were among old colleagues spotted in the crowd; Chris Garland, of a later and more glamorous breed, was there with John once again. It was a short service with two hymns, *For the beauty of the earth* and *O Jesus, I have promised*, prayers and a blessing and brief addresses from four speakers: John's son and youngest child Philip, on behalf of his mother and sisters Julie, Carol, Alison and Linda, and all the family; Ian Blackwood from school; Max Lines, the golfing friend; and the journalist David Foot, who spoke eloquently but nevertheless somewhat bizarrely on behalf of Bristol City Football Club. Bristol City were well represented at the service, in one way and another, but several observers, aware of the professional qualifications and urbanity of some of the directors, were surprised that nobody could be found to speak for the club at first hand.

Philip's speech, over an erratic public address system, struck listeners as poignant testimony to the father of a loving and tight-knit family, one who displayed 'the warmth and compassion which allows growth and individuality to blossom'. On the way out, to the accompaniment of *The red, red robin*, there was the opportunity to make a donation to the coronary care unit at Bath Royal United Hospital. The jaunty organ music was a reminder that this was a life to be celebrated, as well as a passing to be mourned, but it had the opposite effect on his old team-mate Brian Clark. 'I was all right until that *Red, red robin*,' he says. 'That's what did for me.' As the cremation was for family only, that was the end of most visitors' involvement, but large numbers of them stood around talking about the big man for a good while, and Ruth and her children stayed with them as long as they were able. One member of the congregation was quite shocked to look up after half an hour or more and see John's coffin, with its football on top, still waiting to make its final journey in the hearse, apparently forgotten while those who knew and loved him regaled one another with tales of his deeds of old, his heroics in life. To them at that moment, in their reminiscences, he was still what he had always been – the caring schoolmaster, the good companion, the loving family man, the swashbuckling hero in red.

CHAPTER 19

WE WILL REMEMBER HIM

Timing was always crucial to John Atyeo's success, and the cynical might say he got it right again when it came to the naming of Bristol City's new stand, built in the wake of the Taylor report on football ground safety, at the old open end. Work began on it in the summer of 1994, with its opening early in the following season, and it was £1.5 million well spent, offering more than four thousand of City's most vociferous, foot-stamping fans an uninterrupted view of the pitch. With the announcement of the project well within a year of John's death, the decision to call it the Atyeo Stand seemed inevitable, and there would have been a good deal of protest had it not been. 'It's a fitting tribute to a man who simply was Bristol City during his time at the club,' said vice-chairman Mike Fricker. 'This new stand is going to be brilliant, and we can think of no better way of marking the highest regard in which John was held.' John's widow Ruth, who died in 1998, stayed in touch with the club in the few years left to her, and would occasionally attend old players' reunions with Harry Dolman's widow Marina. 'It's a great honour for John to be remembered in this way,' she said when news of the naming of the new stand broke in April 1994. 'He would have been thrilled to know the club were doing this.' At Christmas, 1993, she had written to one of the authors of this book: 'Life is very different, now, but thanks to my marvellous family and their partners, plus some very good friends, I manage to keep pretty busy.' Jantzen Derrick was equally enthusiastic about the Atyeo Stand gesture, though it was with some feeling that he told the *Evening Post*: 'It's just a pity he's not around to appreciate it.'

The supporters' club bar in the main Williams Stand is also named after John and is adorned by a life-sized black-and-white mural photograph of him straining every sinew to reach the ball. It is a familiar but strange image of him in his later years, heavily retouched the first time it went into the newspaper and now blown up a good deal more than it should have been to create an almost eerie aura of a distant era and place. It all looks a long, long time ago, longer than it really was – for those of us who remember him, at least.

At Kingdown School, a tree in John's memory was planted little more than a month after his death, within sight of his window in the maths block, by former pupils Andrew Herbert and Mark Wilkinson. Splendidly named and thoughtfully chosen, it is an *Acer platanoides* or Norway maple 'Crimson King' with deep red leaves, and it still flourishes and indeed is yet to reach its prime. 'Mr Atyeo always had the gift of giving you self-belief when you had none,' Mr Herbert explained. The tree is unmarked by a plaque, as is the sculpture *Atyeo 1986* at Baltic Wharf, a pleasant housing development on the Bristol waterfront in easy walking distance of Ashton Gate. Carved in now weathered pink Verona marble, this substantial monolith was unveiled by the Minister of the Environment William Waldegrave in the year of its creation – the work of Stephen Cox, a distinguished sculptor born in Bristol in 1946 and so exposed to the city's Atyeo lore from the age of five to twenty. Look at the sculpture from many angles, and it is hard to see what he is getting at; indeed, in its early days it was labelled 'Ateo', and the developers put out a statement explaining that it portrayed Bristol and its relationship with the world, or some such. Then, home in on the ball in the instep of a mighty foot, and it is an irresistible symbol of dynamism and power, all in a colour which, like the school's tree, hints at the red of Bristol City. There are two other significant pieces of public sculpture at Baltic Wharf, a graceful top-sail and a large and enigmatic hand, said to be that of a river god. The only one of the three that reflects the life of the city on dry land is Cox's *Atyeo 1986*. Admirers of John will be a good deal happier when both the tree and the stone are marked with simple plaques to explain their presence to this and future generations; in the case of the latter, it can equally be argued that a native son as widely renowned in his field as Stephen Cox is also being sold short by the sculpture's current anonymity.

Two Atyeo Closes are named after the great man, at Dilton Marsh and in Ashton Vale, Bristol, both of them occupying tiny areas. At the time of writing, John's last home at The Avenue, Warminster, was about to be demolished, with half a dozen or so homes built in its grounds, so maybe that town, too, will be commemorating him with a street name. It is the other great City hero whose memory is honoured in a thoroughfare alongside the Ashton Gate ground, though it must be confessed that Wedlock Way is by no means as prepossessing as the roads named after Sir Matt Busby in Stretford, Greater Manchester, Sir Tom Finney in Preston or even Harold Fleming in Swindon; the deeds of that goalscoring legend from the Wiltshire club's earliest Football League days are also celebrated by a bronze statue at the County Ground.

The third tee bench on the West Wilts course ensures that John's golfing friends and those following on in the future will remember him, while a temporary showcase at Westbury Heritage Centre contained various souvenirs, including the civic certificate presented to him shortly after his first England game in 1956. All John's awards, mementoes and souvenirs of any value are safe in a bank vault. The ex-City player Brian Clark swears that if ever Bristol City open a museum, its first exhibit should be John Atyeo's fawn mac.

How else is Big John remembered? On the internet, his story is told on Bristol City websites official and unofficial, as well as on a site dedicated solely to him. Click on 'John Atyeo Home Page', however, and all you get is news from a lecturer in radiation therapy in Sydney, New South Wales. He would doubtless claim that he is doing more for the good of mankind than our John ever did, but nevertheless, we must leave him be. There are the odd florid flights of fancy on the net. City supporter Gareth Calway, the self-styled Bard on the Wire, introduces himself on his site with: 'I am really the love child of John Atyeo and the goddess Aphrodite (conceived, without John's knowledge, during a breath- taking goal he scored in 1955). I was placed at birth with two worthy Anglo-Welsh bystanders. This website is about asserting my true inheritance.' In a similar light vein, John finds himself as a trivia question – the first of four players with a surname ending in 'o' to play for England; he was followed by Ken Shellito, John Salako and Tony Dorigo, who lasted longest and collected fifteen caps between 1990 and 1994. Happily, in Dilton Marsh, the children were reminded that 'Atyeo' is more than a name on a local street sign in May 2002, when the village primary school's 'drama extravaganza' to mark the Queen's golden jubilee presented a series of tableaux depicting scenes from the last 1,000 years of local history. There were the monks working in the marshes, Saxons and Danes, Napoleonic prisoners, Victorian schoolchildren, the Home Guard, the Land Army girls; and there was John Atyeo, resplendent in red, played by a little dark-haired boy called

Nick Brake. Again in the Westbury area, Big John's name is still regularly evoked when the town's sporting heritage appears to be under threat; as recently as January 2005 former deputy mayor Mike Pearce told the Town Council that Westbury would not produce any more John Atyeos or other sportsmen of quality if facilities were not improved: 'They picked up all their basic skills in Westbury, and unless things change we will never see players like that again.'

The authors of this book are surprised, bearing in mind Bristol's reputation for prolific local publishing and accomplished sports journalism, that this is the first publication of any size to be devoted to John Atyeo's life and career. Maybe there will be others. There are doubtless more stories to be told, passed down through the generations, and even some people who are aware of his extraordinary feats on the football field only through the record books will remember him in his later life, as they found him in the classroom or in the grandstand. They will think of him as a good-hearted, community-spirited man whose mischievous sense of humour either masked or illuminated – sometimes it is hard to say which – a personality that veered between something akin to an inferiority complex and an innate and well-justified sense of self-worth.

Bristol City fan Darren Hurley was born two years after the big man hung up his boots, but he still treasures his memory of the one occasion he met him. It was in 1989, after City had played Manchester United in a pre-season friendly. He spotted Atyeo quietly slipping out of Ashton Gate, almost unnoticed, and ran after him with a pen and a scrap of paper to ask for his autograph. As he signed, he wondered out loud what the young man was thinking of, wasting his time on him, when across the car park the likes of Bryan Robson, Steve Bruce, Brian McClair and Mark Hughes were filing aboard their team coach. Why on earth should Darren want *him* to sign?

'Ah,' he replied, 'but you were my dad's hero, and he was your greatest fan.'

'And what else did your dad say about me?'

'He said you were the greatest.'

John pondered that wonderful accolade for no more than a heartbeat. 'Well,' he replied gruffly, with that cheeky old grin of his, 'you just go home and tell your dad he was right.'

STATISTICS

Major International Appearances

Young England v Italy, Stamford Bridge, January 19, 1955
England won 5-1
England: R. Matthews; Foulkes, P. Sillett; Flowers, Trevor Smith, Edwards; Hooper (2), Atyeo (1), Ayre (1), Haynes, Bluntstone (1).

Scotland v Young England, Firhill Park, Glasgow, February 8, 1955
England won 6-0
England: R. Matthews; Foulkes, P. Sillett; Flowers, Trevor Smith, Edwards (3); Hooper, Atyeo (1), Ayre, Haynes (1), Bluntstone (1). Sub used: Anderson.

Scottish League v Football League, Hampden Park, Glasgow, March 16, 1955
England lost 2-3
Football League: R. Matthews; Foulkes, Mansell; Armstrong, Marston, Edwards; Hooper, Atyeo, Bentley (1), Evans (1), Bluntstone.

Football League v League of Ireland, Goodison Park, Liverpool, December 7, 1955
England won 5-1
Football League: Baynham; Hall, Byrne (1); Clayton (1), Wright, Dickinson; Finney, Atyeo (1), Lofthouse, Haynes, Perry (1). Ireland o.g. Mackey.

England v Spain, Friendly, Wembley, November 30, 1955
England won 4-1
England: Baynham; Hall, Byrne; Clayton, Wright, Dickinson; Finney (1), Atyeo (1), Lofthouse, Haynes, Perry (2).

England v Brazil, Friendly, Wembley, May 9, 1956
England won 4-2
England: R. Matthews; Hall, Byrne; Clayton, Wright, Edwards; S. Matthews, Atyeo, Taylor (2), Haynes, Grainger (2).

Sweden v England, Friendly, Solna, May 16, 1956
0-0 draw
England: R. Matthews; Hall, Byrne; Clayton, Wright, Edwards; Berry, Atyeo, Taylor, Haynes, Grainger.

Republic of Ireland, World Cup Qualifier, Wembley, May 8, 1957
England won 5-1
England: Hodgkinson; Hall, Byrne; Clayton, Wright, Edwards; Matthews, Atyeo (2), Taylor (3), Haynes, Finney.

Denmark, World Cup Qualifier, Copenhagen, May 15, 1957
England won 4-1
England: Hodgkinson; Hall, Byrne; Clayton, Wright, Edwards; Matthews, Atyeo (1), Taylor (2), Haynes (1), Finney.

Republic of Ireland, World Cup Qualifier, Dublin, May 19, 1957
1-1 draw
England: Hodgkinson; Hall, Byrne; Clayton, Wright, Edwards; Finney, Atyeo (1), Taylor, Haynes, Pegg.

Goals for Bristol City in major competitions

Season	F. League	F.A. Cup	F.L. Cup	Total
1951-52	12	2	-	14
1952-53	11	-	-	11
1953-54	22	3	-	25
1954-55	28	-	-	28
1955-56	30	1	-	31
1956-57	23	5	-	28
1957-58	23	2	-	25
1958-59	25	-	-	25
1959-60	16	1	-	17
1960-61	19	7	3	29
1961-62	27	3	-	30
1962-63	16	2	-	18
1963-64	21	4	2	27
1964-65	23	-	-	23
1965-66	19	-	-	19
Totals	315	30	5	350

Appearances for Bristol City in major competitions

Season	F. League	F.A. Cup	F.L. Cup	Total
1951-52	44	2	-	46
1952-53	33	-	-	33
1953-54	45	3	-	48
1954-55	46	1	-	47
1955-56	39	1	-	40
1956-57	37	3	-	40
1957-58	42	4	-	46
1958-59	40	3	-	43
1959-60	42	1	-	43
1960-61	37	6*	3	46
1961-62	42	5	1	48
1962-63	30	3	1	34
1963-64	47**	5	1	53
1964-65	38	4	-	42
1965-66	35	1	-	36
Totals	597**	42*	6	645

* Including abandoned game v Leicester City (a)
** Including abandoned game v Queens Park Rangers (h)
John Atyeo scored in neither abandoned game

ACKNOWLEDGEMENTS

The authors acknowledge the help given in compiling this book to those named below, with apologies to any other whose name has been accidentally omitted:

Philip Atyeo, Ernie Barber, Patrick Barclay, Roy Bentley, Joan Biancoli, Jack Boxley, Gerry Brooke, Terry Bush, Lian Chen, Brian Clark, Jack Connor, Paul Davis, Tim Davey, Keith Dawe, Charlie Derrick, Jantzen Derrick, Marina Dolman, David Duffin, Penny Ealey, Pete Farrell, Bob Flicker, David Foot, David Fudge, Steve Fudge, Philip Fussell, Mike Gibson, John Giles, the late Herbert Gilliam, Geoffrey Goatman, Peter Godsiff, Terry Hamlin, Arthur Hopegood, David Hopegood, Edward Hopegood, John Hopegood, Robert Hopegood, Linda Hudson, David Humphrey, Mick Hunter, Richard Jones, Steve Lansdown, John Laycock, Max Lines, John McCann, Geoff Morgan, Quita Morgan, Tom Morgan, Malcolm Norman, Richard Owen, Ken Palmer, Ivan Ponting, Geoff Rose, Graham Russell, Ollie Rogers, Anne Spurr, Roy Spurr, Tony Stedall, Peter Taylor, John Watkins, Alan Williams and David Woods.

Principal books used for research were *The Bristol Babe: The First 100 Years of Bristol City F.C.*, by David M. Woods (Yore Publications, 1994); *Bristol City Football Club: The First 100 Years*, by Leigh Edwards and David M. Woods (Redcliffe Press, 1997); *Football League Players' Records, 1946–1988*, compiled by Barry J. Hugman (Arena Press, 1988); *The Football League, 1888–1988: The Official Illustrated History*, by Bryon Butler (Queen Anne Press, 1987); and various editions of *Rothmans Football Yearbook*.

Other books referred to included: *An Away Game Every Week*, by Ray Kendall (Breedon Books, 2001); *Bristol City Greats*, by Ivan Ponting (Redcliffe Press, 1990); *Bristol Rovers Greats*, by Ivan Ponting (Redcliffe Press, 1990); *C'mon City: A Hundred Years of the Bluebirds*, by Grahame Lloyd (Seren, 1999); *The Complete Book of the World Cup*, by Cris Freddi (CollinsWillow, 1998); *A Wiltshire Football Club: Westbury United, 1920–1995*; *Don't Shoot the Manager*, by Jimmy Greaves (Boxtree, 1993); *The F.A. Book for Boys 1950–51* (Naldrett Press, 1950); *Finney on Football*, by Tom Finney (Sportsmans Book Club, 1960); *Football is my Passport*, by Billy Wright (Sportsmans Book Club, 1959); *League Football and the Men Who Made It, 1888–1988*, by Simon Inglis (Willow Books, 1988); *Pompey: The History of Portsmouth Football Club*, by Mike Neason, Mick Cooper and Doug Robinson (Milestone Publications, 1984); *Sixty Soccer Years*, by Bill Harvey (Nene Lithographic, 1990s); and *Stanley Matthews: The Authorized Biography*, by David Miller (Pavilion Books, 1989).

The authors thank the staff of Trowbridge and Frome Reference Libraries, *The Warminster Journal* and Bristol United Press for help in microfilm research. Newspapers most referred to have been *The Bristol Evening Post*, *The Western Daily Press*, *The Bath Chronicle*, *The Wiltshire Times*, *The Warminster Journal*, *The Frome and Somerset Standard* and the former *Bristol Evening World*. Special acknowledgements to Mike Norton and Chris Bartlett, Editor and Sports Editor of *The Bristol Evening Post* and Terry Manners and Chris Spittles, Editor and Sports Editor of *The Western Daily Press*. The Bristol City programme, in its various guises, has also been a valuable source of information.

INDEX